BAREFOOT

A Memoir

BAREFOOT

A Memoir

Dhirendra Kumar Sahu

All Nations University
2022

Barefoot: A Memoir— jointly published by the Indian Society for Promoting Christian Knowledge (ISPCK), Post Box 1585, Kashmere Gate, Delhi-110006 and All Nations University, Koforidua, Ghana.

Online order: http://ispck.org.in/book.php

Also available on amazon.in

ISBN: 978-93-90569-82-3

Cover Design: Roshan Davina Edda

Laser typeset by

ISPCK, Post Box 1585, 1654, Madarsa Road, Kashmere Gate, Delhi-110006 • *Tel:* 23866323

e-mail: ashish@ispck.org.in • ella@ispck.org.in
website: www.ispck.org.in

To my parents -

Barefoot Pastor Birendra Kumar Sahu & Promodini Sahu

&

Manju, Bibhu, Ashis, Natashia, Agnes, Aavisha, Davinia, Aviella

Contents

Acknowledgements

Distilling memories from life's experiences is not an easy task and cannot be perfect. It can be an even more difficult and complex exercise when one has lived in a different part of the world and worked in diverse institutions. I would not have taken the plunge but for the support of my family and friends, some of whom nudged me along this twisting path. Writing this memoir has been immeasurably rewarding as it has allowed me to gratefully reminisce God's grace and mercy.

I want to give credit to our eldest granddaughter Aavisha, who skilfully sketched the bare feet that adorn the cover page of this memoir. The picture denotes her great-grandfather wearing a *dhoti* and walking barefoot. The *dhoti*, a long loincloth that is traditionally wrapped around the hips and thighs with one end brought between the legs and tucked into the waistband, is a simple garment that commands respect and dignity.

The presence and support of my wife Manju in recording various aspects of life has been incredible. She has been a constant source of support from the day we got married, sometimes with punch lines to awaken me from slumber and other times counselling me to be content and grateful. Bibhu and Ashis are our family consultants. They have stood in solidarity with us during times of joy and sorrow, cheering me on to write this memoir for posterity. Aavisha, Davinia, and Aviella are our three angels who have brought us joy. Davinia challenged me that anyone could write and Aviella, at the age of seven, questioned me whether I knew how to write a book review.

I want to thank Rev Dr Samuel Donkor, Senior Pastor of All Nations Full Gospel Churches International, Toronto, Canada and President of All Nations University (ANU), Koforidua, Ghana for his friendship, for encouraging me to write the memoir, for penning the Foreword, and for permitting me to include 'An African Story by Africans' in the section 'African Exploration' in this memoir, apart from ANU being a joint publisher with the Indian Society for Promoting Christian Knowledge (ISPCK). I also want to express gratitude to Dr Sunil Chandy, Former Director of Christian Medical College, Vellore, Rev Dr Ravi Tiwari, Former Registrar of Senate of Serampore College, and Mr Dilip Mukerjea for their comments and suggestions on the first draft.

I am indebted to my parents for teaching me the virtues of simplicity and humility not only in words but also through an exemplary lifestyle. They poignantly lived out the principle of not retaliating in adverse situations but leaving it to God, who is the best judge.

■■■

Foreword

Barefoot is a theological memoir of Bishop Sahu's inspiring journey of faith; a faith that began with his father, Pastor Birendra Kumar Sahu, who was christened the 'Barefoot Pastor'. A legacy of sacrificial love, service, and devotion to Christ is the hallmark of Bishop Sahu's life. It exemplifies Paul's statement to Timothy, '*When I call to remembrance the genuine faith that is in you, which dwelt first in your grandmother Lois and your mother Eunice, and I am persuaded is in you also*' (2Timothy 1:5). His faith that grew from humble origins in Odisha, India has touched several lives across Asia, Europe, North America, and Africa today through selfless service to the body of Christ.

I met Bishop Sahu in 2015 when he was serving as the Dean of the Gospel and Plough Institute of Theology at Sam Higginbottom University of Agriculture, Technology and Science, Allahabad, Uttar Pradesh, India. I initially went there to train faculty for All Nations University, Koforidua, Ghana but eventually enrolled as a student in the School of Theology and Bishop Sahu became my PhD thesis supervisor. Later, he was invited to Toronto, Canada to minister where he not only ministered to the congregation in Toronto, but also to the All Nations Full Gospel Church congregations in Calgary, Edmonton, Ajax, Hamilton, Windsor, and Ottawa. Bishop Sahu also shared his vast repertoire of experience with the ministers-in-training at the All Nations Bible College. Those in Toronto attended in person while others watched the live-stream from different locations across Canada.

Bishop Sahu took the students on a journey of faith; from believing God for sponsorship to study theology in India to gaining a full scholarship for studies at the University of Oxford and Birmingham University in the United Kingdom. His life story and experiences challenged and motivated the ministers. His commitment to serving the church faithfully in rural locations along with his wife, eventually placed him at the helm of Serampore College, Church of North India (CNI) and the National Council of Churches in India (NCCI). As an astute scholar, Bishop Sahu has impacted many young ministers through education.

This memoir examines several perplexing theological subjects that ministers, Christians, and people in general, deal with in life. The wealth of knowledge and insight in these pages will not only inspire the reader but also resolve any profound dilemmas they may be facing. It will challenge ministers both young and old to a life of faith in a true and faithful God who never fails to meet His own at the point of their need. This memoir of stories, papers, and selected sermons, embedded in Bishop Sahu's life experiences, will indeed serve to preserve the history of one of the giants of faith in India.

May God increase your faith as you read this book.

Samuel H Donkor, PhD, DMin, DD
Senior Pastor of All Nations Full Gospel Churches International, Toronto, Canada
President of All Nations University, Koforidua, Ghana

■■■

1

On Being a Servant

'Life is not what one lived, but what one remembers and how one remembers it in order to recount it'.

Gabriel García Márquez

It is aptly said that at the age of seventy-one, one lives on borrowed time. In the evening of my life, I have desired to put within the pages of a memoir, some thoughts on my journey of faith as well as excerpts from my papers and selected sermons. Fundamental thoughts and themes recur and, in certain places, they are embryonic or anticipatory. This memoir is an attempt to understand myself, my relationship with God, family, and friends. The mystery of life can step free from the chaos to form a story, making the contingencies of life intelligible and meaningful. Life has been wonderful with memories both sweet and sour. I am still attempting to comprehend how I ended up being a servant of the Servant King. Graham Kendrick puts it eloquently, *'From heaven you came helpless babe, entered our world, your glory veiled, not to be served but to serve, and give Your life that we might live, this is our God, the Servant King, He calls us now to follow Him'.*

I am the eldest son of Birendra Kumar Sahu, well-known in Odisha as the 'Barefoot Pastor' and also lovingly called '*Budhia Bhai*' (Budhia brother). '*Budhia*' means intelligent, but my father never received any formal education. He was ordained as the honorary pastor of my home church—Khordha Baptist Church—and served there for thirty-three years. It was difficult to understand him as he travelled barefoot regardless of the cold in winter or heat in summer when the mercury would rise to 45° celsius. It was not only symbolic to walk barefoot but an act that translated into his lifestyle, a rare virtue today among church leaders. Therefore, my memoir is titled *Barefoot* and theologically explores this theme. *Barefoot* is a search for identities in multiple layers. Sometimes it is easy to understand, theologically explicable with jargon, and sometimes it ends in mystery, beyond understanding, leaving several unanswered questions.

In 2018, I had the privilege of visiting Toronto and Oxford with my wife Manju for business and pleasure. The London visit was to meet our granddaughter, Nora, son Ashis, and daughter-in-law Rosy. At Oxford, I attended a seminar at Regent's Park College—my alma mater—on the occasion of two hundred years of the Serampore Mission in India and to preach in the College Chapel at Regent's Park College on a Friday and at New Road Baptist Church on a Sunday where we had worshipped before for seven years. The Toronto visits included ministry at the All Nations Full Gospel Church. There I was requested to recount my testimony again as I had done during my previous visit in 2016. On our return to India, I received a note from my friend, Samuel Donkor, 'You have drawn enough experiences in ministry. The rich spiritual legacy can benefit others only through your writings, for that shall benefit both current and future generations'.

Memoir is from the French word 'memoire' meaning reminiscence. The literary technique narrates the story of one's life, usually around a specific theme. It can be categorised as a sub-genre of autography. While autography spans a person's entire life, including intricate details, a memoir is more specific and focused. In the words of Valson Thampu, former Principal of St Stephen's College, Delhi, 'most of the time, our consciousness lies buried deep under the burden of the body. The life of the body, says Albert Camus in the Myth of Sisyphus, begins before the life of the mind. He is sort of right. And wrong too. The life of my body may have begun with me. Not the life of my mind. The life of my mind began, if psychoanalysts are right, a long time before the life of my body. A human being is more like a stretch of flowing river than a square inch of ivory. The past flows into us, and out. The future beckons us, as the portrait-in-waiting does in the flowing unpredictable touches of the artist'.[1]

Reading *Hannah's Child: A Theologian's Memoir* by Stanley Hauerwas, was inspiring.[2] A loving, hard-working, godly couple had long been denied a family of their own. 'She had heard the story of Hannah praying to God to give her a son, whom she would dedicate to God. Hannah's prayer was answered, and she named her son Samuel. My mother prayed a similar prayer. I am the result. But I was named Stanley'. In 2001, Time Magazine named Stanley Hauerwas the 'best theologian in America'. The story of Hauerwas' journey into Christian discipleship is captivating and inspiring. With genuine humility, he describes his long struggle to understand the God of the Bible within the context of being an apprentice bricklayer, a student, a teacher, a father, and a husband to a mentally-ill wife. His struggle to live with his wife forms the main conflict of his story – how do you love someone who cannot receive your love? How do you live with someone so delusional she might kill you in your sleep? For twenty-five years, Hauerwas dealt with this conflict as he continued to publish and dedicate his works to a wife who gradually hated him more and more.

Return to India is another powerful memoir by Shoba Narayan that explores the themes of family, culture, and identity. It describes the trajectory of immigrant life grappling with hyphenated identities. She discusses why she yearned for America, became a citizen of the land, but eventually left. It is about family, identity, and the quest for a place called home. 'Home: a word filled with loss and longing. Snatches of music bring to mind a mother's song. Smells in restaurants conjure up a kitchen back home. A face in a crowd looks like a relative'.[3] The book resonates with what it means to be an immigrant in a foreign country and what propels immigrants to return to their homeland.

Elie Wiesel's Night is one of the most widely read and acclaimed Holocaust memoirs. Wiesel recounts the unimaginable horrors of life in Auschwitz and Buchenwald and the loss of his deeply-held religious faith. 'Never shall I forget that night, the first night in camp, which has turned my life into one long night, seven times cursed and seven times sealed. Never shall I forget that smoke. Never shall I forget the little faces of the children, whose bodies I saw turned into wreaths of smoke beneath a silent blue sky. Never shall I forget those flames which consumed my faith forever. Never shall I forget that nocturnal silence which deprived me, for all eternity, of the desire to live. Never shall I forget those moments which murdered my

God and my soul and turned my dreams to dust. Never shall I forget these things, even if I am condemned to live as long as God Himself. Never'.[4]

Raised in an orthodox family in Sighet, Transylvania, Wiesel was liberated from Buchenwald at age 16. In unsentimental detail, Night recounts daily life in the camps, the never-ending hunger, the sadistic doctors who pulled gold teeth, and the Kapos who beat fellow Jews. On his first day in the camp, Wiesel was separated forever from his mother and sister. At Auschwitz, he watched his father slowly succumb to dysentery before the SS beat him to within an inch of his life. Wiesel writes honestly about his guilty relief at his father's death. In the camps, the formerly observant boy underwent a profound crisis of faith. Night was one of the first books to raise the question – where was God at Auschwitz?

Memoirs have been around since ancient times. Perhaps Julius Caesar, who wrote and depicted his personal experiences about epic battles, was the first memoirist. Eventually, it became a popular and acclaimed literary genre. Memoirs serve to preserve history through a person's perspective. Through memoirs, the writers reveal their life story, their struggle in seeking normalcy, their experiences—both good and bad—while attaining certain life goals, along with eye-witness accounts of particular events. A memoir provides a window into the lives of other people. The assertions made in the work are factual. Many of the best stories come from everyday instances and events. Stories are always interesting. You can always find somebody, somewhere who will want to hear your story. Michael Margolis says, 'The stories we tell literally make the world. If you want to change the world, you need to change your story'.

I have attempted to recount my story in a manner that is true to me, relying primarily on my memory. But memory is a tricky business that cannot be flawless. I have endeavoured to be honest about myself, my friends, and also friends who betrayed me. Some may find some sections immodest, but, after all, I am human. The conversations in this book come from my recollections and do not represent word-for-word transcripts. Rather, I have retold them in a manner that evokes the feeling and meaning of what was said and, in all instances, the essence of the dialogue is accurate. My attempt was to discover amid the fragments that constitute my life, a pattern around the theme of going barefoot; it is a theological exploration.

Theology is not merely a cerebral activity disconnected from the Christian life. Hence, my memoir interweaves pieces of my life story. It begins with our three granddaughters, who are part of our journey as a source of joy, inspiration, and gratitude to God for His love for us. Then it moves to the roots of our joint family, the dreams dreamt, the lessons learnt from five institutions, selected sermons, and finally ends with an exploration of African Christian Theology that includes a lecture on African Christianity by Rev Dr Samuel H Donkor and the story of All Nations Full Gospel Churches International (ANFGCI) and All Nations University (ANU) by Dr Cynthia Gyimah. The similarity between India and Africa, home to two billion people, is an exhilarating account of deep-rooted empathy and solidarity that is key to the continued vibrancy of reconstructing theology.

'What to write', 'When to write', and 'Why to write' were three questions that lingered with me despite having published articles, a doctoral thesis, a Festschrift when I turned sixty, and edited a book 'A Conversation on Health and Healing' on the Centenary Year of Medical Education (1918-2018) for Christian Medical College, Vellore.

Endnotes

[1] Thampu, Valson. On a Stormy Course. Hachette India, 2018, p.1.

[2] Hauerwas, Stanley. Hannah's Child. William B. Eerdmans, 2010.

[3] Narayan, Shoba. Return to India: An immigrant memoir. Jasmine Books, 2012, Prologue.

[4] Wiesel, Elie. Night. New York: Bantam, 1982, p. 32.

■■■

2

Stories

'I have fought the good fight, I have finished the race, I have kept the faith. Henceforth there is laid up for me the crown of righteousness, which the Lord, the righteous judge, will award to me on that day, and not only to me but also to all who have loved his appearing'

(2 Timothy 4:7-8)

The plaque, in memory of my father's dedicated service, on the wall of Khordha Baptist Church, Odisha cites the passage from 2 Timothy 4:7-8. It is a memorial to his thirty-three years of barefoot ministry and the formation of his identity as a barefoot evangelist cum pastor. Although he was ordained in the Baptist Church of Khordha he had no formal education or seminary training. He was also not on the payroll of the church or any organization. Instead, he lived out a 'tent-making ministry' for thirty-three years, fashioning his profession and ministry into his vocation. The image of Isaiah in 52:7, 'How beautiful upon the mountains are the feet of him who brings good news' was my father's vocation, and his goal was to finish the race in 2 Timothy 4:7-8.

'Take your sandals off your feet, for the place on which you are standing is holy ground'. (Exodus 3:5). Being barefoot is not an objet d'art but the reality of life in India. Bare feet stories are multi-layered and multi-faceted. The reader must have a particularly sensitive perspective to observe the reality of everyday life in India. The Bible narrates Moses' barefoot encounter at the beginning of the exodus. It is where he was commissioned to return to Pharaoh and lead the Israelites out of Egypt into the Promised Land (Exodus 3:7-10). Joshua's encounter occurred after he had brought God's people into the Promised Land, having led them miraculously through the Jordan just as Moses had through the Red Sea forty years earlier (Joshua 3:13).

'And the commander of the Lord's army said to Joshua, "Take off your sandals from your feet, for the place where you are standing is holy." And Joshua did so' (Joshua 5:15). In Exodus 3:2, the One who spoke to Moses is 'the angel of the LORD' who is no ordinary angel but is identified as the Lord Himself. He does not merely speak for Yahweh; He speaks as Yahweh. When this 'angel' speaks, He says, 'I am the God of your father(s)' (Exodus 3:6), following the same pattern we witness with Hagar (Genesis 16:7-13) and Jacob (Genesis 32:24-31).

Joshua was the man chosen by God to be Moses' successor (Deuteronomy 31:1-8). He was charged with leading Israel into the Promised Land after Moses. Given the clear parallels between the two, it is understandable that God would give Joshua a similar command when encountering him. Indeed, assuming Joshua was familiar with Moses' experience at the bush, hearing this command would likely have served to strengthen his faith in God's promise: 'Just as I was with Moses, so I will be with you' (Joshua1:5). God promised to be with Moses and the children of Israel, guiding them to a land flowing with milk and honey. God says, 'Behold, I send an angel before you to guard you on the way and to bring you to the place that I have prepared. Pay careful attention to him and obey his voice; do not rebel against him, for he will not pardon your transgression, for my name is in him' (Exodus 23:20-21).

Being barefoot is not an uncommon sight in India. One unforgettable image is the story of Dharavi, a locality in Mumbai, India, which is considered to be one of Asia's largest slums. Dharavi has an area of just over 2.1 square kilometers and a population of about 1,000,000.

Dan McDougall, in an article for The Guardian International Edition and The Observer on Sunday 4th March 2007[1] states, 'These slum dwellers use their imagination and work hard to make something out of the day-to-day objects others leave behind, yet have been abandoned by the government; Survival in a slum rarely means adhering to the law. Barely 10 percent of the commercial activity here is legal. Most of the workshops are constructed illegally on government land, power is routinely stolen and commercial licenses are rarely sought. There is just one lavatory for every 1,500 residents, not a single public hospital, and only a dozen municipal schools.Dharavi remains a land of recycling opportunities for many rural Indians. The average household in Dharavi now earns between 3,000 and 15,000 rupees a month... The new money through recycling has in effect, spawned a new slum gentry. Certain corners of Dharavi have even gone upmarket with bars, beauty parlours and clothing boutiques. A new estimate by economists of the output of the slum is as impressive as it seems improbable: £700m a year'.

The book Born to Run by Christopher McDougall is stimulating. At the heart of Born to Run lies a mysterious tribe of Mexican Indians—the Tarahumara—who live quietly in canyons and are reputed to be the best long-distance runners in the world. In 1993, one of them, aged 57, came first in a prestigious 100-mile race wearing a toga and sandals. This is as much a memoir as it is a story about running. Born to Run begins with a simple question: Why does my foot hurt? In search of an answer, Christopher McDougall embarks on a journey to locate a tribe of the world's greatest long-distance runners and discover their secrets, and in the process reveals that everything we thought we knew about running was wrong. The aim of this book is not to agree with every point he raises, either as a Harvard graduate or subsequently as an American author and journalist, but to observe the questions raised. To quote him: 'That was the real secret of the Tarahumara: they had never forgotten what it felt like to love running. They remembered that running was mankind's first fine art, our original act of inspired creation'.

'Every morning in Africa, a gazelle wakes up, it knows it must outrun the fastest lion or it will be killed. Every morning in Africa, a lion wakes up. It knows it must run faster than the slowest gazelle, or it will starve. It does not matter whether you're the lion or a gazelle-when the sun comes up, you'd better be running.[2] 'You do not stop running because you get old; you get old because you stop running... Isolated by the most savage terrain in North America, the reclusive Tarahumara Indians of Mexico's deadly Copper Canyons are custodians of a lost art. For centuries they have practised techniques that allow them to run hundreds of miles without rest and chase down anything from a deer to an Olympic marathoner while enjoying every mile of the journey. Their superhuman talent is matched by uncanny health and serenity, leaving the Tarahumara immune to the diseases and strife that plague modern existence'. [3]

Born to Run is a 2016 Indian Hindi-language biographical sports film directed by Soumendra Padhi. It is based on the life of Budhia Awooga Singh, who is from my district of Khordha, Odisha, India, was born in 2002 and is a distance runner by instinct. 'His father had died at an early age. As a consequence of their poverty, his mother, Sukanti Das, sold him at the age of two to a vendor for Rs 850. Biranchi Das, a local judo coach, and the president of the Salia Sahi Slum-dwellers Association, repurchased Budhia at his mother's request and the child came to live with him and other orphans at a local judo hall. One day, Das caught him being a "saucy lad". He punished him by making him run, but then forgot about him; he returned after five hours and Budhia was still running. After a medical check-up, his heart was found to be normal even after running for several hours. He then began to train him to run marathons. He ran from Puri to Bhubaneswar at the age of five covering 65 kilometres (40 miles) in seven hours and two minutes and was listed as the world's youngest marathon runner in the 2006 edition of the Limca Book of Records, an Indian records book. He was given a Rajiv Gandhi Award for excellence in 2006. Budhia was admitted to the SAI sports hostel in Bhubaneswar. However, he "felt like he was lodged in a jail". After staying in the hostel for almost nine years, Budhia is now at home, living with his mother, Sukanti Singh, and his sisters. His coach Biranchi Das instead of being applauded for spotting and nurturing a prodigious talent was accused of exploiting a child and was shot dead at B.J.B College on the evening of 13th April 2008 when he was sitting inside the judo centre with friends after a training session at the time of the attack'.[4]

Since feet were easily soiled, removing one's footwear was a sign of eliminating the dirt, thus indicating holiness in worship. Additionally, to shake the dust off one's feet meant complete rejection of a location. When sending out the 12 disciples, Jesus told them, 'And if anyone will not receive you or listen to your words, shake off the dust from your feet when you leave that house or town' (Matthew 10:14). 'But they shook off the dust from their feet against them and went to Iconium' (Acts 13:51). A verse frequently quoted in the New Testament is Psalm 110:1: 'Sit at my right hand until I make your enemies a footstool for your feet', which implied putting someone 'under your feet' (Romans 16:20; 1 Corinthians 15:25). Moreover, 'to fall at someone's feet' indicated humble submission, often when one had a request (1 Samuel 25:24; Luke 17:16).

The highest theological thought is revealed in the lowest human extremity. The barefoot is the essence of human innocence. The messenger becomes beautiful because of the value of the message being delivered (Isaiah 52:7). They are a symbol of the effort required in bringing the Good News (Gospel) to others. In earlier times, with unpaved roads, feet were easily sullied and had to be washed often. I have witnessed my father washing his feet when he returned home every day. From earliest times, hosts offered to wash their guests' feet (Genesis 18:4), a task usually performed by the lowliest servant (John 13:3-14). High honour was paid by anointing another's feet (Deuteronomy 33:24; Luke 7:46; John 12:3). Origen suggested that we interpret Scripture allegorically when plain sense is problematic. One might allegorize the Mountain, the Golden Calf, and Moses' shining face, but the one element of the narrative impossible to allegorize or demythologize is the perfect bareness of Moses' feet. John Calvin provides the correct interpretation: 'If any prefer the deeper meaning (anagoge) that God cannot be heard until we have put off our earthly thoughts, I object not to it; only let the natural sense stand first, that Moses was commanded to put off his shoes, as a preparation to listen with greater reverence to God'.

***

Why O God?

'Eloi, Eloi, lama sabachthani? My God, my God, why have you forsaken me?'
(Mark 15:34)

One of life's most difficult questions is 'Why O God?' Tragedies do occur. Young people die, loving people suffer from crippling diseases, neighbours and relatives live with mentally-ill children for years, natural calamities and pandemics destroy millions of lives. Pain is the price we pay for being alive. Dead cells cannot feel pain. In the 23rd Psalm, which is perhaps the most cherished Psalm in the Bible, the Psalmist does not pretend that life is easy but rather offers a guide to living in the world with faith and courage – 'The Lord is my shepherd'. So what do we do with our pain and suffering?

Rabbi Harold Kushner in his book When Bad Things Happen to Good People narrates what God can mean to a person who has been hurt by life – by death, illness, rejection, or disappointment. Where does one turn for strength and hope? When his three-year-old son was diagnosed with a degenerative disease that meant the boy would only live until his early teens, he had to ask the difficult question: Why God? He writes,[5] 'We discovered that the local paediatrician was doing research in problems of children's growth, and we introduced him to Aron. Two months later, the day our daughter was born - he visited my wife in the hospital, and told us that our son's condition was called Progeria, i.e. 'rapid ageing'. He would never grow much beyond three feet in height and would look like a little old man while he was still a child and would die in his early teens'.

Elie Wiesel was born in Sighet, Transylvania in 1928. He was 15 years old when the Nazis sent him and his family to Auschwitz. He and his two older sisters were the only members of his family who survived. His father died before the camp was liberated in April 1945. When the war ended, Elie studied in Paris and became a journalist. 'Wiesel had written a lengthy manuscript in Yiddish, Un di Velt Hot Geshvign (And the World Kept Silent); published in Argentina but that had attracted little notice. In an interview, (François) Mauriac spoke of his admiration for the Jewish people and spoke at length about Jesus, the Jew from Nazareth. Wiesel regarded that interview as an "impassioned, fascinating monologue on a single theme: the son of man and the son of God, who, unable to save Israel, ended up saving mankind. Wiesel spoke in atypically harsh terms to Mauriac. While waiting for the elevator, he felt a hand on his arm. It was Mauriac, asking him to return. So, he did: "And suddenly the man I had just offended began to cry…wordlessly, never taking his eyes off me, he wept and wept." Mauriac wanted no apologies; to the contrary, he wanted to know why Wiesel hadn't written about his experiences in the

Holocaust. Encouraged by Mauriac, Wiesel brought the French version to Mauriac, who helped him find a publisher and contributed the foreword of the internationally acclaimed memoir Night:

"What did I say to him? Did I speak of that other Israeli, his brother, who may have resembled him—the Crucified, whose cross has conquered the world? Did I affirm that the stumbling block to his faith was the cornerstone of mine, and that the conformity between the Cross and the suffering of men was in my eyes key to that impenetrable mystery whereon the faith of his childhood had perished? The Jewish nation has been resurrected from among its thousands of dead. It is through them that it lives again. We do not know the worth of one single drop of blood, one single tear. All is grace. If the Eternal is the Eternal, the last word for each one of us belongs to Him. This is what I should have told this Jewish child. But I could only embrace him, weeping".[6]

Wiesel in the memoir wondered where God was when His people were being murdered. 'Behind me, I heard the same man asking: "For God's sake, where is God?" And from within me, I heard a voice answer: "Where He is? This is where – hanging here from these gallows...What are You, my God? I thought angrily. How do You compare to this stricken mass gathered to affirm to You their faith, their anger, their defiance? What does Your grandeur mean, Master of the Universe, in the face of all this cowardice, this decay, and this misery? Why do you go on troubling these poor people's wounded minds, their ailing bodies?'[7]

The Bible says 'And at the ninth hour, Jesus cried with a loud voice, "Eloi, Eloi, lama sabachthani?" which means, "My God, my God, why have you forsaken me?"' (Mark 15:34). These words are an Aramaic quotation from Psalm 22. The story refers to the crucifixion, but it resonates with us at some point in our journey of faith. Two of my granddaughters—Aavisha and Davinia—can relate to this cry of dereliction very personally as they lost the love and care of their mother in childhood.

Aavisha is a Hebrew name, meaning 'Gift from God'. Aavisha, or 'Tia' as she is lovingly called at home, is now 18 years old. Davinia, originating from a Hebrew name meaning 'Cherished' or 'Adored', is called 'Kyra'; she is now 12 years old but quite mature in her thinking. Aavisha and Davinia have a younger cousin—our third granddaughter—Aviella. Aviella, also of Hebrew origin, means 'my father is God'. We call her 'Nora' and she is now seven years old. 'A rose by any other name would smell as sweet' is a popular quotation from William Shakespeare's play 'Romeo and Juliet', in which Juliet seems to argue that it does not matter that Romeo is named 'Montague', and belongs to her family's rivals – the Montagues. Charles Wesley puts it differently: 'Jesus! The name that calms our fears, that bids our sorrows cease. It's music in the sinner's ear; is life, and health, and peace! What a beautiful name Jesus is!'

I do not know why our two sons—Bibhu and Ashis—decided to give Hebrew names to their daughters who were born at different times: 17th March 2003, 19th May 2009, and 25th May 2014. It was a revelation to us when they decided to give Hebrew names with such profound meanings. Children are usually named after other family members, to carry on legacies, or they are named after great heroes of the past. These names, however, carried with them an element of identity and intentionality. Naming in the ancient world was significantly different from the way we think about naming today. It was particularly this way in the Bible, and especially so with God. God was the first Person to give names and His naming carried significant weight in shaping identity. In a perfect world, God named a thing and it became what it was supposed to be.

Leonard Wallmark explains: 'In contemporary Western culture, a name rarely possesses significance beyond that of a highly sentimental, perhaps aesthetically conditioned response on the part of proud, doting parents to the intoxicating joy of a new arrival. Not so in the Bible. There a human name typically reflects character and mission anticipated in life, which may turn out for either good or ill. It may embody the spiritual vision of parents for their child's future. In other instances, it is prophetic of future outcomes or events. On the negative side, it may typify a life come to ruin.'[8]

God's names reveal His will for the thing named. In the Old Testament, God's act of naming is both creative and authoritative. We see this reality occurring at the beginning of the creation narratives. God called things into existence and gave them names. The created things functioned exactly as God called them to function: 'And God said, "Let there be light," and there was light. And God saw that the light was good. And God separated the light from the darkness. God called the light Day, and the darkness He called Night. And there was evening and there was morning, the first day' (Genesis 1:3-5). 'He called the dry land "Earth" and the waters gathered together "Seas"' (1:10). God named His created world and it became whatever He named it, perfectly. It was all 'very good' (1:31).

Throughout history, the act of 'naming' something has often been linked to the exertion of power over the thing named. This concept is found in almost all cultures. Naming is a sign of authority. The one doing the naming has authority over the thing that is named, and such a relationship is perfectly realized when God named a thing, 'And it was so' (1:29). God even bestows a version of this authority upon humans. Adam (the human) is tasked with naming all the creatures that God brings before him. The author of Genesis writes, 'And whatever the man (human) called every living creature, that was its name' (2:19b). Adam even named his wife, 'woman' (2:23).

One classic example in the Bible is Israel. Israel comprises Abraham's physical descendants while the New Testament depicts the Church as his spiritual heirs. God fulfilled His promise to make Abraham 'the father of many nations'. Abraham's faith in God's promises was 'credited to him as righteousness' (Genesis 15:6) and this holds true for anyone who places their faith in Jesus (Romans 4). Paul stresses that all believers—Jews and Gentiles—legitimately stand as Abraham's offspring (Romans 4:16). From the time of the monarchy in Israel's history, the temple is seen as the centre of worship. Here, God's presence dwells visibly and priests intercede before Him on behalf of the people with offerings and sacrifices. In the New Testament however, believers are the temple of the Holy Spirit (1 Corinthians 6:19) and the living God (1 Corinthians 3:16-17). They are its living stones and a holy, royal priesthood (1 Peter 2:5). Christ is building up believers into a spiritual house – a temple.

The stories of Aavisha and Davinia have not only been educative but also a theological milestone in our journey of faith. Aavisha, our eldest granddaughter, arrived on 17th March 2003 in the comfortable climate of Shillong, in Meghalaya. We were then in Darjeeling as I was consecrated as the Church of North India (CNI) Bishop of the Eastern Himalaya Diocese.

We visited Shillong before and after the birth of our first granddaughter, before and after our trip to the U.K. in 2003. A girl in our family was most welcome from both our perspective as well as our son's. To understand why, let me go back a few years.

My wife and I were married on 15th April 1975. Interestingly, I was ordained a CNI Presbyter in the Cuttack Diocese on 13th April 1975, was married on 15th April 1975, and subsequently transferred to Kondmal in Odisha on 1st May 1975. Perhaps it was naiveté or cultural conditioning, but I wished that our first child would be a boy whom we could name Bibhudutta. Bibhudutta is not a Hebrew name but a typical Odia name, meaning 'God-given'. My desire to have a son was twofold – to maintain the family identity as well as financially being able to afford to raise a son with a pastor's salary. Although, my wife always wished to have a daughter, that desire was never fulfilled as our second child was also a boy whom we named Ashis (called Babi at home) an Odia name, meaning 'blessing'. While Bibhudutta (called Bubu) was born on 8th August 1976 at Moorshead Memorial Mission Hospital, G. Udayagiri, Kandhamal, Odisha, Babi was born on 16th May 1981 in Oxford, UK. There is a twist in the story of the birth of our two boys. When Bubu was born, I was serving as the Chaplain of Moorshead Memorial Hospital, which was adjacent to our bungalow in G. Udayagiri. When my wife was admitted in the early hours of 8th August, the lady doctor told me, 'You can go to our home and spend the day with my husband as your presence is not needed at the Hospital'. However, in Oxford, when my wife conceived and we went to the GP, the doctor asked me if I would be available when the time came. On the day she was admitted into John Radcliff Hospital, Oxford, I stayed with her in the labour room until the baby was born. I remember that when our son was born, in her excitement, the gynaecologist told my wife that it was a baby girl, but, unable to control myself, I cried, 'How can that be? I see a boy there'.

We have three granddaughters in our family. In India, the abuse and atrocities against girl children and women are based on false assumptions. There is an underlying preference for sons because the cultural institutions in India, particularly those of patrilineality – inheritance through male descendants, and patrilocality – married couples living with or near the husband's parents, play a central role in perpetuating gender inequality and ideas about gender-appropriate behaviour. The law of inheritance has now been modified, giving equal rights to sons and daughters. The cultural concept of parental preference for a son springs from their importance as caregivers for parents in old age. The dowry system, involving cash or in-kind payment from the bride's family to the groom at the time of marriage, is another institution that disempowers women. It has resulted in dowry-related violence against women by their husbands and in-laws if the dowry is considered insufficient or as a means to demand more payment.

Our elder son married Natashia Deka Kharkongor, a Khasi girl. Meghalaya, a North Eastern state in India, is home to three tribes that practice kinship based on matriliny– the Khasi, Garo, and Jaintia communities. A matrilineal society is one wherein the lineage or ancestry of a society is traced through the mother; it is not to be confused with matriarchy. The youngest daughter of the family, the 'Ka Khadduh', inherits all ancestral property. After marriage, the husband lives in the mother-in-law's home and the children take the mother's surname. Although the entire state of Meghalaya follows a matrilineal system, most people tend to misuse the word 'matrilineal' and often times, mistake it for matriarchy. In the case of the Khasi community however, this is not true. The husband is still the head of the family and older men have a vital role to play in society. Even now, in the Meghalaya Legislative Assembly or village councils or panchayats, the representation of women in politics is minimal. As of 2013, in a Meghalaya Legislative Assembly of 60 members, there were only four women. In the male-centric 'Dorbar Shnong', which is the basic political arm of the tribes, women are not permitted to hold office. However, women feel that they are better financial managers than men and they enjoy economic freedom.

The marriage of our elder son was held in the Chapel of St. Paul's School, Darjeeling and the reception was at the Bishop's Lodge in Darjeeling on 26th May 2001. It was a simple ceremony but the support of the leaders and people from my diocese was overwhelming. The happy couple had two children. Their second daughter—Davinia—was born in Pune, Maharastra. I used to say, and still maintain, that the elder daughter is the photostat copy of her father while the second daughter, of her mother, not only in appearance, but also in character. They were a lovely family with two little darlings, living a simple life. I am proud to say that while our two boys had the best of both worlds in India and the UK, they inherited the quality of being content with whatever they had. To our pleasant surprise, both our two daughters-in-law also possessed and cherished this quality without it being imposed upon them after marriage. Life seemed to be blessed with love and care.

***

Caregiver's Cross[9]

The story *Caregiver's Cross* is penned by our elder son Bibhudutta when cancer shattered all our hopes and dreams. The story beautifully narrates the love, pain and memory of his wife Natashia and was part of a consultation on Health and Healing that I organized for the Centenary Year of Medical Education 1918-2018 at Christian Medical College (CMC) Vellore, and also published thereafter. The story is not only heart-breaking, but also a revelation, personally. Therefore, I resolved to include a portion of the same story here as a lesson on care and compassion.

'Welcome to my state of mind, as my world came crashing around me at 22:30 on the 25th of May 2013, two hours shy of our 12th wedding anniversary when my wife succumbed to lung cancer. Coming back to the place where the journey of the biggest loss and lesson of my life began may very well be a part of the process of gaining closure and healing. It set in motion a cascading motion of events that I could not have predicted in my wildest dreams. But those are a series of stories for another day and may not be suitable for all ears.

My wife, Natashia D. Kharkongor, was diagnosed with Stage 4 Adenocarcinoma (lung cancer) and as the diagnosis suggests, cancer had spread to multiple locations in the body with no practical recourse to combat the disease. My wife was a picture of health for all the years of our marriage, did not smoke, ate well and was tenacious in her fight against any minor illnesses the family members went through. It is a frightening scenario to encounter, an abyss of sorts, given the positive disposition of both the patient and the caregiver. Have no doubts, it is a death sentence without any appeal for mercy.

A Caregiver's Cross is both a blessing and a burden for the bearer. To be able to dedicate an entire portion of your life to the well-being of your loved one, amidst the finality of the situation, is the struggle of heroes but also the abode of spiritual peace. A cross, by virtue of the word, signifies a sacrifice and the weight of the world on one's shoulders. At the same time, in the context of Christ, it conveys a stronger message of love intertwined inextricably with liberation so beautifully, that it is hard to argue otherwise. We have all been called upon to make innumerable sacrifices and faced many losses but none can compare with the loss of a loved one who has been under one's care for a considerable period. This is the common narrative of many a mother, father, sister, brother, husband, wife, daughter and son, and the conflicting world of choices and, while convincing oneself that it was carried out with a clean conscience.

With the passage of time, the sequence of events gets a little foggy but the stark reality is that my wife and I landed in CMC Vellore with no idea of the world that was about to unfold in front of our eyes. Within a span of 2 weeks, our world went spiralling from that of a twisted nerve in the shoulder to full-blown lung cancer. I recall very vividly the restless pacing up and down the corridors of the 4th floor of the 'A' Block hoping for the best and preparing for the worst. We had left our daughters back in Shillong, Meghalaya with their grandparents and extended family. This was going to be the first of many sojourns back and forth in the bleak hope of a miracle.

As a caregiver, I was faced with the challenge of instilling hope and confidence while battling my own apprehensions. There have been many times that I have gazed out at the twin hillocks and imagined the outline of a cross as the sign of delivery from this ongoing struggle. I have paced the passageways of the A-Block (a FitBit might have been a great help at that time) fervently talking with God and looking back on my life to identify the decisions I could have made to avoid this prevailing predicament. The self-flagellation combined with the passionate requests for swapping places with my wife because I knew in my heart and head, that she would have made a much better single parent than I, in raising our two beautiful daughters.

The rude interruptions in my conversations with God would jolt me back to the physical world and there would be a need for my services to turn the lever to raise the bed, call the nurse, check the drip, listen attentively to the doctor as he came on his rounds, etc.

The fire to fight back was extinguished in the eyes of most of the visitors and that in itself can be quite a downer. Contrast this to the environment in Shillong and Vellore and one will notice the upbeat approach to tackling the beast that is cancer. There are prayer meetings, regular visitors, words of encouragement, and stories of life-changing experiences that provide food for the soul. These nuggets of spiritual upliftment work wonder for the patient as well as the caregiver. It must be understood that the patient and the caregiver are almost inseparable and share a bond that familiarizes them with each other to the extent of becoming predictable. They depend on each other for physical, emotional and spiritual sustenance.

Religion is irrelevant but faith is. The chapel itself is located in the heart of the building and is the place where my wife and I would visit to regain our strength for the coming week. The hymns and the contributions from the various departments would satiate our emotional well-being even though uncertainty prevailed. This chapel and the chaplains provided a means of selfless service for the masses and personal relief for all the weary souls. It was across religious phenomena, and you got a sense that this was a family of caregivers, each playing their roles in earnest. The pastors wouldn't confine themselves to the chapel but would drop in regularly in the wards to offer a prayer or two. A caregiver's cross weighs heavily on the shoulders of the bearer at the end of the journey and it is a burden that raises a million questions of what if's and but's. My wife had fought such a weary battle throughout that I truly believe that she fought just to stay alive because we wanted her to. She would be embattled with thoughts concerning the well-being of her daughters. I think that somewhere in the back of her mind, she didn't harbour much hope in my parenting skills. And being very honest, I would have had to agree with her… at the time. On the evening of her passing away, I had gone to the local market to purchase a few clothes as my current lot was worn out. It was one of my very rare days off from hospital duty. During my shopping visits, I received a call from a very close friend of mine who had visited Natashia that afternoon and suggested that I give my wife permission to move on. It was a bitter pill to swallow but the pain and her unresponsive nature must have been unbearable for her as much as for her loved ones. She was fighting for each breath and doing so every day. I might have laughed off the idea at the time but the idea played on and on in my mind, causing a sense of uneasiness and a clash of priorities. Unless God himself performed a miracle that night, I might have been tempted to stave off the notion of letting her go. But it is no wonder that God didn't rise up to the challenge of saving my wife that night. At 22:00 hrs, as we prayed over her, I silently and reluctantly released her from her earthly obligations and submitted her to the life beyond. It was within 30 mins that she breathed her last after a protracted battle to stay alive amidst the pipes being thrust down her throat and drops of blood that were emerging from the suction pipe. What if I hadn't taken the decision to let her go and/or I hadn't allowed the nurse to insert the pipe? The caregiver is always struggling with the ramifications of his decisions which can take a lifetime to resolve'.

Natashia left us on 25th May 2013 after battling for nearly two years. In 2019, I decided to attend the birthday of Kyra, which falls on 19th May. The memory was very fresh as it happened to be a Sunday. As a family, we went to the CNI Cathedral in Shillong that morning, where I was privileged to preach and partake in communion. The former CNI moderator Most Rev Purely Lyngdoh celebrated Kyra and she was blessed with the congregation's prayer. After the service, we visited the cemetery with her other grandfather, Mr Deka Kharkongor. I understand that my son and his two daughters visit the cemetery every Sunday. My son wrote in his blog:

'We stood there, as we do every Sunday without fail, in silence and stillness. But this was no ordinary Sunday as it is your 45th birthday this year. The irony is that it falls a day after you gave me a replica of yourself in the form of Kyra... Her birthday followed by yours... You planned it out to the tiniest of details. The three of us wondered, while standing and emotions welling up inside, what life would have been like if you were still with us physically... We can only wonder! But we know for sure that it would have been a lot easier! Happy Birthday to you @ Natashia Kharkongor. Thank you for the years you gifted me with pure companionship and love that transcended every challenge that we faced. Thank you for these two wonderful and almost too good to be true daughters that are by far inspiring me more than the other way round. You prepared the foundation so that I wouldn't have to struggle... Kyra never fails to place two flowers, one either side of the cross'.

Children grow and leave their parents to start their families and career. Typically, conversation revolves around what will happen when children fly the nest and settle down in the cities of their dreams. 'It was Kyra, without hesitation, who promptly stated that she would take the entire plot that you occupied with her wherever she went so that she would never miss a Sunday visit... That's the biggest and most heartfelt gift you've given me in the form of Tia and Kyra... More of you to me... Love you forever ...'My son said that while celebrating 'A Decade of the Dancing Princess Davinia (Kyra)'. Sometimes the unexpected moments turn out to be the best treasures you can cherish... Great health and no relapse. On her birthday, when she turned 10, Kyra surprised us with autographed copies of a booklet[10] she had authored bearing the name 'W.H.E.L. Have an Adventure'. She writes 'Meet Willow, Hania the Dragon, Evelyn and Lavender (W.H.E.L.). They are four friends who ran away to a forest and live there; they meet many friends and have some enemies. But their friendship is very strong and they care for each other dearly. And that is why it makes them stronger day by day. So come join W.H.E.L in their adventures, hard times, fun times and sad times'.

***

Exhilaration

Aviella's story is different from the earlier one. We lovingly called our youngest granddaughter 'Nora'. My son Ashis, (Babi) and his wife Agnes (Rosy) called us one day from South Africa to inform us that they were returning to Allahabad—now called Prayagraj—to stay with us for a while. The timing was apt. We were still coping with the fact that our two granddaughters had been deprived of their mother and that our eldest son had become a single parent. Therefore, their homecoming was welcome news for us. Eventually, I suggested that Rosy do a Bachelor in Education (B Ed) programme, which she did. It seemed to be a perfect plan - she would complete her B Ed in one year and then be able to return to the UK. However, God had other plans. One fine morning we were given the news that we were to become grandparents. The story began with the arrival of our third granddaughter Nora - the cutie. They had come to stay for one year but with the arrival of the baby, my wife insisted that the family stay until she was one year old. Our lonely house in the Sam Higginbottom University of Agriculture, Technology and Sciences (SHUATS) campus suddenly became a hive of activity, particularly for the grandmother.

Rosy came into our family via a different route than the one taken by Natashia. With Natashia, one day, our son told us that he wanted to marry a girl whom he had met in Mumbai where both of them were doing post-graduate studies. That was how our son introduced Natashia to us. Eventually we met her parents and their marriage became a part of their history. While we were all expecting Ashis to do the same, perhaps find a girl either in the USA or UK, it was not to be. When the time came, he gave us the task of finding a girl for him. Easier said than done; the task was herculean. Proposal after proposal came pouring in and we became a panel of two whose job was to screen each one. Our son had told us that he would choose from the final two options that we would give him. Eventually, the four of us—my wife, our two boys, and I—visited two families in Cuttack. Traditionally, we are supposed to convey our proposal a few days later. However, on our return trip, I overheard my sons and wife talking, 'Why delay the process, he has already made a choice out of the two'. We welcomed our daughter-in-law to our home in Khordha. The marriage was held on 27th December 2011 at the Oriya Baptist Church in Cuttack and the wedding reception in Stewart School, Bhubaneswar on 28th December 2011. It was a perfect choice and by God's grace she has been a blessing to all of us.

Nora's birth and her stay with us for one year was truly memorable for us as grandparents. Some moments of joy in our day-to-day life are remarkable, they are 'special' extraordinary experiences where we are lifted out of our daily routines and everyday concerns. I remember the day we experienced this joy. My wife and I with our son, his mother-in-law, Smruti

Smith (Mani) who had come from Cuttack to stay with us for the delivery, and her son Akash, whose stay with us in Allahabad was quite amusing, and sometimes, hilarious; hilarious in the sense of enjoying his choice of foods as being the youngest in their family with two sisters. Obviously, he has now grown to face the reality of the world as he has started working in Kolkata. We were eagerly waiting in the clinic in Allahabad for the arrival of the baby, imbued with anxiety as well as joyous expectation. When the doctor came out of the operation theatre and said 'a baby girl' our smiles were radiant. In hindsight, it was an unforgettable experience because all of us had a sense that something special had occurred. What I call 'joy' was almost an epiphany, and was, in effect, a quiet realisation. These moments of joy attend experiences of disembodiment that seem to have a crystallising power that enables one to perceive a more enduring reality.

These realisations of joy are embedded in quiet afternoons during Christmas break when my wife and I see our three beautiful grandchildren truly enjoying each other's company when they are home. We are recipients of a deep sense that 'all is right with the world'– or, more specifically, all is right with our world in such moments, and that hopes and dreams are being realised. I can recall experiencing joy while enjoying a meal with my wife at home, something we have done as a daily ritual during forty-six years of married life with exceptions while pursuing higher studies and visiting our parents and relatives in Odisha: breakfast between 8-8.30 in the morning, lunch between 12.30-1.00 p.m. and dinner 7.30-8.00 p.m. I also recall with a sense of joy, wonder and fulfilment when I think about the lady who chose to marry me and has stayed by my side for the last forty-six years despite knowing that the beginning of married life was to be on a meagre pastor's salary of just Rs 300/- per month. There is a sense of fulfilment when we have a conversation with Nora—now seven years old—via Skype on Sunday evenings. Recently, when I asked her to show us some books that she reads, she immediately ran and picked up her Bible, a Children's Study Bible, and a prayer book. We were delighted to know that our family values are cherished and maintained even today and we pray that she will grow in the love and nurture of her parents and more importantly, in the wisdom and fear of God.

We have experienced a kind of grateful astonishment, a sense of being on the receiving end of nothing short of grace. Joy is relational. In a relational context, joy emerges from a sense of resting on someone who gives; in such a context, having received—being a recipient—is not a debt but rather the basis for joy. It presupposes recognition of one's finitude, one's 'indebtedness'. In an interview[11] with Religion News Service, theologian Miroslav Volf, the principal investigator of Yale Divinity School's project on the Theology of Joy and the Good Life, defines it as[12] 'A theology of joy is a kind of theological endeavour that tries to determine the nature and the place of joy in human life. We study it from the perspective of the Christian account of the good life and the place joy has in that account'. Then he explains that 'happiness generally is today understood as a kind of pleasurable feeling of whatever sort that I might get. Joy has something specific about it. We rejoice when we are united with the object of our love, with things that we love. Joy is elicited when something good comes our way and, for the most part, when that good is unbidden, when it comes in a kind of gratuitous way'.

He refers to a biblical story. 'One of the signature stories of the Bible is the story of the prodigal son. When the prodigal returns, there is great rejoicing. It's a central story in the Gospel of Luke. At the beginning of the Gospel of Luke, you have an angel declaring that the coming of the saviour is the one that brings joy. At the very end of the Gospel of Luke, when Jesus Christ is resurrected and ascended to heaven, the disciples leave him and, though they were despondent when he died on the cross, they go with joy to return back to Jerusalem. The whole Gospel of Luke, you can say, is framed by the theme of joy'. There are people as joyous persons, that is to say, people who are capable in various situations of discovering the good over which they can delight and over which they can rejoice. So, in that sense, joyfulness is a disposition and joy is kind of a virtue. The interesting part of the parable of the Prodigal Son is that he who leaves his father's house also returns forgiven, but the brother who stayed at home is the most bitter of all. Not only did he never celebrate with his friends, but also he feels no joy when his lost brother returns. On the contrary, he is angry.

***

A Story Remembered

A story, affectionately remembered and written by our granddaughter Aavisha is about what it means to have a pet. My wife is a lover of animals both in our home and even those on the street. She always reminds me of their faithfulness in contrast to the ingratitude of human beings. Our granddaughters have watched how she takes care of them. For most of us so-called dog lovers, it is an inexplicable bond that begins the moment those puppy eyes set their gaze upon us. They step into our lives – fluffy and bumbling. Their soft canines nibbling away our daily burdens; ears perked up to catch the first letter of their name, which we so lovingly distort and then drop. In no time, they rightly claim the house we live in as their home.

'The 14th of February 2004 was and is always going to remain a memorable day for our grandparents. We were told that our family pet called Snowy had run away from home, never to return. Subsequently, a friend of my grandparents, Mr N R Pradhan from Kalimpong sent two lovely German Spitz puppies. One was sick and needed immediate medical attention from the local veterinarian. After an ordeal of observation for forty-eight hours, the happy, memorable journey began with Snoopy and Sandy. We, the grandchildren, have been introduced to the two new members of the family at different stages in our lives. Although we were not around always, we were entertained and enthused by their presence during the holidays when we would visit our grandparents.

They travelled with my grandparents in the flight from Siliguri to Nagpur in 2005. The family grew to be 13 in the course of time, and ten of them were given for adoption to different families after careful scrutiny. Three of them stayed with their parents making a family of five pets at home. They travelled again by road from Nagpur to Khordha in Odisha in 2010. One of them passed away, but a physically challenged pup adopted from the roadside, took her place. Five pets travelled again by road from Khordha to Allahabad in two cars in 2013 passing through the states of Odisha, Bengal, Bihar and UP.

Snoopy was the head of the family and was ferocious, territorial, possessive, ill-tempered, wary and scary in his youth. No one other than Tatama (grandmother) dared pet him. You could say that Snoopy was a son to Tatama, often referred to as 'dil ka tukda' (piece of the heart). Out of the three pups left with them, Chunama and Jeeta left the world on 27th November 2011 and 6th June 2013 respectively. An unfortunate accident occurred on 8th March 2015, International Women's Day, when Sandy, mother of 13 and Snoopy's life partner, was attacked by our neighbour's German Shepherd in Prayagraj after managing to jump over the fence. She succumbed to her wounds on the 9th of March 2015. It was distressing and difficult to come to terms with it at that time. Sandy and Snoopy have been a part of our lives. They were a great source of comfort to Tatama (grandmother), when she was alone. All of us remember how fierce he was, but he mellowed down as the years passed, eventually allowing us, the grandchildren, to pet him freely, although, he scratched me when I first tried. He was as soft as a cotton ball. His fur was a stark contrast to his growl. Looking at him often reminded us of royalty. He also looked like a wolf, which probably made me wish, more than once, to ride him.

As the head of the house, he often took strolls, patrolling the area to check if everything was all right and in place. This routine continued even as he got older. With the arrival and adoption of a new pup, Snowy II, he had to resume the role of a parent and bear all the tantrums all over again. Snowy II's favourite hobby was to irritate Snoopy, often leading to nasty snarls. Snoopy and his daughter Joy bore the emptiness they felt after Sandy's death, together. Snoopy was the darling and a spoiled gentleman who was part of our life in a special way. He was the prince of our home and our hearts. He would not leave the bedroom if either of us were in bed and the first one to respond when either of us entered the house. We were fortunate to have good vets both in Nagpur and in Prayagraj who took thorough care of the pets.

Snoopy did not suffer much and left the world on 15th January 2020 without an alarm and without any expectations. He slipped away into the night knowing full well that he was surrounded by the ones who loved him the most. He was the angel of hope and companionship in our family. He spent 16 years as part of the family, sprawling in front of the fireplace and eating bones from Uncle Babi's hand. He took kindly to aunty Rosy and patiently bore Nora's bullying. We have all had our moments with this strong and cute member of our family, and he is missed dearly. The last one of Snoopy's family was Joy, who was 13 years old. On Tuesday 13th October 2020, the youngest and only survivor of Snoopy and Sandy's dynasty, passed away at 5.15 a.m. A chapter of love and care given to me by my Tatama for the last 16 years came to a close. They were not only loving and sensitive but understood feelings and emotions. I wish they could teach us in a language that humans can understand, the virtue of being faithful and grateful!

The story of Tatama's love and care is not confined to her pets alone. It embraced the ones on the street as well. One of their neighbour's German Shepherd called Tiger, was old, lonely, and literally on his last legs when he walked out of his 'home' into Tatama's home. The handsomeness of the once stately German Shepherd was now visible only in his bleary eyes. If you are wondering why this house opened its doors to a dying pet, the answer perhaps lies in the following months. Tiger's initial cries of pain or longing began to diminish as the lady of the house started pouring her love on him, despite having three other pets to look after. Thus began a daily routine of cleaning, feeding, and comforting. Chronic infection, age, and low immunity made Tiger an easy target for maggots but Tatama was determined to not only cure his wounds but also revive his crushed spirit. There were days when she snatched him from the clutches of death simply by holding him close to her heart.

Tiger lived an extended life. He weathered a rough winter, which he could never have survived on his own, in his new house full of warmth. He strode out every day from his room to bask in the sunny grace of new life. He ate and slept like a baby, secure in the promise of unconditional love for the rest of his life. Eventually his journey came to an end. Tiger breathed his last on the evening of 27th May 2020. That morning he would not let the lady of the house move outside his line of vision even as she walked across to talk to her neighbour. From his room he hollered like an indulged family member.

***

Prayer & Patience

The story of prayer and patience is a mixture of experiences that describe a learning process in the midst of theologising. My wife, Manju, often reminds me of the virtue of prayer and patience. Sarcastically, she also quotes Jonathan Morris, 'Patience is a virtue, possess it if you can, seldom found in a woman, never found in a man'. I am sure she not only professes this virtue but also practices it every day especially in those moments when there is a difference of opinion between us. She does not revert with counter arguments but instead, will adopt a period of complete silence. She inherited this quality from her mother, Pritilova Sahu. It was amazing to observe this trait in my mother-in-law, who lost her husband, Udayananda Sahu, on 22nd October 1969, when my wife was only 17 years old. She had to look after her, as well as my youngest brother-in-law Chittaranjan Sahu whom we lovingly called 'Babu Bhai'. Despite being physically challenged from birth, he was gifted with a sharp memory. We watched and experienced the patience and care of my mother-in-law for her son for almost fifty years till she passed away on 26th November 1995. The mantle then fell on my eldest sister-in-law Snehalata Das, who had cared for both mother and younger brother for almost 20 years at the cost of her privacy and comfort. Incredible are the stories of love, care, patience, and not the least, prayer. My brother-in-law passed away on 10th October 1999.

My father suffered from dementia, which was very difficult to watch. Every afternoon, when it was time for his regular house visits for prayer, he would don his white dhoti and kurta as he had been doing for many years. My mother became a caregiver but after my father's demise, she suffered from breast cancer. By the time we discovered this, the cancer had advanced to the fourth stage. My younger brother Dillip (Tunu) and his wife Sarita (Jhumpu), who lived with our parents, deserve the credit for caring for our parents as we—the four brothers—were away from home. My father passed away on 3rdJanuary 1998 and my mother on 9th June 2005.

Prayers, and the quality of patience, are embodied in the lives of many around the world, a phenomenon that is both inspiring and educative. Those stories are multi-faceted and sometimes do not emerge into the limelight since our world defines and perceives success from a single perspective alone. One such story is *Arthur's Call*, a profoundly moving theological memoir on parenting, love, and disability by Frances Young, the former Edward Cadbury Professor of Theology at Birmingham University, UK.[13] *Arthur's Call* is a brilliant theological and pastoral memoir that is excellently reviewed by Krish Kandiah.[14] The memoir conveys what it is like to live with a child with a severe learning disability. The story of Arthur begins with Young, having successfully defended her PhD thesis at Cambridge University, a few weeks earlier, giving birth to Arthur, and then being told that he was 'brain-damaged, microcephalic' that is with an abnormally small head. That would mean he would likely be dependent on her for the rest of his life. The memoir explores the pain and challenge this meant for the mother, from 'the daily difficulties arising from feeding him, to the attachment Arthur made to a plastic hammer that he still uses 46 years later'. It is an emotional lesson on wrestling with God.

Krish Kandiah makes a good observation that 'when reflecting on the phenomenon of miraculous healing, Young explores the fact that such healings arising from the kind of genetic abnormalities that her son lives with are unheard of, and indeed she wonders whether supernatural healing would rob her son of his very identity, the essence of who he truly is. This is a fascinating point to ponder upon but Young's conclusion is that "extraordinary things may happen, but the definition of a miracle as a breaking of the laws of nature is surely theologically suspect".

She argues that modernity has left no room for God because it was humanistic and optimistic. Modernity thought suffering was eradicable if humanity could simply come up with the right formula. Post-modernity has not shifted our assumption that life was meant to be perfect and thus "the biggest problem for religious belief remains the issue of arbitrary suffering". Reflecting on this, Young observes that having read a great deal of Christian literature from earlier centuries, she found a "lack of concern with this problem". Despite the ubiquitous experience of suffering, Young concludes that in earlier centuries there was a greater understanding of the nature of creatureliness and our dependence on God. Young's argument is that it is "through tragedy that we discover what is most deeply life-giving, and the clue is provided by the Cross, along with lives like Arthur's". Young raises questions about the classical, evangelical and liberal approaches to the atonement: "the whole approach to atonement offers a moralistic and individualistic gospel. The question remains: what relevance has this to Arthur? Is he not so limited as to be innocent as a baby?"

In the chapter on Arthur's vocation, Young gives us a rich reflection on not just Arthur's call in the world but how all of us, no matter how broken, fallen or damaged, can be useful in God's purposes. Young writes of Arthur, "might not he and others like him have a vocation to enable the shift in values… away from individualism, dominance, competitiveness, to community, mutuality". Her conclusions are very profound, especially as someone who regularly brings children from vulnerable backgrounds, many of whom also have learning difficulties, to church...They point to a broken yet beautiful creation, the majestic power of the Cross, to include all people and how tragic circumstances somehow draws the best out of the community...Her honesty and humility, as she wrestled with the joys and challenges of caring for Arthur, alert us to pastoral, practical and theological concerns we may well have ignored'.

***

The Fascinating Story of Job[15]

The book of Job opens with the words: 'There was a man in the land of Uz whose name was Job, and that man was blameless and upright, one who feared God and turned away from evil. There were born to him seven sons and three daughters. He possessed 7,000 sheep, 3,000 camels, 500 yoke of oxen, and 500 female donkeys, and very many servants, so that this man was the greatest of all the people of the east'. Satan appears before God and God says to Satan, 'Did you notice my servant Job? That there is none like him on the earth, a blameless and upright man, who fears God and turns away from evil'. Satan answers God, 'of course Job is pious and obedient. Take away those blessings and see how long he remains Your obedient servant'. So God accepts Satan's challenge.

The book of Job is a fascinating narrative that has been read and reread. It is probably the greatest and most profound discussion ever written on the subject of good people suffering. Job is important in the story because he appears to be the pretext, someone like us who gives voice to the arguments we would make. Job does not claim to be perfect, but says that he has tried, more than most people, to live a good and decent life. The dialogue with his friends become heated, even angry. After three cycles of dialogue in which we alternatively witness Job voicing his complaints and the friends defending God, the story comes to a thunderous climax. God responds—He appears and speaks—and Job is almost blown away. 'Where were you when I laid the foundation of the earth?' (38:4) 'Have you an arm like God?' He demands (40:9). Then, in a rolling Magnificat, He names the things He has created: the earth, the sea, the night, the light, the constellations, the clouds, the winds, the dew, the rain, the snow, the hail, the frost, the thunder and lightning. He goes on to the animals: the goats, the asses, the hinds, the peacocks, the ostriches, the grasshoppers. In two celebrated passages, He describes with pride the monsters He created: the Behemoth (40:15-24) and the Leviathan (41), the Behemoth's counterpart in the sea. 'His breath kindles coals, and a flame comes forth from his mouth'. (41:21). God's description of the warhorse is even more exalting. Likewise, the eagle: 'On the rock he dwells and makes his home, on the rocky crag and stronghold. From there he spies out the prey; his eyes behold it from faraway. His young ones suck up blood' (39:28-30).

Job immediately apologises for challenging his maker: 'I despise myself, and repent in dust and ashes' (42:6). Now God addresses the three friends, 'My anger turns against you and against your two friends, for you have not spoken of me what is right, as my servant Job has' (42:8). God then rewards Job. The Book of Job seems to claim that all wrongs can be righted with material things. If everything was taken away from Job, the problem is settled by God's giving it all back, mostly twofold—14,000 sheep for his 7,000 et cetera. Job had seven sons and three daughters in place of ten dead children, and the new daughters were more beautiful than any other woman in the land.

HOW SUFFERING REFUTES RELIGIONS

Reading the story of Job from a perspective outside the community of believers is very interesting as well as alarming but can be an opportunity for theological engagement. Arun Shourie, an Indian economist, journalist, author and politician, in his book Does He Know A Mother's Heart: How Suffering Refutes Religions, brilliantly and insightfully takes his specific personal situation and transforms it into a discussion on the larger questions that humankind has been grappling with over the ages. In a devastating dissection of the scriptures, he says: 'Your neighbours have a son. He is now thirty-five years old. Going by his age you would think of him as a young man, and, on meeting his mother or father, would ask, almost out of habit, "And what does the young man do?" That expression, "Young man", doesn't sit well as he is but a child. He cannot walk. Indeed, he cannot stand. He cannot use his right arm. He can see only to his left. His hearing is sharp, as is his memory. But he speaks only syllable by syllable...The father shouts at him. He curses him: "You are the one who brought misery into our home...We knew no trouble till you came. Look at you—weak, dependent, drooling, good for nothing." Nor does the father stop at shouting at the child, at pouring abuse upon him, at cursing the child. He beats him. He thrashes him black and blue...As others in the family try to save the child from the father's rage, he leaps at them. Curses them, hits out at them. What would you think about that damned father? Wouldn't you report him to the police or some such authority that can lock him up? Wouldn't you try everything you can to remove the child from the reach of the father?'[16]

However, what if the father is The Father? That is, what if the 'father' in question is 'God'? Shourie asks a pertinent question. Why does our reaction and response change if the 'father' in question is 'God'? Does He Know A Mother's Heart? is centred on the deep bond of love in the Shourie family and the answers he seeks while caring for his son Aditya, who has cerebral palsy, and his wife Anita who is diagnosed with Alzheimer's after an accident in her 40s. Aditya's premature birth precipitates him being placed in an incubator that has insufficient oxygen, which causes cerebral palsy and other complications. Nevertheless, despite blow after blow, the child gushes with love and gratitude towards those around him.

He says that all suffering in India is blamed on bad karma, the sins of a past life. 'One immediate consequence of this is that God is let off the hook. Karma is "a convenient fiction", thus, not just in "explaining" what has happened to an individual but also in getting God off the hook', writes Shourie, borrowing the phrase from writer and philosopher Eliot Deutsch. Karma, inextricably linked to rebirth, is then nothing more than a clever intellectual invention. God, godmen, and religious scriptures are but mere props. 'One must realize that no cosmic purpose is served by our suffering or that of those dear to us, just as no cosmic purpose is served by our birth or death. This is because there is no cosmic purpose to begin with'. Having arrived at this realisation, Shourie believes you should accept your circumstances and find salvation by serving others. 'Even if our circumstances prevent us from serving those who are in pain, we can serve those who are serving them: all of us have the ability to be the servant of servants'.

Shourie asks: 'Does the Quran explain the matter?' Job appears in the Quran as Ayyub, where he is as virtuous as he is in the Bible. In fact, Allah is said to inflict suffering in accordance with one's capacity to endure. In 21:83, no reason is given as to why distress and suffering have fallen on Job. Yet, in 38:41, he cries out to Allah, 'The Evil One has afflicted me with distress and suffering'. Nevertheless, unlike the Old Testament, the Quran is clearer on why Allah decides to relieve Job's suffering. In 21:84, Allah says, 'So we listened to him'—that is, he alleviated Job's pain and tribulation in response to the prayer of a faithful devotee 'as a grace from ourselves and a thing of commemoration, for all who serve us'. Referring to the Old Testament, Shourie sarcastically remarks, 'Once Job surrenders, God restores his animals, riches, as well as his children. Job lives for 140 years. A Bollywood ending'.

FAITH SEEKING UNDERSTANDING

Elie Wiesel began lecturing about Job as early as 1946. He considered the Book of Job a great text and great torture. For many, Job epitomized the suffering of the Jews during the Second World War and their perceived response to it. 'As God played dice with his life, Job grieved and protested, but he did not take any action[17]. This interpretation anguished Wiesel. Wiesel, in his *Messengers of God: Biblical Portraits and Legends* (1976), argued that, contrary to the usual reading, Job did not submit when God told him that he must. You can tell, Wiesel says, because, in the text that we have, he submitted so fast. He was just pretending. The true ending, Wiesel preferred to believe, was lost. But later Wiesel settled on the idea that Job merely chose silence, not submission. Job, he wrote, had learned that he lived in a world that was cold and cynical—a world without true friends but one, nevertheless, in which God seeks to join man in his solitude. Wiesel has had many heirs, speaking not necessarily for the Jews but for other suffering people. With Job, the danger was that human beings could legitimately ask God why he ran the world the way he did. But objections to Job's capitulation came from many ideological quarters. The American rabbi Richard Rubenstein has said that we should think not just of Job, who was able to have his argument with God and be saved, but also of his barely mentioned children, slaughtered because of God's bet with Satan.

Harold Kushner suggests that the author of the book of Job takes the positions which neither Job nor his friends take. He believes in God's goodness and in Job's goodness. Our misfortunes are none of His doing and so we can turn to Him for help. Our question will not be Job's question "God, why are You doing this to me?" Rather "God, see what is happening to me. Can you help me?" We will turn to God, not to be judged or forgiven, not to be rewarded or punished, but to be strengthened and comforted'.[18]

The authors of the book Biblical Interpretation[19] succinctly state, 'It would be religiously foolish to sacrifice "the valley of the shadow of death" in Psalm 23, or "I know that my Redeemer lives" (Job 19:25) to the scruples of philologists. Philology is the study of language in written historical sources; it is a combination of literary criticism, history, and linguistics. The Jews and Christians both appeal to the Hebrew Bible but understand it somewhat differently. The Bible as the scripture of a community is important for a community's self-definition. It helps to preserve the community's identity by being constantly read and reread within a tradition of interpretation. The confusion arises when tradition is equated with the event of revelation or guidance of the Spirit in the present context. While in biblical interpretation a variety of methods is necessary, the interpreter has to transcend the boundary of only intellectual interest. If Christian theology has a foundation in scripture, the devotional and liturgical life of a believer is nourished by the Bible.

Robert Polzin in an interesting article[20] addresses 'A Structuralist to the Book of Job'. The framework of the story then is a work of genius. By means of its remarkable resources, it takes the reader on a journey, the beginning of which may be described as equilibrium without insight and whose conclusion is appropriately equilibrium within sight. The genius of this journey is that insight is conferred not by the avoidance of contradiction and inconsistency but precisely by the courageous integration of contradiction and resolution. In other words, the story is a paradigm. What is on the surface a diachronic linear treatment of a problem reveals itself as containing an underlying or latent synchronic structure'.

'Mark Larrimore[21] provides a panoramic history of this remarkable book, traversing centuries and traditions to examine how Job's trials and his challenge to God have been used and understood in diverse contexts, from commentary and liturgy to philosophy and art. Larrimore traces Job's obscure origins and his reception and use in Midrash, burial liturgies, and folklore, and by figures such as Gregory the Great, John Calvin, Immanuel Kant, William Blake, and Elie Wiesel. Is there such a thing as disinterested faith? Will people go on believing in God if they are not rewarded – indeed, if they are unjustly punished? And why should they be faithful to a God who allows the wicked to triumph and the innocent to suffer?'

'Behold, the fear of the Lord, that is wisdom and to turn away from evil is understanding' (Job 28:28). Cambridge theologian David Ford, who was my PhD thesis supervisor and guide, 'in a complex but rewarding way argues for a "wisdom" model of "doing" theology and living before God in the modern world. Wisdom has on the whole not had an easy time in discussion. The wisdom texts of Hebrew Scriptures address the practices of ordinary life more than the great events of history and they attend to those who suffer.

David Ford has sought to answer the question by defining theology in terms of wisdom.[22] The Book of Job is central to his project, and he treats Job 28 as a summary of the book's teaching on wisdom. Building on the work of Susannah Ticciati, Ford reads verses 1-11 as an allegory of the moral self (of

Job and the reader) who searches to embody integrity in life under God and who, in turn, is probed by God. He shifts attention from what is most often seen as the burden of the book – the problem of evil or unjust suffering, to its central concern of obedience, sanctification or transformation of self before God. He brings Barth's theological commentary in to engagement with a wide range of current critical work on Job, allowing the divergence between these approaches to stimulate critique and enrichment on both sides. The reading finds its focus in an emergent understanding of Job's self, which is at once biblical, psychological, philosophical, historical and theological. David Ford says that theologians should listen hard to cries of suffering, joy, bewilderment, and gratitude. Theology should operate in all five moods: indicative (affirming what we believe), imperative (calling to obedience), interrogative (struggling with hard questions), subjunctive (exploring possibilities, as Jesus' parables do so well), and optative (desiring in hope). Theologians have too long limited themselves to the indicative and the imperative. As an alternative to Barth's identification of God as "the One who loves in freedom", Ford speaks of the "God of blessing who loves in wisdom". He thinks that Barth focuses too much on knowledge and not enough on wisdom, too much on indicatives and imperatives, not enough on interrogatives, subjunctives, and optatives'.

Peter Ochs introduces David Ford's 'wisdom' as both superabundant (the object of desire) and discerning (the activity of reasoning, shaped by the Word). Wisdom is forged out of affliction Job 3:20–26, 'Why is light given to one in misery and life to the bitter in soul, who long for death but it does not come... Why is light given to one who cannot see the way, whom God has fenced in?' [Ford:] 'Job cries from out of the depths of the worst imaginable, the fulfilment of what he has dreaded most...What response can possibly be made to this comprehensive and intensive suffering?... [The] book of Job is about wise living before God in the face of extreme testing (90–91)'. The first words of Chapter 3 introduce the condition for a non-idolatrous theology of the cry, fully recognizing the cry as not just any cry, but a cry of Job ('from out of the depths of the worse imaginable'), of Jesus on the cross, and of the Shoah. The biblical word Shoah (שואה), meaning 'calamity' in Hebrew, is the standard Hebrew term for the 20th-century Holocaust.[23]

In a similar way, Michael Polanyi[24] set out on a quest 'to stabilize knowledge against scepticism' which was ironically produced by the program of comprehensive doubt employed by Descartes and his heirs. He was a Hungarian polymath, who made important theoretical contributions to physical chemistry, economics, and philosophy. He argues that positivism supplies a false account to knowing, which if taken seriously undermines our highest achievements as human beings. As a distinguished physical chemist and philosopher, Michael Polanyi, demonstrates that the scientist's personal participation in his knowledge, in both its discovery and its validation, is an indispensable part of science itself. 'Knowing' is an art, of which the skill of the knower, guided by his personal commitment and his passionate sense of increasing contact with reality, is a logically necessary part. In the biological and social sciences this becomes even more evident. The tendency to make knowledge impersonal in our culture has split fact from value, science from humanity. Polanyi wishes to substitute for the objective, impersonal ideal of scientific detachment an alternative ideal that gives attention to the personal involvement of the knower in all acts of understanding.

Polanyi did not speak of wisdom per se, but of 'skill' in a way that over laps remarkably with ancient Near Eastern conceptions of wisdom: by inhabiting a tradition of superior knowledge and by submitting to this tradition as an apprentice to a master, the knower integrates knowing into skilful performances which both arise from and continue to produce the tacit forms of knowledge 'we can know more than we can tell' which characterize that tradition. The framework of knowing thus becomes a part of the knower who inhabits the framework, integrating what Descartes had thought of as two realms—the objective and the subjective. Skill, furthermore, is not something that is reflected upon at a theoretical level, but something which is embodied and enacted.

Exploring Polanyi's thoughts, Bishop Lesslie Newbigin extended Polanyi's work into another realm by suggesting that it points to knowledge of reality which is 'only fully explicable by reference to a personal being'. That is, Polanyi's concern to 'reconnect human knowing with reality may be construed in theological terms in which a personal knower engages with a personal deity. He applies the question of 'Where is wisdom?' to contemporary efforts to speak about truth, beauty, and goodness in an age of epistemic scepticism'.[25]

The wisdom commended in the final verse of Job 28 is not just a kind of thought or emotion, but something which is embodied in action. This tenet is also foundational to the rabbinic midrash - a method of interpreting biblical stories, which is a form of wisdom-seeking concerned with how to put the text into play in human life. Jesus says 'wisdom is justified by her deeds' (Matthew 11:19) and 'wisdom is justified by her children' (Luke 7:35). The intimate connection is between knowing and doing. The rabbinic saying that 'when two sit and there are between them words of Torah, the Shechinah (הניכש) (divine presence) rests between them' reflects the experience as recorded in Matthew18:20 'where two or three are gathered in my name, there am I among them'. While Judaism and Christianity agree about the identity of God and share some of the same scriptures, they fundamentally disagree whether the decisive revelation of God is in the Torah or the Lord and Messiah Jesus who was crucified.

A human being cannot avoid the reality of suffering, evinced from the death or impending death of someone. Swiss-American psychiatrist, Elisabeth Kübler-Ross, in her 1969 book On Death and Dying, was inspired by her work with terminally-ill patients and introduced the proposition that human beings pass through five stages of grief: denial (and isolation), anger, bargaining, depression, and acceptance. This revelation grew out of Dr Kübler-Ross's famous interdisciplinary seminar on death, life and transition. She provides us with a better understanding of how imminent death affects the patient, the professionals who serve the patient, and the patient's family, bringing hope to all who are involved, and that death with dignity is what should be the mandate for the extinguishment of life. Before coming to terms with the possibility of their dying, or of having lost a loved one through death, the grieving process encompasses the above mentioned five stages – denial, anger, bargaining, depression and, finally, acceptance. She clarified that these were not chronological stages and that people may experience them concurrently or switch between them during the process of grieving.

On the eve of the failed attempt to assassinate Hitler that eventually led to his execution, Dietrich Bonhoeffer on 21st July 1944 wrote to his friend Eberhard Bethge: 'I thought I could acquire faith by trying to live a holy life…I discovered later, and I am still discovering right up to this moment, that it is only by living completely in the world that one learns to have faith. One must completely abandon any attempt to make something of oneself, whether to be a saint, or a converted sinner, or a churchman, a righteous man or an unrighteous one, a sick man or a healthy one. By this - worldliness, I mean living unreservedly in life's duties, problems, and successes and failures, experiences and perplexities. In so doing we throw ourselves completely into the arms of God, taking seriously, not our own sufferings, but those of God in the world - watching with Christ in Gethsemane'.[26]

The words of the authors of the same book Biblical Interpretation are worth quoting: 'some interpreters spread the word so that it yields fruit thirty, sixty or a hundred fold. Others keep it in the culture's intellectual banks, where at least it creates interest and at present interests are high. Yet others hawk it about for their own profit – a salutary warning to all who make a profession out of the Bible and its interpretation. Books about interpretation are no more a substitute for interpreting than recipes are a substitute for cooking but the final test is not whether they stimulate further methodological reflection: it is whether they encourage good cooking'.[27]

Endnotes

[1] https://www.theguardian.com/environment/2007/mar/04/india.recycling

[2] https://www.goodreads.com/quotes/292417-every-morning-in-africa-a-gazelle-wakes-up-it-knows

[3] McDougall, Christopher, Born to Run: A Hidden Tribe, Superathletes, and the Greatest Race the World Has Never Seen, Profile Books, 2010

[4] http://www.indiatimes.com/news/india/here-are-some-mind-boggling-facts-about-budhia-singh-the-world-s-youngest-marathon-runner-257082.html

[5] Kushner, Harold, S., When Bad Things Happen to Good People, Anchor Books, New York, 2004, p 4

[6] Boys, Mary C., When Elie Wiesel Met François Mauriac: learning from a historic Jewish-Catholic encounter, America, the Jesuit Review, 6 July 2016

[7] Wiesel, Elie, Night. New York: Hill & Wang, 2006: 65-66

[8] From Baker's Evangelical Dictionary of Biblical Theology

[9] Sahu, Bibhudutta, Caregiver's Cross, In: Conversation on Health and Healing, Eds: D.K. Sahu & Arul Dhas T, ISPCK, 2019, pp. 277-290

[10] Kharkongor, Davinia, W.H.E.L. Have an Adventure, 2019

[11] Interview by Adelle M. Banks, Religion News Service, 22 May 2018

[12] Volf Miroslav, et al, Joy and Human Flourishing: Essays on Theology, Culture, and the Good Life, Fortress Press, 2015

[13] Young, Frances. Arthur's Call: A Journey of Faith the Face of Severe Learning Disability, London, SPCK, 2014

[14] The book review by Krish Kandiah, 23 February 2016, was originally produced for Anvil Journal and the Journal is currently transitioning to a new partnership with CMS. During this phase, book reviews are being published by Fulcrum.

[15] Sahu, D.K., Interpreting the Interpreted: Story of Job, Allahabad Theological Journal, 2015

[16] Shourie, Arun, Does He know a mother's heart? How Suffering Refutes Religions, Harper Collins Publishers India, New Delhi, 2011, p 1

[17] Acocella, Joan, Misery: Is there justice in the book of Job? The New Yorker, 8 December 2013

[18] Ibid, p 50

[19] Morgan, Robert & Barton, John, Biblical Interpretation, OUP,1989, p 291

[20] Polzin, Robert, The Framework of the Book of Job, Interpretation, 28 no 2 April 1974, p 182-200

[21] Larrimore, Mark, The Book of Job: A Biography, 2013

[22] Ford, David, Christian Wisdom: Desiring God and Learning in Love, CUP, 2007

[23] Ochs, Peter, Christian Wisdom, David Ford, Cambridge: CUP, 2007, Reviews and Author Responses Focus on Scriptural Reasoning, p 134-146

[24] Polanyi, Michael, Personal Knowledge: Towards a Post-Critical Philosophy, Chicago: University of Chicago, 1958, p 245

[25] Newbigin, Lesslie, Proper Confidence: Faith, Doubt and Certainty in Christian Discipleship, Grand Rapids: Eerdmans,1975, p 47

[26] Bonhoeffer, Dietrich, Letters and Papers from Prison, SCM Press, London, 1971, p 369

[27] Morgan, Robert & Barton, John, Biblical Interpretation, OUP,1989, p 296.

■■■

3

Roots

Alexander Murray Palmer Haley was an American writer who is best known as the author of Roots: The Saga of an American Family. It tells the story of Kunta Kinte, an 18th century African, who is captured as an adolescent, sold into slavery in Africa, and transported to North America; it follows his life and the lives of his descendants in the United States, down to Haley himself.

The story is fascinating. 'When he was a boy in Henning, Tennessee, Alex Haley's grandmother used to tell him stories about their family – stories that went back to her grandparents, and their grandparents, down through the generations all the way to a man she called 'the African.' She said he had lived across the ocean near what he called the "Kamby Bolongo" and had been out in the forest one day chopping wood to make a drum when he was set upon by four men, beaten, chained and dragged aboard a slave ship bound for colonial America.'

Haley began to search for documentation that might authenticate the narrative. 'It took him ten years and half a million miles of travel across three continents to find the truth, but finally, in an astonishing feat of genealogical detective work, he discovered not only the name of 'the African"—Kunta Kinte—but the precise location of Juffure, the very village in Gambia, West Africa, from where he was abducted in 1767 at the age of sixteen and taken on the Lord Ligonier to Maryland and sold to a Virginia planter.' Kunta was sold in Annapolis to John Waller, from whom he tried to run away four times, and after the fourth attempt, a part of his right foot was cut off. Later, he was bought by his master's brother, William Waller, where, working for him, he became a gardener and eventually his master's buggy driver. He married Bell, a slave in 'the big house', and together they had a daughter, Kizzy. 'Kizzy's childhood as a slave is as happy as her parents can make it. She is close friends with John Waller's daughter Anne, and she rarely experiences cruelty. Yet her life changes when she forges a travelling pass for her beau Noah, a field hand; when he is caught and confesses, she is sold away from her family at the age of 16. Kizzy is bought by Tom Lea, a farmer and chicken fighter who rose from poor beginnings. He rapes and impregnates her, and she gives birth to George, who will later be known as Chicken George, who eventually becomes his master's cockfighting trainer'. When Tom Lea loses all his money in a cockfight, he sends Chicken George to Europe for several years to pay off the debt, and he sells most of the rest of the family to the Murrays.

'The Murrays were generally kind masters who treat the family well. When the Civil War ends, however, the Murray slaves decide that rather than sharecrop for their former masters, they will move from North Carolina to the town of Henning, Tennessee, which is looking for new settlers. They eventually become a prosperous family. Tom's daughter Cynthia marries Will Palmer, a successful lumber businessman, and their daughter Bertha is the first in the family to go to college. There she meets Simon Haley, who becomes a professor of agriculture. Their son is Alex Haley, the author of the book'. Alex relates his journey back to Africa to find his roots and to discover as much about his family as he can. Eventually, Alex goes to Juffure, the very village that Kunta came from 200 years before.

Reading the novel as well as watching the documentary, generated recollections of my own roots, including events and elements that are sometimes forgotten, and often unacknowledged by future generations. We, as children were told the story of our family originally being from a nondescript village called Tentuliapada in Bhusandpur in the then district of Puri in Odisha. We were told that our grandmother, Netramani Sahu with a little baby boy called 'Budhia'—Christian name Birendra Kumar Sahu—second son of Somanath Sahu, arrived in Khordha. The date and time of birth are a matter of oral history as there is no record of these facts. My grandmother used to say that Budhia was born during the harvest season. The benevolent Pastor of our church, Dayanidhi Sahu, gave her shelter and a 'one room' home for the family. She became a 'house helper' in the Christian sahi (street) of Khordha as a means of obtaining a livelihood, and was also a church bearer in our mother church—Khordha Baptist Church—which was established in 1878. She would clean the church and ring the church bell, a ritual she performed faithfully until the end of her life.

Our roots are very humble. My family comprised five brothers and two sisters, but the two sisters passed away prematurely at a tender age. I was the eldest. My brothers are Surendra Kumar Sahu (Sanu), Prasant Kumar Sahu (Manu), Dillip Kumar Sahu (Tunu), and Pradeep Kumar Sahu (Bulu). We all carry two names: one is the family name endorsed in our school certificates for official records and the other serves as a nickname by which we are known to our relatives. The five of us grew up together in the love and care of our parents in our family home, which was a thatched cottage: one room was for my parents, the other for us five brothers, and the third for a tailoring shop with an open courtyard and a kitchen. One cannot help but be amazed at how happy and content we were in those humble beginnings. 'In all of us, there is a hunger, narrow deep, to know our heritage...Without this enriching knowledge, there is a hollow yearning no matter what our attainments in life' - Alex Haley.

***

History Revisited

Dr Taradatt, IAS, Chief Editor wrote a well-researched article, which brought back many memories associated with my birthplace, school, college, and its importance within the larger context of the history of my home state of Odisha.[1] Khordha is one of the new districts carved out of the former Puri District on 1st April 1993. It was the first place to rise against the British soon after their occupation of Odisha. The name of the district was changed from Khurda to Khordha in 2000. It covers a geographical area of 2813 square kilometres, which comprises 1.80% of the state.

Khordha is now the district headquarters formerly known as Jajarsingh. The word Khurda is derived from two Odia words - 'Khura' and 'Dhara', meaning razor and edge, probably because the soldiers of Khurda were as sharp and dangerous as a razor's edge. History narrates that in years gone by, the area was densely populated by the Savaras, a tribal community still found in some pockets of the district. Khordha ascended to eminence and glory during the reign of Ramachandra Deva the first King of the Khordha Dynasty, who made Khordha the capital of his kingdom in the latter part of the 16th century. This was a strategic decision given its ideal location with Barunei Hill on one side and dense forest on the other. Despite repeated onslaughts from the Maratha and Muslim cavalry, Khordha managed to maintain the glory of its independence as a royal fort until 1803. Therefore, out of respect and reverence, the Royal Fort is called 'Khordhagada', the last independent fort, which remained free from the clutches of the East India Company for the longest period from 1757, the year of the Battle of Plassey, until 1803, when the East India Company established company rule in Bengal.[2]

Khordha, however, was only fully occupied by the East India Company in 1827. The delay was a consequence of fierce revolts by the Paikas of Khordha that greatly affected the Company's administration in this region. History witnessed the strength and bravery of the Paikas of Khordha during the Paika Rebellion of 1817 – 18 under the command of Bakshi Jagabandhu. Our High School in Khordha was named after this hero as the Bakshi Jagabandhu Bidyadhar High School (B J B High School), where we five brothers studied till class XI. The school stood directly in front of our home just across a playground. I remember how we would come home for lunch during the break, as it was barely a five-minute walk away. When we were young, school education spanned the period from class I till class XI, followed by another year known as Pre-University, after which three years were dedicated to either Pass or Honours undergraduate studies. In high school, we had to choose one optional subject to span the period between class IX to Class XI. Not knowing what would be the best for my eventual vocation in life, I opted for Mathematics like every other good student. We had to do one compulsory and one optional paper on this subject, and I passed my matriculation examination with a First Class!

British historians recorded the Odia resistance movement as the 'Paik Rebellion', which was, in fact, the first War of Independence in India. It originated on Khordha soil and spread to other parts of Odisha in 1817, well ahead of the historical Sepoy Mutiny of 1857. Walter Ewer recorded his views in his 1818 report, an excerpt of which reads: 'Now there is no need of assistance of Paiks at Khordha. It is dangerous to keep them in the British armed forces. Thus, they should be treated and dealt as common Ryots and land revenue and other taxes should be collected from them. They must be deprived of their former Jagir lands (rent-free lands given to the Paiks for their military service to the state)'.

'In 1804, the English soldiers seized the fort of Khordha for three weeks and razed it to the ground with cannon fire. They proclaimed Raja Mukund Dev-II a rebel, dethroned him, and made him a prisoner of war. Raja Mukund Dev-II submitted an appeal to the British authority, stating that as per the instruction of Jayee Rajguru, he had fought with them and he was in no way responsible for the battle. Considering the appeal, the British pardoned him and offered him the responsibility of managing the temple of Jagannath. He was also ordered to remain in Puri. Jayee Rajguru, being the kingpin of the Khordha Rebellion of 1804 was sentenced to death, and hung from a banyan tree at Baghitota in Medinipur. The gruesome murder of Jayee Rajguru by the Company authority caused much discontentment among the Paiks of Khordha, who thereafter under the leadership of Bakshi Jagabandhu Bidyadhar, rebelled against the Company'.[3]

Although the Indian National Congress (INC) was founded in 1885, it was only after the efforts of Utkalamani Gopabandhu Das that the INC entered and established itself in Odisha in a meaningful way. Gopabandhu Das and Jagabandhu Singh mobilised the people of Khordha and the students of Khordha High School played a significant role in the non-cooperation movement. On 21st January 1921, student leaders of Khordha High School such as Nrusingh Charan Samanta Singhar, Laxmidhar Pattanaik, Shyam Sundar Senapati and Balaram Patra, proceeded to the seacoast to manufacture contraband salt during the Civil Disobedience Movement. When the civil disobedience movement was resumed after the second Round Table Conference, Prananath Patnaik along with others was arrested for picketing before the foreign cloth shops in Jatni. Therefore, it is no coincidence that after completing schooling from B J B High School, we five brothers joined Khurda College, now called 'Prananath College' after its founder.

In college, I was advised to study Economics for an honours degree with Philosophy as a minor. The college—erstwhile Khurda College now Prananath Mahavidyalay—was about three kilometres away from home and was affiliated to Utkal University in Bhubaneswar. My dream of attending college came with a rider: my father opined that while he could provide my food and lodging, he could do no more as he had to pay for the educational expenses of my four younger brothers too. I would have to find my own resources to sustain myself. I received this news with a measure of aplomb because I had been awarded a post-matric scholarship, and additionally, I knew I would also be able to garner some funds by giving morning and evening tuitions daily. My income would not only cover my expenses but also my younger brother's, helping him complete his graduate studies. As it transpired, despite all the industrious labouring I had to undergo, the outcome was a happy one for all of us.

My final BA examinations in 1974 were conducted during a period of student unrest; it was bizarre in the way the other students brazenly went about copying answers from their textbooks. I stayed resolute in my values and was the only student in the college who desisted. Despite my fears that the others would surpass me, I fared brilliantly. Thirty-five years later, I received a phone call announcing that the college had decided to honour me as one of their distinguished alumni! This nomination in my favour was submitted by one of my former teachers who while testifying during an enquiry into the incidents of 1974, revealed that there was a lone Christian student who had not copied his answers during the final examinations that year. Incredible are the ways of God!

***

Home & Hospitality

The little boy (Budhia) grew up to become a master tailor after apprenticing for a couple of years with a famous tailor in the same town. Nobody ever thought that one day he would be able to buy a small piece of land adjacent to the Kolkata-Chennai National Highway, where he would build the thatched house that would become our home. As children, we often observed my father and his elder brother, Haribandhu Sahu, conversing under the large banyan tree in front of our home. Presumably, my father was urging him to come inside, but Haribandhu never opted to eat with us at our home because we were Christians.

One day, my father sent me to attend a marriage ceremony involving their family, in the village. I was welcomed warmly and treated to delicious snacks in the early evening, but I was careful not to overeat as dinnertime was approaching. What I did not realise was that the marriage feast is served only after the completion of the wedding ceremony, which to my shock, was to be conducted in the middle of the night! I nodded off to sleep on a mat on the verandah, but was woken at 2 a.m. to come and have dinner, which was served on the road in front of the house, where I had to sit cross-legged while the food was placed on a banana leaf! We once requested our father to take us to the village. It was a maiden visit as a family with my parents, my wife, and my younger brother and sister-in-law to our ancestral home in Bhusandpur. Our elder cousin brother Gopinath Sahu and his family welcomed and served us a banquet despite our having arrived without prior notice. Nevertheless, that is Indian hospitality.

We were close to the maternal side of our family. My maternal grandfather, Jibulen Behera was from a village called Bahilipada, from the Puri District of Odisha, but being a South Eastern Railway employee, he was based in Kharagpur, West Bengal his entire career. I was also born in Kharagpur, as my mother went to her parents' home for her first delivery. We used to visit Kharagpur during the summer vacations with our mother and thoroughly enjoyed the hospitality of our maternal grandmother, Paria Behera, who was from a village called Pipili, from Puri district, which is famous for filigree work. One of our uncles, Farendra Behara (Fana Mamun), was very gregarious; he would visit us often especially before Christmas, with gifts for all of us.

Recently, I was inspired to trace my family roots. One way of doing this was through the family surname - Sahu. Thankfully, our parents did not change our names to John, Peter, or Jacob as it is very important to retain one's identity. The other option of tracing my roots was through the various Sahu professions. There are two kinds of Sahus - the first are Gudia—Guda in Odia means molasses—and they are the traditional confectioners of Odisha, while the second are Teli—Tel in Odia means oil—and they are involved in the edible oil business of Odisha and are mostly referred to as Sahoo. Traditionally, Gudias prepared a variety of confectionery products from rice, cheese, sugar, etc. specially during festivals and on religious occasions. We remember my father telling us how our grandparents were confectioners in their small village.

Odia-speaking people express their ideas in, what may be called in Latin, the infinitive. They use appropriate verbs and nouns and twist the language according to the expression they wish to convey. This language is based on older grammatical development, even on classical Sanskrit and Indo-Aryan languages, which can be combined with the ancient Sanskrit that was spoken in Vedic times. In the rural pockets of the district, most of the houses were built of mud and timber with a thatched roof, just like ours, which my father built in 1956. Traditional houses were generally divided into three compartments: first a verandah, second a dandaghar or entry room, and third a bedroom. Most of the entry rooms in the village were to house domestic animals such as bullocks, sheep, goats, cows, etc. The family used the bedroom, while guests were received in the verandah. Most traditional houses had ceilings (attu) made of bamboo and mud.

We tried to locate our ancestral home through the family surname 'Sahu' and the Gudia (confectioner) profession in the village, using clues from the past to guide us, such as noting that some of the houses still had a small earthen chullah to cook in the front verandah. During a visit to Odisha in the summer of 2018, my elder son Bibhu, my younger brother Surendra, and I went on an expedition with my son as the driver that day.

However, the landscape of the entire area had changed drastically and we could not locate the place despite meticulously searching each street and exploring some probable homes. I made a second attempt after a while with my youngest brother Pradeep Sahu, but ended up in another village with no success. Later my brother Dillip, his wife Sarita, and I made a third attempt. We tried to locate our elusive ancestral abode through land records and by speaking with a few elderly people, but once again without success. In desperation, I entrusted the work to my brother Dillip who is a journalist. He made another visit with one of his friends from that area and collected some information, tried to coordinate matters, and visited the Tehsil Office, which is the land record office. Yet again, these efforts were to no avail. Still, he didn't give up and told me to make one last attempt, and if that failed, to close the chapter. Finally, the miracle occurred and we were able to identify my grandmother's ancestral home. We discovered that the eldest son of my father's older brother who was called Gopinath Sahu, was still alive and living there. What a joy it was for us to be able to trace our roots!

When we discovered the address of our ancestral home, I wanted to visit the family, but the COVID-19 lockdown delayed matters for about a year. My wish was eventually fulfilled on 14th April 2021, when my wife, our elder son, and I visited our ancestral home. We received a warm welcome and met the oldest survivor, Gopinath, his son, their cousins, and their wives with small children. Conversing with them gave us a glimpse of our family history. We were lovingly served an excellent vegetarian lunch inside the house where we sat cross-legged on a bed. Gopinath Sahu, who was 80 years old, suffered from a slipped disk and thus unable to walk. However, he used to receive a pension of INR 500 per month and about 30 kg rations of free rice per month. It was a privilege that we could meet him and he shared his story and feelings. He passed away on 27th March 2022. His eldest son, Ravi Narayan, lives with his family a little distance away from the home and runs a teashop. One son is studying in class XII while the other son, Kabiraj works in Himachal Pradesh, although his wife Mamata stays at home with their child and cares for her father-in-law. Gopinath's nephew Dhaneswar, his wife Sumitra and his mother also live in the original house. Dhaneswar supports his family by selling snacks, while commuting on his bicycle around the village. Dhaneswar with his wife, mother and sister-in-law were able to do a reciprocal visit to our home in Khordha in February 2022.

Home was where we learnt the meaning of hospitality, via heart and hearth, where mirth and merriment reigned as the focus of hospitality. Despite our limitations, I never saw anybody being turned away from home, even if they arrived uninvited at lunch or dinnertime. We were all married from the same home and celebrations were organised in the same small place. In contrast, nowadays we look for a place to rent for the reception to welcome our guests. I still remember when my marriage was arranged; we had very little money to spend. My father invited about 400 people since he was a pastor to most of the families in our town and nearby villages. I asked him how we would meet the expenses. As was normal, his response was that God would provide. We somehow managed to pay for the prior arrangements with our meagre savings, except the main reception. Once the reception was over, the first thing we needed to do the next morning was pay the butcher who had arrived exactly on time to collect his dues. So, we calculated the monetary gifts we had received from friends and relatives and found that the amount was exactly sufficient to pay him first! Who says that miracles do not happen. Eventually, four of us brothers except one were able to build our own homes, two of us near our ancestral home and the other two in the city of Bhubaneswar.

The story of our own house is an interesting tale. My father had emphatically told me never to buy mission land for building a home. Therefore, we bought a piece of land just adjacent to our parents' home, about 100 yards away. His dream was that I build a home for my family, but he wondered how I would do it given my meagre pastor's salary. However, my wife sold the ornaments she had received from her mother and with that money we were able to purchase a parcel of land. She declared that the priority was to establish our home first rather than adorning herself with jewellery, therefore this was a good investment. She also made the effort to regularly travel from Serampore to supervise the construction since only a tenuous labour contract had been formalised. My father too would visit, to oversee and administer the construction work that was taking place, being vigilant in ensuring each phase was going according to plan. Finally,

15 years later, our home was inaugurated during the Christmas vacation when every one of us was present. After the New Year celebrations, all my relatives left except for my wife, our children, and I. We were supposed to return to Serampore after a few days, but my father requested us to spend a few nights in our new home, so we acquiesced, much to our mutual joy and contentment.

Our new home soon became the focal point of a fateful convergence, a meeting of destinies. A couple of days later, there was a knock on our door in the middle of the night; it was my mother summoning us to come quickly because my father was 'restless'. We rushed to his bedside, and he asked to lay his head upon my lap. I held him gently, but heartbreakingly for too short a time. He breathed his last with his head still on my lap. This was early morning on Saturday, 3rd January 1998. My brothers had always proclaimed reassuringly that they lived close enough to attend to our father should anything untoward transpire, since I lived in Serampore. Yet, as fate would have it, it was I who was present with him in his final moments, who had to call my brothers with the news of our beloved father's demise.

***

Family

We come from a time and place when family prayers—either in the morning or evening—were the foundation of the Christian life followed by Sunday school and youth fellowship at church. An evening stroll down our Christian sahi (street) would feature the song that would be sung during our family prayer times. Every day, both in the morning and in the evening, a song would be sung, a scripture passage read, and our father would pray. Later, when father left for his pastoral family visits in the evening, our mother would be with us and we too learned how to pray. Today the Christian sahi has become a commercial retail street, while some people have sold their ancestral property to move to the city.

The most difficult lesson to learn was the Lord's Prayer, not as much to recite but to practice. Our only livelihood was the income from the tailoring shop where my father was the master tailor. In our town, he was known to be a good Christian tailor. However, the net of the two employees in the shop, left very little for household expenses, which had to be managed with great dexterity. In my 21 years of staying at home, we never knew what we would eat tomorrow. The rations had to be purchased daily. I remember my grandmother doing that; later the job was transferred to me. In all sincerity, I failed to understand my father's rationale for not buying our household provisions one day in advance so that we would not have to indulge in a daily scramble. Once, being curious, I summoned the courage to ask him about this; his reply, according to the precepts of his theology, was to read the Lord's Prayer properly, which categorically says, 'Give us today our daily bread'. If you pray, then why are you worried about tomorrow? He believed and practised that quite literally. Astonishingly, as far as I can recall, we never went a day without food!

He wanted to instil sterling values in me from when I was in school. In the process, he would take me with him to distribute tracts during festivals, where he would sell gospel portions. After I completed school, he chose to send me alone on these trips to engage with the crowds and respond accordingly to queries about Jesus. However, the difficult part was that he would only give me adequate money to cover travel expenses and one meal. As for the remainder of my financial needs, he expected me to sustain myself via earnings from the sale of the gospel portions, which were priced at a subsidized rate provided by the Bible Society of India. After my baptism on Sunday,14th April 1968, during my first year in college, he suggested that I visit some churches in Odisha and preach during the summer break. He sent postcards to seven churches in different parts of Odisha and without receiving any confirmation, he told me to go on my maiden trip as an 'itinerant preacher'. He paid the exact bus fare to the first stop of my journey and said God would provide the rest. This was a continual act of amazing faith that imparted a training of a different kind, one which I had never experienced during my seminary career. In fact, after the first stop, I received the travel fare for the next stop, and likewise, thenceforth. At every location, I availed the opportunity to preach in a church or before a community audience in a village in the evening shade. One of those places that I visited was G. Udayagiri. Never in my wildest dreams did I think that would be the first place I would be posted after my ordination – to work in Kandhamal in Odisha where I was accompanied by my wife and our journey began in 1975.

During my college days, in addition to preaching in our Khordha Baptist Church, my father would take me with him to visit the village churches where he ministered. We both would ride on one bicycle – I would pedal while he would sit comfortably as the passenger. He would dismount at a church and ask me to proceed to another. In the evening, we would return together. This was the practical training I received from my father prior to joining a seminary for formal theological education. In addition to this extended routine, he assigned me to clean and sweep the floor of our church every Saturday and ring the church bell if I was there on Sundays.

We, as human beings, live with hopes and dreams that we like to accomplish in life. However, sometimes, we may experience a situation that may be so far removed from our ideals that we may be unable to achieve our dreams. We might call those unfulfilled dreams. Going through hard times, we often ask the question why did my dream not come to pass? Robert Schuller writes, 'Someone once said, "Hope you live to see all your dreams fulfilled". I replied, "I hope not, because if I live and all my dreams are fulfilled, I am dead". It is unfulfilled dreams that keep you alive'.

***

Theological Studies

We had a local pastor who left the Baptist church to join the Pentecostal movement in the 1960s. It was an urban movement in Odisha where the Baptist Missionary Society (BMS) missionaries had begun their work. The scale, scope, and sweep of this mission was like a tidal wave that advanced with a definiteness of purpose. It also coincided with the church union movement in north India, which was predominantly a round table movement, not filtered to the grassroots level. The decision to join the CNI was taken at the Council level, the news being conveyed, without delay, to the people in our congregations. The CNI was formed on Sunday, 29th November 1970; this resulted in most of the Baptist churches who owed allegiance to the BMS, joining the union. Some, however, left the union to form another group, which has found expression in various forms up to the present.

The decision to undertake theological studies was not an easy one. My father was a close confidant of the local Pentecostal pastor, who believed that a good pastor did not need theological education, and doing so would result in a loss of faith. This was not uncommon advice in some circles. However, God heard my prayer and my father did not follow that advice. Still, the question remained about who would sponsor my studies. My godfather Rev Norman Outlaw from the BMS was our district missionary. Both he and his wife were a source of encouragement to me from my school days. He was the one who baptised me in a pond in my town. The baptism certificate was handwritten by him in the Odia language, which I still have with me. The pastor in my early school days had helped me purchase an Odia bible and the missionary gave me a Thompson Reference Bible as a gift after my baptism. I had to choose whether to go to an evangelical theological college such as the Union Biblical Seminary or Serampore. My first option was to go to UBS.

So, I went to meet the famous Odia evangelist, Rev Subodh Sahu, in his home. He was very kind and advised me to go to UBS. However, regarding sponsorship, he said he could only pay ten rupees per month for my personal expenses and beyond that I would have to pray to find some other source of financial sustenance. I was naturally a little disappointed, but did not lose hope. God's plans are marvellous and unique, and my faith in Him remained undiminished. One day, a message arrived from Bishop Jugal Kishore Mohanty of the Diocese of Cuttack, confirming that the Diocese would sponsor my studies in Serampore. He asked me to come and fill up the admission form, which I duly did while seated on the floor of his verandah. Unbelievably the sponsorship by the Diocese included my tuition fee, accommodation, hospitality, twice a year visits to my home, and not the least, ten rupees personal expense money per month from 1971-1974.

I recall the day when the Rector of the Theology Department at Serampore called me to his office to say that perhaps I would have to come back with my application a year later unless proof of my success in the B.A. Honours degree in Economics could be confirmed latest by 31st August 1971, the last day for registration with the Serampore Senate. At this juncture, no exam results had been released. I was anxious about my prospects as I knew that I was the only candidate in the 1971 batch at P N College, Khordha, who had not succumbed to the temptation of copying in the examinations, whereas the others, having no such scruples, might have fared better. I resolved to calm my nerves and go eat some dinner in the dining hall. Once again, with supernatural benevolence, providence graced me with glad tidings to ease my apprehensions: my friend, and senior, Amarendra Pradhan, who later became the CNI Bishop of the Diocese of Marathawada, charged into the dining hall with an open telegram in his hand, exclaiming with joy that I had passed my exams with Second Class Honours in Economics! My exultation matched his and, dinner forgotten, I raced along to the home of the Rector with this news of my academic success. He too was excited and congratulated me most heartily.

***

Foundation of Ministry

The first year of my ministry (1974-75) was served directly under Bishop Jugal Kishore Mohanty of the Diocese of Cuttack, and my work entailed preaching in the local city church, visiting four village churches (Minchinpatna, Bahilipada, Ashryapur & Banamalipur) within the district, and working in his office. The first task that he gave me in the office was to translate the CNI constitution into Odia. My joining date was Wednesday, 1st May 1974, and my first preaching assignment was at the Church of Epiphany on the first Sunday of June 1974. I received my first salary of INR 150/- on a Friday morning, had lunch in my single room at the Bible School Hostel, and then went to the office. When I returned, I found the back door of my room open and all my belongings, including INR 150/-, stolen. Still, the thief was truly considerate because he left my kerosene stove and utensils so that I could cook, my bed sheet and the mosquito net so that I could sleep, and my towel and lungi so that I did not need to worry about my nightclothes. I washed my only pair of clothes on Saturday, which dried immediately in the summer sunshine, and then on Sunday, I preached at the Church of Epiphany in my standing as a graduate from Serampore. To my surprise, I was delighted to see Rev Subodh Sahu seated in the pew. How marvellous was my first Sunday in the ministry?

My next opportunity to preach was at the Odia Baptist Church, one of the largest churches in Cuttack and considered a privilege as they had withdrawn from the church union. The following week, I was in the office at my usual seat in the back room of the bishop's office, when I was asked to leave and return in the afternoon. I eventually came to know that this was because a delegation of three Baptist church elders had come to the bishop with a request to deputise me as Pastor at the Odia Baptist Church. The bishop refused to accede to their request, but allowed me to preach there when invited.

My ordination was on 13th April, wedding on 15th April, and a transfer order to join the Pastorate in Kandhamal on 1st May 1975. My pastoral responsibility under the Area Superintendent, Rev Sudhanshu Naik, comprised teaching in a mission school, being chaplain in Moorshead Memorial Christian Hospital, and looking after the Boys Hostel. It was the beginning of a different kind of experience, unique in that my wife and I had to live in a big mission bungalow with frequent disruption of electricity for days, depend on kerosene lanterns, and draw water from a well in the garden. My wife was only 22 years old and was often alone given my pastoral visits. She eventually began to teach in the mission school, which had recently been initiated in one of the old mission bungalows adjacent to our home. To work in the church was not without tension as we were from the so-called plains and were now working among tribal people. Despite sincere attempts to integrate, the demand was to entrust the responsibility to local leaders and establish a separate diocese. During a Diocesan Council meeting, as recording secretary I had to minute the demands of the people for a separate diocese. Their dream was eventually fulfilled in 1997.

I never thought that I would visit G. Udayagiri, the scene of my first rural ministry, 29 years later as the General Secretary of the National Council of Churches in India. The scene was devastating after the riots in Kandhamal. The murder of Swami Lakshmananda Saraswati and four others on Saturday, 23rd August 2008 in Kandhamal was shocking. The former Hon'ble Prime Minister of India, Dr Manmohan Singh termed the violence in Kandhamal, 'a national shame'. Church leaders across the country condemned the brutal act and appealed for restraint and harmony in Kandhamal. Memories of the violence there on Christmas Eve 2007 were still fresh in everyone's mind. The twelve-hour bandh on Monday, 25th August called for by the Viswa Hindu Parishad-Bajrang Dal (political parties in India) to protest the killing, witnessed several churches and prayer halls being burnt, ransacked, and desecrated, Christian houses being burnt, and educational institutions and orphanages attacked. People had to flee to the forest. The law-and-order situation in Odisha was volatile despite the efforts of the state government to control the situation. Curfew was clamped on Phulbani, Baliguda, Tumudibandh, G. Udayagiri, Nuagaon, Raiki, and Phiringia districts. I met the Chief Minister and the Governor of Odisha to appraise them about our concerns as a minority community.

The National United Christian Forum requested Christian schools, colleges, and other educational institutions be closed on Friday, 29th August 2008 as a mark of solidarity for the suffering brothers and sisters in Odisha and to protest all acts of communal violence and atrocities on innocent people and the Christian community. We appealed to declare Sunday, 7th September 2008 a day of prayer and fasting, hoping that all churches and related institutions would hold prayers and memorial gatherings, highlighting the need for solidarity and prayer with all those who were facing trying and difficult times.

***

Walk the Talk[4]

The world loves the bold, the beautiful, the brilliant, the successful, and the rich. That is visible in advertising, news, and on the stage. We are surrounded by their images and trappings and the noise of public applause. We are also supposed to admire and emulate them. In contrast, Paul writes that '...for consider your calling, brothers (sisters): not many of you were wise according to worldly standards, not many were powerful, not many were of noble birth. But God chose what is foolish in the world to shame the wise; God chose what is weak in the world to shame the strong; God chose what is low and despised in the world, even things that are not, to bring to nothing things that are' (1 Corinthians 1:26-28).

Hospitality, for instance, dismantles the overarching sin of hostility. The generosity and vulnerability of hospitality are intricately bound together. We must be generous with our space. We must be vulnerable in sharing our stories and even the mess in our lives. It is very difficult to be generously vulnerable. Nevertheless, the demand and challenge are to step out of our comfort zones and take the risk of sharing our mess. A true community built on this foundation creates and fosters a 'welcoming hospitality' when we intentionally step out of our comfort zones; it may be called 'intentional vulnerability' or in the words of Paul 'self-emptying'. Thomas E Reynolds offers a theology that focuses on hospitality toward persons with disabilities. These theological reflections come from his experience as a parent of a son with disabilities.[5] He states that the Christian story is one of strength coming from weakness, wholeness emerging from brokenness, and power in vulnerability.

A perspective on 'Walk the Talk' is quite appropriate in the healthcare profession as many are found in the 'Talk the Talk' queue but not the 'Walk the Talk'. It means behaving differently from what one says. People tend to preach what they themselves do not wish to act upon. If people would base their lifestyles on the saying – 'actions speak louder than words', then the world would be a better place. 'Walk the Talk' is a distinctive storytelling technique employed in film and television wherein several characters have a conversation enroute. The most basic form of 'walk the talk' involves a pacing character who is then joined by another. On the way to their destination the two converse. Variations include interruptions where new characters join the group and one of the original characters leaves the conversation, while the remaining characters continue walking and talking. It also serves the purposes of smoothing transitions from one location to another and adding visual interest to what might otherwise be static 'talking head' sequences.

One may define hospitality as welcoming the stranger. By implication, it means a boundary is already fixed. Yet, a boundary cannot be so rigid as to exclude the other completely. The fear of differences can be overcome by acknowledging our commonalities, including the healthy and the sick. Therefore, hospitality is the art of setting vulnerable boundaries that can be fluid as well as prudent depending on the biblical affirmation of self-emptying. It leads to the power of discernment. To understand as clearly as possible the Imago Dei i.e. the 'image of God' in the other and ascertaining how their need and aspirations are fulfilled. It requires power to discern genuine and artificial needs. Power normally leads to domination rather than equity, but true power alone gives up what one has.

Hospitality in the modern world has become a minimal moral component and tends to become a nice 'extra' if one has time and resources. It falls within the discussions on presence, practice, tolerance, success, failure, and strangers within the kingdom of God. Hospitality also fully engages the absurdity of prosperity theology, failure of ecological stewardship, racism, and sexism. The Christian story is a story of God's love, which continues to pour into our world, astounding our cultural expectations and defying our theological assumptions. The One who creates, knows, and loves, simultaneously calls each one of us by name to join the ongoing redemptive work of God's hospitality in the world. God's welcoming love and care for each one of us becomes the invitation and calling to welcome the stranger into the kingdom of God.

Vulnerability is a virtue in medicine because in healthcare one does not treat a disease, but a person. It is possible to shed tears after giving a difficult diagnosis, hug a patient after a medical triumph, or share with a colleague the feeling of an emotionally draining day. Overall, it is life together and it is possible to see and treat a patient more than simply a disease. The word vulnerability comes from the Latin root vulnus meaning wound. To be vulnerable means being capable of being wounded. Patients come so that they may be healed of their wounds, but in seeking care, they open themselves to being wounded again both physically and emotionally. Being a patient always entails physical as well as emotional pain, uncertainty, and loss. Patients expect and allow doctors into their stories before they can know if someone will respond with compassion and understanding or if their stories will be brushed aside or if they will be made to feel shame. By not having anyone hear their already wounded stories, patients are open to the possibility of sustaining further wounds. It is only through telling their stories and trusting doctors and nurses that they can join the healing process with God's blessings. Therefore, vulnerability is a prerequisite for healing. The best teachers are patients. There is a lot to learn from patients about the power of vulnerability.

A caring doctor or nurse strives to show signs of compassion, empathy, respect, professionalism, and confidence while applying their medical knowledge to figure out a diagnosis while being part of the healing process. For a doctor, there is also the pressure to do this within a 15-minute visit while answering questions faster than an internet search. It is and can be overpowering. All of us have had vulnerable moments in our lives, and most would agree it is not a good feeling. The redemptive work of God as cited in Philippians is an act of extreme vulnerability. 'Christ Jesus, who, though he was in the form of God, did not count equality with God a thing to be grasped, but emptied himself, by taking the form of a servant, being born in the likeness of men. And being found in human form, he humbled himself by becoming obedient to the point of death, even death on a cross' (Philippians 2:5-8). One basic question of human existence is whether we can find a home with others who recognise us, value us as we are, and empower us to truly become ourselves i.e. in the image of God. The Christian response to otherness is nothing but hospitality rooted in vulnerability.

***

An Inclusive Hospitality

One of my favourite theologians is Dietrich Bonhoeffer, who shared extraordinary insights through his letters and papers from prison before his execution in 1945. It is an example of sheer confidence in adversity and the search for truth and wisdom. In the 21st century, we continue to experience the demands of basic human needs, friendship, warmth, empathy, healing, and collective experience within our communities. There appears to be a void in some of our mainline churches which generally do not meet the emotional and social needs of all including the physically challenged. Therefore, people search for 'instant-do-it-yourself' spirituality to meet their immediate needs. There is a world out there crying out for hospitality; a world torn apart by discrimination and marginalisation, a world broken by wars, oppression, prejudice, and injustice; a world destroyed by floods, tsunami, hurricanes, earthquakes, and pandemics.

There is an urgent need for a greater and deeper theological understanding of hospitality today. Most of the search for a theological basis has arisen from a response to events and an insight into a particular period. Such contextual theology is called 'local theology', which is of immense importance because it is formulated for the need of the hour and satisfies that need in the context of the best possible theological insights of the time. Hence, there is an urgent need to understand and develop hospitality for people with disabilities in the wider sense of including everyone in our journey of faith to experience God. It is a call for a paradigm shift from hostility to hospitality.

We define bodies in different metaphors: black, brown, white; male, female; young, old; beautiful, broken, able-bodied and disabled bodies. Our bodies explain our past and write the future of our stories. The pertinent question to ask is whether our bodies per se determine the story or whether the way in which we construct our bodies as a society shapes our stories?

Bodily differences have existed for centuries and they determine social structures by defining certain bodies as able and defining those which fall outside the norm as 'disabled'. The degree of 'disability' is defined by the extent of variation from the norm. In doing this, we have created an artificial paradigm of humanity into which some fit neatly and others fit very badly. Life outside the paradigm of 'able' is likely characterised by discrimination, isolation, and abuse. The story of people with disabilities is a story of a life lived on the margins and more particularly a story of silence. It is difficult to know where our construction ends and reality begins. Perhaps these stories and constructions that might have created different realities are selectively forgotten. Models of inclusion demand that disability needs to be accepted as being normal. The silence needs to be broken by re-creating a culture that celebrates and embraces differences.

In Judeo-Christian tradition, the roots of understanding bodily differences have been grounded in Biblical references, the consequent responses and impacts of the Christian church, and the effect of the enlightenment underpinning the modern era. These embodied states were seen as the result of evil spirits, the devil, witchcraft, or God's displeasure. Alternatively, such people were also signified as reflecting the suffering Christ, and were often perceived to be of angelic or beyond-human status to be a blessing to others. Therefore, themes that embrace notions of sin, sanctity, impurity, wholeness, undesirability, weakness, care, compassion, healing, and burden have formed the dominant bases of conceptualisations of and responses to groups of people who, in a contemporary context, are described as people with disabilities. In the past, however, they were labelled crippled, lame, blind, dumb, deaf, mad, and feeble.

In pre-industrialisation nomadic or agrarian societies, time was cyclic. People with limitations often lived with their families. They were ascribed roles and tasks in line with their capabilities, which fulfilled the co-operative requirements for corporate survival. Others, however, could not stay with their families. Some were ostracised and their survival threatened because of a popular conception that such persons were monsters and therefore unworthy of human status. Others became homeless and displaced for reasons such as poverty or shame. Religious communities, often within the local confines or parishes, responded to these groups of people in various ways such as the promotion and seeking of cures by actions such as exorcisms, purgings, and rituals. They provided care, hospitality, and service as acts of mercy or charity and the duty of Christians to strangers.

However, important changes occurred with the evolution of the modern era, which was profoundly influenced by the enlightenment and industrialisation. Religious values and models were challenged by the uprising of reason and rationality. Medical and scientific knowledge expanded profusely. The doctor and the scientist replaced the priest as custodian of societal values. Work and produce became commoditised and time became linear. Human worth was thus determined by perceived work value and profitability. Lifestyles and lives were dictated by mechanistic practices and institutions of the nation-state. Normality was determined by the ideal of the white, youthful, and able. Differences were redefined as deviations commanding control.

This had a major impact on the lives of those with bodily limitations with them being reduced to little more than a medical label and their futures defined by a medical prediction. Thus, people with disabilities became a class requiring physical removal from the able-bodied norms of what constituted urbanised society. Some commentators note this as the era when cripples disappeared and disability was created. Certain groups of people came to be viewed as unproductive and incapable, so institutions were established as places with a dual purpose where such people could be placed while other family members could be trained to become productive members of society.

There was also an increasing emphasis on the roles of special institutions shifting from agents of reform to agents of custody for social control. Institutions became the instruments for the facilitation. Care for people with disabilities became depoliticised and professionalised, predicated on notions of tragedy, burden, and helpless dependency. Disability came to be defined and signified as a power-neutral, objectively observable characteristic of an 'afflicted' person. It was the individual and not society who had the problem. Different interventions were aimed to provide the person with the appropriate skills to rehabilitate or deal with it. However, in a culture supported by modern medicine where the body is objectified and controlled, those who could not control their bodies were seen as failures.

There was also a trend since the 1970s, wherein the locus of individualised conceptualisation shifted from state-run public institutions to community-based facilities and care. However, the medical perspective of disability remained wedded to the economy, whereby personal capacity and ability were often assessed as incapacity and inability to determine a person's eligibility for financial assistance, benefits, and access to personal resources. An economic view narrowed the complexity of disability to limitations and restrictions. Lack of access to adequate material resources perpetuated a charity discourse that depicted certain people as objects of pity, in need of help, personally tragic, and dependent. It was a discourse of benevolence and self-sacrifice. It was similar to the responses of early Christian communities with a discourse to serve a complementary relationship between perceivably helpless people as instruments for good and virtuous works of mercy and compassion by the more 'privileged' members of society.

Currently, the discourse on disability has come to be conceptualised as a socio-political construct within a rights-based approach. The emphasis has shifted from dependence to independence as people with disabilities have sought a political voice, demanding human and civil rights against casteism, sexism, and racism. From the mid-1980s, some have enacted legislation that embraces a rights-based discourse rather than a custodial discourse, which seeks to address issues of social justice and discrimination. The legislation also embraces the conceptual shift from disability being seen as an individualised 'medical problem' to being about community membership and participation with access to regular societal activities such as employment, education, recreation, and so on. Where access is inappropriate, inadequate, difficult, or ignored, advocacy processes have been initiated to address situations and promote the people's rights. This rights-based discourse has become a means of constructing disability by locking people with disabilities into an identity that is based upon membership of a minority group. Therefore, the conceptual barrier between 'normal' and 'abnormal' goes unchallenged.

***

Discourse in India

Concerns regarding the rights of the disabled in India became visible in the public domain in the 1990s when a cluster of legislation was enacted by the Parliament. These were the Rehabilitation Council of India Act 1992, Persons with Disabilities (Equal Opportunities, Protection of Rights and Full Participation) Act 1995, and National Trust for Welfare of Persons with Autism, Cerebral Palsy, Mental Retardation and Multiple Disabilities Act 1999. Additionally, the Indian Lunacy Act of 1912 was replaced by the Mental Health Act of 1987, which came into effect in 1993. The rise of the disability rights movement and the protective role of the United Nations propelled these legislations and laid the foundation for disability jurisprudence in the country.

The concept of disability prior to the legislative enactments fell within the ambit of mental health, which was a recurrent issue across various legislative domains such as marriage, divorce, adoption, guardianship, property, and criminology. Underlying this was the undisputed understanding of a disabled person being incapable of looking after themself and their non-person status. The most dramatic development was the adoption of the Convention on the Rights of Persons with Disabilities (CRPD) by the United Nations General Assembly on 13th December 2006, which was ratified by most member states including India. The core principles of CRPD are autonomy, self-determination, equality, and non-discrimination. It proposes an inclusive paradigm of legal capacity compatible with rights rather than welfare, to be actualised through reasonable accommodation, informed consent, and freedom of choice.

The objective of the current disability discourse centres on a wider paradigm to achieve equality between the disabled and the non-disabled. Notions of formal and substantive equality are used to explain the issue. The formal approach to equality is concerned with equal treatment, i.e. likes must be treated alike and unlike must be treated differently. Difference justifies differential treatment even if it is unequal in effect. Like segregated educational facilities for disabled children would be immune from an equality challenge under the formal approach since there is an objective difference between disabled and non-disabled children. Substantive equality on the other hand focuses on the actual impact of the law. The debate shifts from the question of sameness or difference to the issue of disadvantage owing to the difference. Here any equality analysis considers the context of systematic and institutional exclusion or subordination and attempts to remedy it substantively. This implies considering both the social barriers to participation as well as the limitations posed by the body (impairment). However, it does not mean that questions on sameness or differences are irrelevant, but in fact, entails recognising and actively engaging with a difference for a different purpose. The difference is accommodated rather than ignored or assimilated. So, the question on how differences are appreciated, conceived, and accommodated in the law is central to achieving equality between the disabled and non-disabled. Therefore, medical discourse is instrumental in validating and quantifying the differences and facilities such as ramps, access to transport and buildings, and other infrastructural modifications become central to the enforcement of equality.

***

Discourse in the Bible

Hospitality is a major theme in the Bible. In nomadic times, hospitality was a matter of survival. When the Lord appeared to Abraham by the terebinth trees of Mamre in the company of two others, Abraham welcomed them according to the custom of the desert. He brought water for their feet and for their thirst, while Sarah prepared a great feast for them. Referring to this, the writer to the Hebrews wrote 'Do not neglect to show hospitality to strangers, for thereby some have entertained angels unawares' (Hebrews 13:2). This hospitality inaugurated a great nation with the prediction that Sarah would give Abraham a son. At the other end of the spectrum, we also read the story of the kind of hospitality given to the two angels who appeared at Lot's doorstep and how that hospitality culminated in hostility and the destruction of Sodom and Gomorrah.

The story of the four lepers in chapter seven of the book of II Kings is very simple but interesting. Elisha foretells abundant relief to the besieged inhabitants of Samaria. Four lepers, perishing with hunger go to the Syrian camp to seek relief and find it totally deserted. Verses 3-5 tell how the Syrians were alarmed and fled. The lepers begin to take the spoil, but then resolve to carry the good news to the city instead. The king, suspecting some treachery, sends some horsemen to see whether the Syrians have set up an ambush. They return and confirm the report that the Syrians have fled. The people go out, resulting in the provisions becoming as plentiful as Elisha had foretold. The unbelieving person who is in charge of the gate is trodden to death by the crowd.

The most interesting part of the story is the efforts of the four physically challenged individuals. They say, 'If we say, let us enter into the city, the famine is in the city, and we shall die there; and if we abide here, we shall die. And now come; let us fall away to the camp of the Syrians: if they save us alive, we shall live; and if they put us to death, we shall but die' (II Kings 7:4). The contrast of the story is the indecisiveness of the able against the decisiveness of the disabled. 'And they rose up in the dusk to go to the camp of the Syrians, and they came to the extremity of the camp of the Syrians; and behold, there was no man there. For the Lord had made the army of the Syrians to hear a noise of chariots, and a noise of horses, a noise of a great host; and they said one to another, Behold, the king of Israel has hired against us the kings of the Hittites, and the kings of the Egyptians, to come upon us. And they rose up and fled in the dusk, and left their tents, and their horses, and their asses, the camp as it was, and fled for their life. And those lepers came to the extremity of the camp, and they went into one tent, and ate and drank, and carried silver and gold and garments, and went and hid it, and they came again, and entered into another tent, and carried thence, and went and hid [it]. And they said one to another, we are not doing right; this day is a day of good tidings, and we hold our peace: if we tarry till the morning light, the iniquity will find us out; and now come, let us go and tell the king's household' (II Kings 7:5-9).

The Church's hospitality is rooted in Israel's festivals originating in the 'Passover', which celebrates their release from slavery in Egypt. In the New Testament, Jesus inaugurates the kingdom of God as a feast. From the beginning of His ministry, He became the medium for hospitality. At the wedding at Cana, with the feeding of the five thousand and numerous other occasions, and finally, at the Last Supper we see this theme in His ministry. His mere presence created hospitality for the tax collectors and other socially unaccepted people. Peter, Paul, and the other Apostles extended this hospitality to the gentiles and all of humanity. Therefore, one major emphasis in Christianity is moving away from hostility to hospitality as people of God. The invitation to God's great banquet is open to all. The tragedy of the Church is that the gatekeepers of our faith always attempt to deny people entrance to this hospitality at the table. To have a vision of the feast of the kingdom of God and to experience a foretaste of it now, needs to be our focus. In Ephesians 1:10, the writer describes a vision that speaks of 'a plan for the fullness of time, to gather up all things in Christ, things in heaven and things on earth'.

A community is constituted by sharing meals. The significance of the meal lies not only in the fact of sharing food and drink together but also the celebration, love, and care of fellow human beings. In sharing meals, we affirm the values and beliefs that are of central importance to the community of faith. The meal is an expression of friendship and hospitality. It is at the heart of the Church as well as society. To break bread with another is to share something of that person's life. Jesus accepted many invitations to meals and much of His teaching was also given in the context of a meal. Several parables feature a meal or banquet theme. The vision is again expanded when people come to sit down at the table from north, south, east, and west, which is a joy that no present community can contain. In Psalm 15, the Psalmist asks, 'God, who gets invited to dinner at your place? How do we get on your guest list?' 'Walk straight, act right, tell the truth. Don't hurt your friend, don't blame your neighbour, despise the despicable.

Keep your word even when it costs you, make an honest living, never take a bribe. You will never get blacklisted if you live like this'.

Perichoresis is a Greek term originally describing the circling and interweaving of a dance. It was daringly adopted by the early Church fathers to describe what occurs in the very life of God. The story of our faith is that the God of Abraham, Isaac, Jacob, and Moses is the God who raised Jesus Christ from the dead and poured out the Holy Spirit. The Crucifixion, Resurrection, and Pentecost are at the heart of how God is known and worshipped. Thus, it became vital to identify God in terms of Father, Son, and Holy Spirit in their interrelationship. This interrelationship was best expressed in worship using the language of the Trinity before the controversial grammar of the trinity became frequent in our doctrine and subsequent practice. The Trinitarian God is neither male nor female nor neuter. The issue is giving an implicit message of the superiority of one over the other. The answer is neither using only female or only neuter pronouns nor avoiding all pronouns completely. The issue is how less distracting one could be in the usage of the language. The solution could be in de-absolutising anyone who may become unhealthily dominant. The heart of the vision in perichoresis is a vision of love. God creates out of love and always transcends creation. God is committed in love to creation and history to the point of self-involvement in the human person of Jesus Christ and continually overflows in love through the Holy Spirit. It is in the context of communication in movement that is also complementary, that the search for expanding the boundary of hospitality needs to be done.

Disability is a condition without boundaries. In fact, one can say it is a human condition experienced by all in some form at different stages of life. One can even go so far as to say that disability is normal. Bodily differences should not be used to obscure our essential humanity. The problem is that instead of welcoming and embracing the diversity of life, we tend to disconnect the reality. Interconnectivity is the essence of life. The rights-based discourse on disability has brought some entitlements to people with disabilities but the question regarding the way in which disability is constructed and the effect of legislative changes, remains. New challenges of genetic and reproductive technology threaten to further alienate the whole and integrated person from the medically diagnosed 'person'. The emergence of a genetic model of disability is a revamped medical model. It promises to expand the population of people with disabilities to include those whose impairment is their 'bad' genes and their disability is the social responsibility of avoidance, discrimination, and even elimination. Thus, the rights-based discourse fails to meet these challenges and rather than seeking to dismantle the entire concept of disability, actually relies upon the construction to support its claims for rights and entitlements.

In this context, there is a real need to understand the importance and place of theology in the life and faith of God's people. The genius of a living theology is to observe how scripture, tradition, witnesses, and reason can be in agreement in creating God's kingdom here and now. This is a way of providing hospitality for seekers of spirituality. This should remove the hostility and resentment associated with discrimination and exclusion. We should be moving towards creating much-needed eucharistic hospitality at the Lord's Table. The early Church practised the fellowship of 'community hospitality' as recorded in the second chapter of Acts. They had a sense of community where everyone in need was cared for. Unfortunately, we have lost that sense of community and solidarity.

There is a driving force at the heart of the story of the Good Samaritan that Jesus narrated. Accepting a stranger as one's neighbour involves opening our hearts to the person we encounter. This is a great leap of faith that removes fear, suspicions, and prejudices and creates an opportunity for a healthy relationship. One way of looking at this is to think of 'hospitality' as grace-driven and to place God at the centre of this extravagant compassion. As we draw closer to God, we draw closer to each other. It is God's love, which births neighbourliness in us.

Endnotes

[1] Taradatt, IAS, Chief Editor, Gazetteers & Director General, Training Coordinator, Government of Odisha, Khordha, Gopabandhu Academy of Administration (Gazetteers Unit)

[2] https://khordha.nic.in/history/

[3] https://khordha.nic.in/history/

[4] Sahu, Dhirendra, Minority Within Minority: If we Talk the Talk, we have to Walk

the Walk, in: Sahu D K & Dhas Arul Eds. A Conversation of Health & Healing, ISPCK, 2019.

[5] Reynolds, Thomas E., Vulnerable Communion: A Theology of Disability and Hospitality, Grand Rapids, 2008.

■■■

4

Dream Dreams

'Dreams are today's answers to tomorrow's questions'.

Edgar Cayce

Understanding dreams is fascinating as well as confusing. It is not my intention to write on the meaning and interpretation of dreams but relate the personal fulfilment of certain wishes however fragmentary they may be. It is said that dreams are also difficult to remember, with no more than 5% to 10% of dreams being remembered the following day. The portions of the dream that are retained the next day may likely dissipate overnight. The word 'interpretation' itself leads to questions about how to measure accuracy because everyone has different ways of interpretation.

Dreaming can be defined as 'a sequence of perceptions, thoughts, and emotions during sleep that is experienced as a series of actual events'. Dreams are one of the most fascinating and mystifying aspects of sleep. Since Sigmund Freud helped draw attention to the potential importance of dreams in the late 19th century, considerable research has worked to unravel both the neuroscience and psychology of dreams. Dreams are a universal human experience that can be described as a state of consciousness characterized by sensory, cognitive, and emotional occurrences during sleep. Nightmares are distressing dreams that cause the dreamer to feel a number of disturbing emotions. People dream in all phases of sleep, from falling asleep to waking, but the characteristics of the dreams may differ in the different phases. Common reactions to a nightmare include fear and anxiety. While neuroscientists are interested in the structures involved in dream production and dream organisation and narratability, psychoanalysis concentrates on the meaning of dreams and placing them in the context of the analytic relationship in accordance with the history of the dreamer and the transference. Despite this advancing scientific knowledge, there is much that remains unknown about both sleep and dreams. Even the most fundamental question—why do we dream at all—is still subject to significant debate.

Freud believed dreams represented a disguised fulfilment of a repressed wish.[1] He believed that studying dreams provided the easiest road to understanding the unconscious activities of the mind.[2] His theories state that dreams have two parts: a manifested content, which is the remembered dream after we wake, and latent content, or the dream that we do not remember which is considered part of the unconscious. He proposed that the latent, or unremembered, dream content is composed of three elements: the sensory impressions during the night of the dream, the residues left from the day before, and the id's drives that are already part of the dreamer. According to Freud's psychoanalytic theory of personality, the id is the personality component made up of unconscious psychic energy that works to satisfy basic urges, needs, and desires. The id operates based on the pleasure principle, which demands immediate gratification of needs. The id is one of the three major components of personality postulated by Freud: the id, ego, and superego.[3]

Carl Jung (1875-1961) was a famous psychiatrist, psychoanalyst, and the founder of analytical psychology. The core idea of analytical psychology is that, for a better understanding of an individual's psyche, one needs to take into consideration the personality type and the power of the unconscious. Carl Jung was one of Freud's apprentices, and many, including Freud, thought that he would be the one to carry on his work. Nevertheless, Jung had his own ideas that were in contradiction with some of his teacher's. He developed his own theories about how dreams are formed. While depth psychology has fallen out of favour in neuroscience, Jung's ideas are still thriving in contemporary psychoanalytic circles. Popular applications directly based on Jung's research include the Myers-Briggs Personality Type Indicator, the Polygraph (lie detector) test, and the 12-step addiction recovery program. People experience the world using four principal psychological functions: sensation, intuition, feeling, and thinking, and most of the time one of these four functions is dominant in a person. The four categories are Introversion/Extraversion, Sensing/Intuition, Thinking/Feeling, Judging/Perception.

The basic idea behind Jungian dream theory is that dreams reveal more than they conceal. They are a natural expression of our imagination and use the most straightforward language at our disposal: mythic narratives. Jung rejected Freud's theory of dream interpretation that dreams are designed to be secretive and did not believe dream formation is a product of discharging our tabooed sexual impulses. Jung believed that the human psyche had three parts: the ego, personal unconscious, and collective unconscious. In the spring of 1957, when he was 81 years old, Jung undertook the telling of his life story. He had conversations with his colleague and friend Aniela Jaffé, and collaborated with her in the preparation of the text based on these talks. He continued to work on the final stages of the manuscript until shortly before his death on 6th June 1961. The following passage from the chapter entitled 'Life and Death' is interesting:

'Our age has shifted all emphasis to the here and now, and thus brought about the demonisation of man and his world. The phenomenon of dictators and all the misery they have wrought springs from the fact that man has been robbed of transcendence by the short-sightedness of the super-intellectuals. Like them, he has fallen a victim to unconsciousness. But man's task is the exact opposite: to become conscious of the contents that press upward from the unconscious. Neither should he persist in his unconsciousness, nor remain identical with the unconscious elements of his being, thus evading his destiny, which is to create more and more consciousness. As far as we can discern, the sole purpose of human existence is to kindle a light in the darkness of mere being. It may even be assumed that just as the unconscious affects us, so the increase in our consciousness affects the unconscious'.[4]

He succinctly wrote in the opening prologue – 'My life is a story of the self-realisation of the unconscious. Everything in the unconscious seeks outward manifestation, and the personality too desires to evolve out of its unconscious conditions and to experience itself as a whole. I cannot employ the language of science to trace this process of growth in myself, for I cannot experience myself as a scientific problem. It was due to the limitations that science offers. The story of life begins somewhere, at some particular point we happen to remember; and even then, it was already highly complex. We do not know how life is going to turn out. Therefore, the story has no beginning, and the end can only be vaguely hinted at. Life has always seemed to me like a plant that lives on its rhizome. Its true life is invisible, hidden in the rhizome. The part that appears above ground lasts only a single summer. Then it withers away, an ephemeral apparition. When we think of the unending growth and decay of life and civilizations, we cannot escape the impression of absolute nullity. Yet I have never lost a sense of something that lives and endures underneath the eternal flux. What we see is the blossom, which passes. The rhizome remains. In the end, the only events in my life worth telling are those when the imperishable world irrupted into this transitory one'.

Is it a dream or fantasy when as a child, one wishes to be somebody? One often wonders how far back one can remember. I do not remember but was told that my parents rented one room with a kitchen, which was our home. The school was not too far away, and I would do the 15 minutes' walk with a slate in the bag. During family conversations, I was told that my parents had dedicated me as a child to be in full-time ministry. To me, it was simply to become a Pastor in the church. Our elder son obviously had his own dream of life. He narrates his dream after his wife's demise: 'Should I say wish! On a lighter note, my daughter and I were reminiscing on our times in Christian Medical College, Vellore and we both agreed that there were very few to compete against the chocolate and coffee on offer at the vendors stall within the campus. My humble submission to my daughters: Last but not least, I dream of the day when I shall sit and watch the sunset one last time and in that gentle breeze, I shall feel her presence guide me as I slip away to the other side. For, as her caregiver, I bear that badge with pride and would do it again and again'.[5]

On the other hand, every Sunday, whether in lockdown or not, we have been in conversation with our youngest granddaughter over 'Skype'. Normally we talk to her during her lunchtime in London. I have been watching her grow as she was born in Prayagraj and stayed with us for one year before moving to London. One day I asked her what was she doing. The reply was immediate. 'Tatababa (Grandfather), do you know that I am doing a Book Review'. A six-year-old girl holding a four-page storybook. I told her that if she could teach me how to do a book review then it would be helpful for me as I teach students here. She just smiled. It was quite refreshing.

***

Finding a Life Partner

One of the discussions among my friends at the Theological College at Serampore was about the future. What kind of ministry we would be involved in, where, and when. However, there was also a lighter debate on finding a life partner in ministry after completing theological studies. The debate became very intense when the discussion came to dowry. Dowry was and still is an issue today in North and South India except the North-East. In fact, in a tribal community, the story is different as the groom is required to give a 'Bride Price'. Dowry is also not an issue among Christians in North India although there is a subtle expectation of gifts in kind to be given to the bride by her parents. In the South, the amount of dowry expected depends on the groom's profession and the bride's family's status. The Church remains silent on this issue citing various excuses like the equal inheritance rights of both the boy and girl.

In our case, it was not the issue of dowry but a beautiful girl and an affluent family. How could such a girl marry a boy who was expected to be a Pastor with a low salary and no ancestral property? In addition to that, both families had a say in an arranged marriage. The difference between an arranged marriage and love marriage is a point of discussion. In one case you marry and then fall in love and in the other you fall in love and then marry. However, which one is the best has not been proven since generalisations are not the answer. In our case, it was not the issue of love or arranged but getting the consent of both families. Neither of us wanted to marry without the consent of our parents. The whole story is now history, and the one-act play ended happily when we got married on 15th April 1975. However, it was not in a church as my father had obviously expected. My brother-in-law was stubborn and he wanted to demonstrate his disapproval by coordinating and arranging the marriage ceremony in a remote village where he was posted in the police station. Our wedding was conducted under a shamiana but, providently, by Rev Suryakanat Behera who had taught me how to write my first letter in the Odia alpthbet when he was our Pastor.

Twenty-five years of your life you spend with your brothers and parents: one family - one kitchen - shared food. My father made our home famous for its hospitality despite limited provisions. The first lesson I learnt after marriage was by my wife on tithing. In those days, I used to preach and receive quite good preaching engagements in churches. That year in G. Udayagiri was interesting. One preaching assignment was in a nearby village church called Bulusuga about two-kilometre walk from home that involved crossing a small stream. We had to remove our footwear and wade through the stream which was not too deep. The church consisted of lepers, who set up a weekly vegetable market and also had a small patch of land to grow them. My preaching was alright, but when the time came to conduct communion with people with disfigured fingers, feet, and faces, I was challenged. This was my first experience worshipping and celebrating communion with broken people. I later came to know that in that pastorate, the offerings in proportion to the members of the church were the highest. That was when my wife asked, 'If such people can give the best, why can't we give tithe even if our income is not too high'? God has honoured that decision till today and it has been a proven blessing. We had to adjust and send a little money to my parents, yet the first lesson on tithing was something my wife taught me. She has followed this implicitly for the last 46 years of our life together as a married couple.

***

Higher Theological Studies

My dream of joining a Liberal Arts College came true after hard work supplemented by a scholarship and earning sufficient money by taking tuitions to pay my fees and help my younger brother complete his graduation. The Diocese was faithful in sponsoring my bachelor of divinity studies. In the final year of college, I received a call from two of my teachers from Canada: Dr E J Furcha and Ms Alice Findlay to meet them. They offered to sponsor my post-graduate studies in Toronto, Canada after which I could return and join the faculty of Serampore. Excited but cautious, I told them I could agree only if my bishop approved. During the Christmas vacation, I visited him and told him about the offer, but his response was a negative as I was expected to join the CNI Diocese of Cuttack as a Presbyter. Later, the Theology department of Serampore College took a decision to write to my bishop requesting to sponsor my M Th studies in India with a view to me joining the faculty since Indian leadership was the need of the hour. However, my bishop turned down that request also.

The third opportunity came after my ordination when a scholarship was granted through the CNI to go to Toronto as part of an exchange program for a one-year course in theology. Having received the offer, I went to Delhi from Kandhamal to get a visa. I eventually received the visa, but it was a little late so the school in Toronto advised me to postpone my visit to the following year. This opportunity through CNI to provide ministry exposure in a context outside India has been misused by students. While some have availed it and returned to serve in India, others have used it as an opportunity to migrate to the UK or USA. I could thus understand my bishop's hesitation in sponsoring my higher studies abroad.

My responsibility as a CNI Presbyter in the G. Udayagiri Pastorate Union was to conduct pastoral ministry under the Area Superintendent, serve as a part-time teacher in the newly inaugurated high school, and be the chaplain at the mission hospital. In the afternoon, I would usually take a walk on the quiet road in the mission compound. One day, in 1978, I met a visitor from abroad also walking like me, whom I did not know. We met on the road and after I introduced myself, we talked as we walked together. He said he had served as a medical missionary in the mission hospital a few years back and he had returned for a short visit. I was delighted to know that despite having a FRCS from London, he had given 30 years of committed service in a remote hospital in Odisha. He is a source of inspiration and challenge to our Indian medical students, who try their best to get a sponsorship quota at Christian Medical College Vellore or

Ludhiana, but most of them, only complete the bond period in a mission hospital and then get a job either in CMC Vellore or Ludhiana, which is secure and comfortable, or migrate to greener pastures.

During the conversation, he revealed that he knew my father, his committed work, and had visited our roadside home on the way to Cuttack from G. Udayagiri for a cup of tea many years ago. Perhaps I had been a child, running around in my shorts! He inquired about my aspirations. During that walk, I briefly narrated the sponsorship opportunities I had received to Canada and Serampore. He heard my story but only answered, 'I will be in Oxford next year'. The conversation ended and I returned home. When I told my wife about it, she categorically said that she had taken a deliberate decision to marry a pastor despite the many more affluent proposals for marriage she had received and she had not known about these aspirations of mine. She then prosaically reminded me that I needed to take the bicycle and go to the market and buy some groceries. The bicycle—a second-hand one—was my only mode of transport in the village. My colleague had a motorbike but I could not dream of buying one with my salary of INR 280/- which, at that point, was equivalent to £17 per month.

***

Home Away From Home

One fine morning an aerogramme arrived from Rev Dr B R White, Principal of Regent's Park College, Oxford stating that a place would be offered to read theology at the University of Oxford. In order to initiate the process, he inquired how much I would be able to pay towards the maintenance. My dream was becoming a reality and I wrote back saying my annual income was £17 x 12 = £204 per year and I also needed to support my wife and child if I was considering going abroad on that amount. He replied apologising for asking without knowing my situation. The next letter I received offered me a full scholarship from the BMS. Surprise! Surprise! I eventually came to know that the missionary I had met on my afternoon walk—Dr Stanley Thomas—was the President of the BMS and he had initiated the entire process in consultation with the Principal to make my dream a reality. I arrived in Oxford in October 1979, leaving my wife and child with my parents, while the Diocese continued to pay my salary to her for maintenance until they joined me.

After a couple of months at Regent's, the Principal himself said that my family must join me in Oxford. It was a double blessing from God alone. The Principal negotiated everything with the BMS and arranged a family apartment in the college. Manju and our son Bibhu arrived exactly nine months later and that too accompanied from India to London by my bishop as he was visiting the UK at that point. The apartment was allotted but not the key and I was informed that the key would be given to my wife. To our surprise, when we entered, we found that it was fully furnished, perfectly clean, and the kitchen was stocked with Indian spices, rice, dal, flour, and, not the least, a grinding stone brought from London! How can I forget that day - the Fellowship group organised a welcome that evening even ensuring the Principal's younger daughter babysat our son!

Regent's Park College was founded in 1810 when a wealthy benefactor purchased a property in Stepney Green, East London, and the Stepney Academy was launched. This was a time when 'dissenters' or nonconformists were unable to obtain degrees from Oxford or Cambridge—the only English universities—unless they agreed with the doctrines of the Church of England. Baptists were among those who responded by developing their own patterns of education, and a Baptist Education Society was established in 1752 followed by another in 1804 to provide an education for Baptist ministers. Out of these emerged Stepney Academy. The College was part of London University by the middle of the 19th century. It soon began to accept a wider group of students and offered Arts degrees to those dissenters still unable to access Oxford and Cambridge, who wanted to pursue professional careers. In 1856, the College took a lease on what had been a large private house in Regent's Park; subsequently two houses, a garden, plus assorted cottages, and garages were purchased and building work began in 1938. The students had to be matriculated through St Catherine's Society. In 1957, the College applied for and was given the status of a Permanent Private Hall (PPH), fully part of Oxford University.

The original vision of the College was to prepare Baptist ministers to serve the Baptist churches and that was very evident when I was a student. During my stay, it was not only visible but also the focus both in terms of admission and life in the community. One such event was the morning devotion every day. Friday evening Chapel and Monday afternoon ministerial formation class with both sermon appraisal as well as an interactive session among the ministerial students, were regular events. However, during our visit in 2016 and 2018, I noticed a change. Resident ministerial candidates are non-existent and the Friday Chapel is now a minority community although the Formal Hall for dinner on Fridays is still full of life. We visited an old friend in Oxford in 2018, who is now quite elderly and homebound, and she raised a pertinent question, 'What about the training of Baptist ministers at Regent's'?

For us, Regent's Park became a home away from home. The love and care that we received was tremendous. The care of the Principal, Dr B R White and his wife Margaret White was unforgettable during our first stay in Oxford from 1979-82. We used to attend the Indian church in Oxford on Sunday afternoons occasionally, but regularly attended New Road Baptist Church in the morning as a family to worship. Whenever I had to preach and share the story of the church in India on BMS weekends, it was easy for my wife and Bibhu to attend this church as it was only a ten-minute walk on the safe pavements of Oxford. My studies required me to travel on Saturday morning, attend an Indian gathering on Saturday evening to share the story of the church and life in India. The following Sunday I was required to preach both morning and evening in two different congregations and return to Oxford in the night. The experience of staying overnight with another family and meeting people and sharing the word of God was a valuable learning process in my ministry.

The Indian church in south Oxford comprised people primarily from Punjab. Excellent fellowship and dinner at a church member's home was always available without any formal invitation. After service, someone would always come forward and invite us for dinner. Not high tea but rather a pukka Indian meal with rice, chapatti, and chicken curry. It was Indian hospitality at its best! During my final year, the Pastor shared his view that the Asian community needed a leader and would it be possible for me to accept this position. He said he would initiate the process of our staying back in Oxford and doing ministry among the Asian community at large in Oxford, London, and Birmingham. While I was tempted to stay back in the UK and it could have been justified with the excuse of having a broader ministry, my wife reminded me of my sponsorship criterion and my commitment to serve in India. So, we returned to India and landed in Calcutta. In the meantime, the Principal of Serampore had negotiated with my bishop to transfer my services from the Diocese to Serampore. This time wisdom prevailed and providence was translated into reality as I was permitted by the Diocese to join Serampore College.

***

Serampore Journey

When I was young, I remember walking in Serampore College campus, passing by the house of William Carey. I never dreamt at that point that I would return to Serampore to serve the Institution for almost 18 years including study leave for doctoral studies. As a family, we were privileged to stay in William Carey House as well, except for the first year.

One issue that the theology faculty in Serampore faced was a good school for their children as they were all from different states in India. When we arrived in 1982, we found that some children went to Calcutta, travelling in a school bus that took four hours to and from Serampore. It used to pick up and drop children at different points and ours was the first pick up and last drop point. Others used to take cycle rickshaws to the bank of the Hooghly River, cross over in a boat, then take cycle rickshaws again to get to school. The boat journey itself was quite frightening. I remember one day, the boat that used to bring our staff children, capsized. Fortunately, none of the children were in that trip that day. I also remember us going to the church across the river occasionally as a family, and one particular Sunday there was sudden wind and a lightning storm. The boat we were in began to heave in the middle of the river and you can imagine our plight as neither my wife and children nor I knew how to swim at that point;

they learnt to swim when we went back to Oxford the second time in 1988. One can now understand the parable of Jesus sleeping in the boat and the disciples' cry. That day I recalled another story that my father had told me. During summer, when there was a shortage of water in the well, my father would take me along when he went to bathe in a pond in our village. Once, while bathing I slipped and went under water, but fortunately my dad was quick to notice and rescued me, otherwise I could have drowned. Another incident was during the final year of BA when our batch of students went for a picnic at a resort with an artificial lake that was deep enough to drown. Before the meal, someone suggested going on a boat ride to the other side of the lake and we did. Unfortunately, on the return journey, right in the middle of the lake a dark cloud and strong winds rose suddenly. Those who knew how to swim suggested that we jump, but we few who didn't, depended on the benevolence of two friends, who attempted to row the boat and eventually managed to bring us safely to shore. When I read the parable or preach it, the memory of the past returns vividly.

So, the first issue we faced after joining Serampore in 1982, was to find a school for our eldest son in the middle of the academic year as we had arrived at the end of August. The principal's advice was that I put him in a local Bengali medium government primary school. Easier said than done! On the other hand, without a recommendation, it was difficult to get a seat in any good English medium school in Calcutta. However, God had a plan. There were fellowship groups around Serampore where students and faculty went for weekend ministry. One Sunday, I visited a group with some students. The Fellowship meeting went well with sharing the word of God and celebrating communion in a home with two or three families. During the conversation, the host realised our need for a good school. To my surprise, a few minutes before departure, he gave me a closed envelope. I thought it was a monetary gift to cover our expenses. Instead, he told me to meet the Principal of Don Bosco School and to give him the letter. I did likewise. The principal immediately took me to someone in the office and advised him to do the necessary. Within half an hour, the admission process was complete and I received the admission receipt.

We never imagined that we would return to Oxford again and that too as a family of four. The requirement of the Serampore Senate was that one must hold a doctorate degree to teach post-graduate students. So, first, I tried to join a secular university in Pune, where I met the Head of the Department of Philosophy. The process was ongoing and I was expected to register. However, in the meantime, I dared to write a letter to the General Secretary of BMS and my Principal at Regent's expressing my wish to pursue research. The response was positive and overwhelming as they wrote back that BMS would consider sponsoring my studies with a family scholarship that is not usually offered except in rare cases. God's ways are different and sometimes overwhelming. There was a hiccup in receiving a recommendation from the Master of Serampore College Council as he wanted to know bureaucratically the scholarship amount per year. The issue was settled after a response (from) BMS that the policy was need-based and would cover tuition, accommodation, and hospitality.

So, I arrived in Oxford for the second time in 1988 to pursue my graduate studies with the family. Prior to that, I had visited the library at United Theological College, Bangalore, and the CNI Bhavan at New Delhi in search of material regarding the church union movement in North India. The experience in Delhi was quite interesting. I explained to the then CNI General Secretary Rev Pritam Santram, who later became the Bishop of the Delhi Diocese, my interest in the formation of the CNI with a focus on ecclesiology in an ecumenical context. I was looking for primary sources of church union records of negotiation. I had already tried looking through records at Bishop's College Calcutta including the Serampore Library without much success. The General Secretary had a PhD from Cambridge and was a learned person. He sarcastically wondered who would be interested in documenting the church union movement and advised me to search the CNI Bhavan storeroom. There were six trunks lying there coated in dust. I made the effort to clean the room, clear the boxes, and read some letters and notes kept by Bishop Bryan. Not a bad way to begin research!

We decided to stay in Oxford as a family as we were familiar with the surrounding, had support from Regent's family, and could fellowship at New Road Baptist Church. The Principal, Dr B R White was kind enough to give me the privilege of becoming a member of the Senior Common Room, which allowed my wife and I to dine with the faculty and students of Regent's Park College during Formal Hall and attending the evening Chapel service on Fridays. Also, being a former alumnus of the University, I had access to the Bodleian Library including the College and Faculty of Theology Library.

The Principal also arranged a meeting with the Head of the Department of History in Divinity of the University of Birmingham. I had sent my PhD proposal prior to the scheduled meeting. Dr McLeod remarked that it would be proper if a Professor of Theology was my guide rather than a Professor of Church History. During the conversation, someone knocked on the door and entered the room with a racquet after playing squash; that was my first meeting with Dr David Ford. Dr McLeod said that he would be happy to help me as and when necessary, but it would be good if David could look at the proposal. So, I made an appointment to meet Dr David Ford a week later in his office.

My research journey under the supervision of Prof Dr David Ford is not only memorable but unforgettable. The following week when I met him, he simply said he would be interested in being my guide, but never spoke about anything related to my proposal that day. Instead, he pulled a book out from a shelf—The Nature of Doctrine by George Lindbeck—told me to read it and come back after a month to begin the conversation. Quite an interesting way to begin research. He settled all the formalities with the university quietly in consultation with my Principal and the BMS without any of the usual hassles that accompany the registration process in Indian Universities. We used to meet once a month on the condition that I sent all written research work one week prior to my visit from Oxford to Birmingham. He offered me at least an hour and a half of quality time on each visit, including coffee and a sandwich. This journey continued for a year until I heard the news that he had been appointed the Regius Professor of Divinity at the University of Cambridge. I did not know what to do, but immediately visited him, offering my congratulations for such a prestigious post, and waited anxiously to know about the future of my research. He simply stated that he would continue to be my guide despite moving to Cambridge and that I was to meet him at the Divinity School in Cambridge or sometimes at his home for the remainder of the research period.

One aspect that I cherish and share with my students is the relationship between the guide and researcher which is vital. We visited David Ford in Cambridge in 2003 when I was a Bishop in the Diocese of Eastern Himalayas. He reciprocated when he and his family visited us in our Diocese, where he was given a warm welcome, preached at one of our village churches, visited a tourist spot in the forest, went on an elephant ride, and last but not least, visited Calcutta to see Mother Teresa's work. They were all excited and still remember their exposure to India.

The memory of meeting Bishop Lesslie Newbigin in his 80s at his residence was unforgettable. I remember that I made an appointment to discuss my thesis with him. While we were talking, Mrs Newbigin entered and served us sandwiches and tea with a smile. He then suggested that I send him a chapter for his comments. He took the pain to read one chapter of my thesis—approximately 65 pages long—in detail and made comments in the pages, followed later by a fruitful, interactive session. On completing my viva, I rang him to convey the news, and to my pleasant surprise the following day I received a postcard with this handwritten note: 'You are going back to a country of dust and heat but full with abundance of love and hospitality'.

My sons were in classes X and VI during my final year of research. I knew that I had to submit my thesis by May 1992 to face the viva-voce, attend the convocation, and then return to India. My wife was by then working at the then Oxford Polytechnic Library, which is now known as Brookes University. It was an opportunity for her to be out of the house and meet people in the workplace, although it meant that our hospitality grant from BMS had to be reduced since we now had some income of our own. One BMS weekend we both decided to go together, and prior to the evening meeting that Saturday we went to a park nearby to have something to eat. A lady walked up to us and introduced herself saying that she also had come to attend the evening meeting as they were missionaries in Delhi. She inquired about our children, their schooling in Oxford, and possible education arrangements in India when we returned. She suggested that we try Woodstock in Mussoorie, India.

Earlier, we had thought of sending our sons to St Paul's in Darjeeling and had written to the then Bishop of Calcutta. The response was not only discouraging, but also humiliating as it stated that since the school fees was high, only rich parents could afford it. Our next option was Woodstock, where admission was not the question but the fees were exorbitant. The third option was a surprise. I had met the Principal of Eltham College, London once and he graciously offered a place for both our boys with scholarships. He had sent me the forms, which I had filled. However, before sending them I had to consult my wife. This time, it wasn't the bishop but my wife who gave the final verdict. 'We came together and we should go back together. If you want to leave them here at this tender age, then don't regret it when they become westernised, start living together with friends, and do not look after us as Indian parents expect'. I had to listen to her and drop the application forms in the waste paper basket.

However, the lady insisted that we apply a second time to Woodstock for a scholarship. We did and the result was that both boys were admitted with full scholarships in Woodstock. Thus, we were now committed to returning to India despite the possibility of me having a job in the UK and my wife having a job at the library. Later that year, when she gave in her letter of resignation to the Chief Librarian, he advised her to think twice, but her response was that we were going back to India. We immediately called the kind lady who had advised us to apply to Woodstock for the second time about the good news of the admission offer. She was none other than Mrs Elsie Grose who was a board member of Woodstock School. My wife's words of wisdom are now a reality as we look back. Both the boys completed their education at Woodstock.

Our elder son had no desire to go abroad despite having completed his 'O' levels from Oxford. We made arrangements for him to study at Wilson College, Mumbai for his undergraduate and postgraduate degrees. Our younger son, however, was different. Having been born in Oxford in 1981, he had British citizenship to his advantage. We first admitted him in St Xavier College in Calcutta, but he came back home saying that he could be an undergraduate student in a Primary School where the teaching method was completely different from what he was used to in Oxford and Woodstock. So, he decided to take a break for one year and stay with us in Serampore. During that time, he sent several applications abroad and all were positive, but with the rider that he pay the fees, which we could not afford. Ultimately, we thought Madras Christian College would be better for him, so my wife accompanied him to Chennai.

A miracle happened during that time. I received an email from Kansas that Ashis had received admission with a full scholarship. Excited, I conveyed the news to them and both mother and son returned to Serampore. Ashis applied for his visa and went for an interview. I had been elected as the Bishop of the Diocese of Eastern Himalayas and that evening, we had arranged a Fellowship meal with a few friends at home. Before the guests arrived, Ashis returned home from Calcutta, threw his bag on the living room floor, and said that his visa had been rejected. The friends came and we had to entertain them, while my son was quiet and composed. Later that night, we had a long talk until midnight, not knowing what to do next. On the following day, I contacted a friend in Delhi and he said that one had to wait for six months before re-applying for a visa. However, Ashis did not agree. I sent a letter to the Dean of the College to resend a notarised letter explaining the details of the scholarship that would cover his studies. He responded quickly. The day Ashis went to Calcutta to reapply for his visa, we had to go to Delhi to attend the orientation before my consecration as a CNI bishop. There was a phone call around lunchtime and I picked up the phone cautiously, hesitant to receive any negative news. Instead, there was a sudden burst of laughter and an excited statement, 'Dad, the visa is granted'. Ashis then told me that when he entered the room, to his utter surprise he found that the visa officer was the same person who had denied it the previous week. However, she said, 'I have never seen such a persistent boy who came back so soon after being denied. Therefore, visa granted'. He came back home and took the Rajdhani Express from Calcutta to New Delhi, arriving in time for the orientation. Ashis completed his undergraduate studies with magna cum laude from Kansas University. On graduation day, he discovered that it was his teacher, who wanted to remain anonymous till that day, who had financially sponsored his studies. How incredible are the ways of God and that we have such people in our world today?

Memory is a precious gift from God. Imagine for a moment if we lost our memory. We need to recollect the memory of God's faithfulness in the past and hope for His continuing presence in our journey. Some stories are quite inspiring and very helpful in our journey of life. One such story that I came across is the story is of a person born in a poor family, who, with persistence, became the President of Parker Brothers at the age of 33. Then he was told that his services were no longer required. 'After years of unbridled success, I took the news hard'. Within five months he got a new job, making more money than at Parker Brothers. He was fired after five months. He spent 14 months unemployed and said it was a time of humbling. In time he got a job with Lenox that makes fine china. What do you think happened then? He was sitting in his posh corner office when he received a phone call. This time, he wasn't fired but was offered a job that would lead to a huge pay cut, require him to move out of his ten-bedroom house on five acres, give up his Jaguar, and work with the poorest people in the world. He wrote a book called Hole in our Gospel that states that the gospel must include justice for the poor. He is the President of World Vision International. Perhaps we need to tell our younger generation such insightful, inspirational stories.

I was looking at my diary and itinerary. It has 30 overseas trips, some places more than once, beginning with Oxford, then Paris, Singapore, South Africa (Johannesburg & Durban), Myanmar, Geneva, Germany, Sri Lanka, Boston, Harvard, Kansas, Edinburgh, Cambridge, Bangkok, Bangladesh, Nepal, Geneva, Indonesia, Cambodia, Taipei, Brazil, Malaysia, South Korea, Thailand, Nairobi(Limuru), Andaman & Nicobar Islands, Netherlands, Philippines, Canada, Israel & Ghana including seven years residency in Oxford for my studies. The meaningful ministry in the Andaman and Nicobar Islands with a team from CNI was remarkable in discovering the culture, customs, lifestyle, and Christian witness on the islands. The visit to Israel was not merely a holy land tour but I also had the opportunity to attend the Galilee Institute for a management course and visit several historic places. While travelling to the River Jordan, the guide announced that if anyone wanted to be baptised there, a priest would be available. Most of the tourists who were in the bus shouted in unison that they did not need a priest since they had a bishop with them. I had the honour and privilege of baptising about 15 people from Africa, Thailand, and Australia who eventually also wanted me to issue them baptism certificates.

Endnotes

[1] https://en.wikipedia.org/wiki/Psychoanalytic_dream_interpretation#:~:text=Freudian%20theory,-Sigmund%20Freud%20circa

[2] Freud, Sigmund (1953). The Interpretation of Dreams. London: Hogarth Press

[3] Peasant, N., A. Zadra (2001). Working with Dreams in Therapy: What do we Know and What Should we do?. Clinical Psychology Review, 24 (5): 489–512

[4] https://www.goodreads.com/quotes/6621488-our-age-has-shifted-all-emphasis-to-the-here-and

[5] Sahu, Bibhudutta, Caregiver's Cross, In: A Conversation on Health and Healing, Eds: Sahu D K and Dhas Arul T, ISPCK, p 287

■■■

5

Life Lessons

'Fair is foul, foul is fair'. Act 1, Scene 1, Macbeth

The phrase 'Fair is foul, foul is fair' is a dominant theme in Macbeth. It highlights the hypocrisy that people adopt to hide their true intentions. Shakespeare employs this theme to caution us about judging things based on face value. Although King Duncan loves Macbeth dearly, it is Macbeth who ends his life. In a nutshell, things are not always what they seem; the good may turn out to be bad, and the bad may actually be good. However, Shakespeare warns us that whatever our motives may be, in the end, they will come back to haunt us. The phrase '*Fair is foul, foul is fair*' (Act 1, Scene 1) is chanted by the three witches at the beginning of the play. It acts as a summary of what is to come in the tale.

I do not intend to explain 'Fair is foul, foul is fair' theologically, but given my pastoral, academic, and administrative association with institutions both as an employee and in an honorary capacity, the experience has been quite enriching. I call them life lessons. I have attempted to understand ministry in the Church and Christian institutions specifically examining my association with five specific institutions: The CNI; The National Council of Churches in India (NCCI); Serampore College; Christian Medical College (CMC), Vellore; and Sam Higginbottom University with a rider that 'things are not always what they seem'.

Where my experiences were adverse or unfair, I have attempted to overcome my predicament with a smile and in silence. Nevertheless, in this memoir, I have tried to elucidate those moments when I felt a sense of fulfilment, frustration, or betrayal, as the case may be. Memories always come back, either filling us with a sense of fulfilment regarding a dream or with the disenchantment that 'Fair is foul, foul is fair'. One question remains – how does one face lies? In a free and democratic society, it is not difficult to question and expose lies. One interesting reading that I came across was the advice to the Queen by the Prime Minister of UK that Parliament should be prorogued for five weeks at the height of the Brexit crisis. The unanimous judgment from 11 justices was that the Prime Minister's advice was unlawful. In the argument, Mr. Aidan O'Neill QC told the judges, 'The mother of parliaments is being shut down by the father of lies. Rule that this prorogation is an unlawful abuse of power. Enough is enough', referring to the Prime Minister of the UK. I wonder how many of us could say that in our churches and Christian institutions. If we do so, can we bear the consequences?

Our memories are sometimes elated, sometimes disoriented, sometimes disillusioned, and perhaps even prone to despair. That is being human. We may call those moments a 'snare of hope', the mistake of believing that the world marches forward in a straight line of progress. That kind of hope is either an illusion or a failed concept, which is why many forms of hope are rightly criticised for being blind and naïve. That is not the Christian hope. Christian hope is not even possible unless one stares at God hanging on a cross. It is not for the faint of heart, and not for shallow hope-seekers. The first step would then be to examine what we were hoping for and in, and maybe even let most of it go. Then we make space for what is to come. We make space for the pain and the shattering of illusion. I call it doing theology in silence and with a smile.

***

United Vis-À-Vis Uniting

United and uniting is the paradigm of a unique journey of a church that set a discourse in the ecumenical movement as well as several other issues that blur the image of a living church. I was brought up in the Baptist tradition and baptised in the local Baptist church. My application for theological studies was processed through the then Baptist Council known as the Utkal Christian Central Church Council (UCCCC). The Council decided to join the CNI and thus, by default, I became a member and later, on completion of theological studies, was ordained as a CNI Presbyter in the Diocese of Cuttack. I still remember, when the bishop was ordaining me, I asked about the cassock. Instead, he advised me to wear a *dhoti* and white *kurta*, specifically one that had a round neck with buttons. My first time, I asked a Bible school student to help me wear a *dhoti* and the second time was on my wedding day. The third and final time was when I went with my wife to visit my in-laws and my mother-in-law gave me a dhoti with the instruction to wear it before joining them for lunch.

My home church decided not to join the church union and remains so till today. The formation of the CNI is the story of a 40-year journey of negotiation (1929-70) together to discern the will of God. The joyful union of six major denominations—the Church of India, Pakistan, Burma, and Ceylon, the United Church of North India (merger of Presbyterian and Congregational), the Methodist Church (British and Australian Conference), the Church of the Brethren, the Church of the Disciples of Christ, and the churches connected with the Council of the Baptist Churches in Northern India—led to the inauguration of the CNI on 29th November 1970 at All Saint's Cathedral Campus, Nagpur. CNI's jurisdiction covers all states of the Indian Union with the exception of the four Southern states – Andhra Pradesh, Karnataka, Kerala, and Tamil Nadu, and has approximately 1,250,000 members in 3,000 parishes.

As a Baptist, there were two crucial issues regarding baptism and episcopacy. How were we to reconcile these two traditions, which every Baptist valued. Even while joining the church as a Presbyter, I never thought that one day I would become a CNI bishop. Yet, the three-fold ministry of Bishop, Presbyter, and Deacon is accepted as the pattern of ministry in the United Church. It was also envisaged that it would be free to develop an appropriate diaconate. A permanent diaconate would free other ministers, presbyters, and bishops to perform the functions that more appropriately belonged to their distinctive calling. Individuals, who had been accepted for the ministry of the diaconate by the diocesan authorities and had received due training, would serve during their lifetime, which would be different from the normal training for presbyters.

I had the privilege of presenting a paper on 'Permanent Diaconate' at the Bishop's Conference in Gangtok, Sikkim just after my election as the CNI Bishop in the Diocese of Eastern Himalayas in 2001. However, there has been no progress even after 50 years of life in a united church. Episcopacy in the CNI is both constitutional and historic. By constitutional, it means that bishops are appointed and perform their functions in accordance with the constitution of the Church. By historic, it means that the episcopate is in continuity with that of the early church.

Personally, I was fascinated by the story of the negotiation and culmination of the union because for the first time we Baptists joined a church union, accepting episcopacy. My doctoral dissertation was on 'The Church of North India: A Historical and Systematic Theological Inquiry into an Ecumenical Ecclesiology', which was submitted at the University of Birmingham, UK in 1992 under the guidance of Prof Dr David Ford, the Regius Professor of Divinity at the University of Cambridge. My PhD thesis was published in 1994 by Peter Lang of Germany. A shorter version called 'United and Uniting' was published by the Indian Society for Promoting Christian Knowledge (ISPCK) for the CNI people and was released during the CNI Synod meeting at St Stephen's College, Delhi. A brief about the CNI was also published in the Companion to the Anglican Communion.[1]

The participation of Baptists in the negotiation process in North India had to address the question of baptism, but settled it simply with the United Church not subscribing to any one view. Intelligently, the issue was addressed by accepting infant baptism to be followed by a later profession of faith, and accepting believer's baptism to be preceded by a presentation and blessing in infancy, as an alternative as well as an equivalent for entry into the household of God. The declaration of acceptance of Jesus Christ as personal saviour and being baptised with water in the name of the Father and of the Son and of the Holy Spirit was to be made either at the time of baptism in the case of believer's baptism or at the time of confirmation in the case of infant baptism.

The emblem of a united and uniting Church captures Frank Wesley's design of an indigenous but universal church. The circle symbolises eternity that is dominated by a golden cross against a red background symbolising the sacrifice. Behind the cross, there is a lotus dear to every Indian as a symbol of purity rising out of the mud beneath the water. The chalice is set at the very centre to emphasise the point that worship and sacrament are at the centre of Christian living. The outer circle is embedded with three keywords: Unity, Witness, and Service.

The two schemes for the Church union in South and North India were almost parallel but the CSI was inaugurated on 27th September 1947, at St George's Cathedral, Madras with the South India United Church, the union between Congregationalists and Presbyterians, the South India Province of the Methodist Church, and the four dioceses of the Church of India, Pakistan, Burma, and Ceylon. The genesis of discussion on church union may be traced back to May 1919 at Tranquebar. The 33 visionaries, all but two of whom were Indian, including Bishop V S Azariah of the Dornakal Diocese of the Anglican Communion, from different churches issued the Tranquebar Manifesto:

'We believe that the challenge of the present hour in the period of reconstruction after the war, in the gathering together of the nations, and the present critical situation in India itself, calls us to mourn our past divisions and turn to our Lord Jesus Christ to seek in Him the unity of the body expressed in one visible Church. We face together the titanic of the winning of India for Christ - one fifth of the human race. Yet confronted by such an overwhelming responsibility, we find ourselves rendered weak and relatively impotent by our unhappy division - divisions for which we were not responsible, and which have been, as it were, imposed upon, us from without; divisions which we did not create, and which we do not desire to perpetuate'.

The story of CSI and CNI with regard to the unification of ministry is different. The CSI negotiator decided to have a fully unified ministry of ordained Episcopal ministers in the CSI after 30 years of negotiation. However, the negotiators in North India decided that the satisfaction of all bodies regarding the unification of ministry was a prerequisite for the union. Therefore, mutual recognition meant that all the ministers from the uniting churches were brought into the ministry through a common service of unification when the CNI was inaugurated. The difficult task was recognising the episcopate as a witness of God's grace in this form of ministry, without negatively judging others. The uniting churches pledged themselves and fully trusted each other that any bishop or Presbyter officiating in the rite would do so with the sincere intention of placing himself unreservedly in the hands of God, to be used as He wills, as a channel of His grace, commission, and authority.

One story is often told by the late Dr Augustine Ralla Ram, one of the 'founding parents' of the Church Union movement in North India. A traveller entering a city for the first time stopped to ask where the various Protestant churches were located. 'You'll have no trouble in finding them', was the reply. 'The Baptist Church is half a mile down the road, near a large pond. The Methodist Church is opposite the gas works, the Anglican Church next to the laundry, and the Presbyterian Church across the road from the ice factory'. In defining and assessing the fourth plan of 1965, W J Marshall makes a succinct remark that one dominant insight was the Church's dependence on God, which may sound obvious but is usually obscured by divisions in the Church.

The sacrament of the Lord's Supper reaffirms a weakness of witness in our global church history when Christians cannot eat the bread and drink from the same cup in unity despite the clarion call given in ecumenical forums when Protestant-Catholic and Orthodox church members meet for intra-faith fellowship. It is more painful to see that when we meet as members of the World Council of Churches (WCC), despite our elongated talks, negotiations, and publication of the document called 'Baptism-Eucharist and Ministry' (BEM), we cannot share the same table of fellowship. We excel in rhetoric, discussions, articulations, and publishing documents that never reach the pew. Even if they do, congregation members are not bothered to read them. They think it is just the outcome of a discussion paid for from ecumenical grants and organised by professional ecumenists. For some, it is a career while for others it is an ecumenical pilgrimage to attend conferences abroad. Once you enter the club, you can attend meetings in different forums for years. Constantly moving from Geneva, Hongkong, Singapore, USA, Canada, or Bangkok and circumventing tenure takes strategic planning. Only God and our ecumenical partners know the full extent. It is not a vocation but merely a career in greener pastures to avoid struggling in the dust, heat, and insecure environment locally.

One painful memory of the negotiation is the last-minute withdrawal of a major church, namely the Methodist Church in Southern Asia (MCSA), now the Methodist Church in India, which is a reminder that sometimes human frailty takes precedence, even in a church. Even the Juridical Council of the Methodist Church in 1972 declared that the decision of the MCSA in 1970, which reversed an earlier decision to join the union, was beyond its legal authority. The issue was never about faith or order, but one of power, assets, and not least, the salary of the bishops.

***

Table Talk

The CNI in its wisdom decided to be self-sufficient in ministry. Therefore, one program that was initiated by the church was Stewardship. I was given the responsibility of coordinating the stewardship ministry in the Diocese of Cuttack in 1975. Several meetings were conducted to focus on this aspect of ministry without receiving overseas grants, which was to cut 20% each year to make the church self-reliant. The decision was bold and made in faith. It created revival and people began to support the ministry. As a diocesan bishop, the priority was and is to mobilise the resources for pastoral ministry as no overseas grant is now received. However, the urban-rural divide of the congregations within the dioceses, the rhetoric of one united church, and the decision to have an inter-diocesan sharing fund till today remain unresolved. It has brought a division within the Church, similar to the struggles of society in general. It reflects the ongoing struggle between leadership and broad-based participatory community.

The most chronic issue is the style of leadership and corruption that is blurring the witness of a united church. The genesis of these problems lies in our understanding of the basics of being a united church. It is our inability to hear the cries of the people within and a lack of courage in facing the challenges. In a series of postings on Facebook since 29th September 2020, a former CNI bishop of the Diocese of Calcutta had the courage to break the silence of a United Church with the audacious title 'Fascism and its practice in the present day in the Church of North India nearly for three years'. He raised numerous questions regarding the 'Moderator and his coterie that includes Synod Executive and "Yes Sir" executive, the threat of transfer, suspension, long leave, forced voluntary retirement of bishops, security like "Z" category for the Moderator, proposing an amendment to extend the term of office of himself as the Moderator and of the Deputy Moderator and not the least the cronyism and corruption'. Such voices are brushed aside and the issues are swept under the carpet.

The genesis of arm-twisting methods employed by the synod authority goes back to the earlier regime in a very subtle manner. Once, I was invited to lead a three-day retreat for the staff and students of a theological seminary. As per protocol, I informed the local diocesan bishop since I was visiting his diocese. The local bishop extended the invitation to preach on Sunday and celebrate communion with him as co-celebrants. It was very meaningful and fruitful. However, to my surprise, a while later, when I fell from grace, I received a letter from the then General Secretary to meet the moderator as he had received a complaint regarding my previous visit to the same diocese. The allegation was that I had caused disturbances during my visit although the Principal of the college had accompanied my wife and I everywhere when we were there. I obeyed the 'diktat', went to the CNI Bhavan, and met the Moderator. When I entered his room, he said, 'Do not worry. *Aisa hi hota hai* (this is how it usually happens). Go in peace'. My question was, 'Why is there so much arm twisting despite knowing full well that this complaint was a lie?'

Perhaps, the then Moderator remembered expressing his helplessness in chairing the Synod meeting the previous day in that very same room. Earlier, on the last day of the Synod meeting, which I was attending as a diocesan bishop, drama unfolded when there was a sudden move, without any agenda item, to remove the General Secretary and the Treasurer. There was a storm and then silence, after which everybody left. Coincidentally, I had stayed back because I had planned to stay in Delhi for a short break. The following day, I visited the CNI Bhavan, which seemed to be in mourning. That was when the Moderator sought my advice and help. My stand was not that they both remain in office, but whether the right process had been adopted in the Synod to remove them. I asked for permission to access the old minutes, then showed him the references with the suggestion that the decision would be his in consultation with all the bishops. I told him that even if they were removed, it must follow due process. We must not set a precedent that engendered anarchy.

Eventually, both of them were reinstated, and while one of them retired with dignity after the completion of his tenure, the other incumbent, not only completed his tenure as Treasurer but returned as the General Secretary and stayed for another seven years. I am grateful to the same person for the goodwill and support he extended during the process of my becoming the Bishop of the Eastern Himalayas Diocese. He was a very good friend but the relationship turned sour when the post of General Secretary became vacant. The Search Committee was entrusted with the task of finding a General Secretary. I received a call from one member of the committee to consider the General Secretary post and was advised to attend the Search Committee. When I did, I told them that I would accept the General Secretary post if I received an invitation. To my surprise, I found that the entire process was nonsense and the then Moderator was a pawn in the hand of the Treasurer who had been reinstated through my intervention. To my dismay I found that the Moderator, who had categorically told me that the Treasurer must leave when his tenure was complete, supported him in selecting him as the General Secretary. One must learn to live with such hypocrisy.

The correspondence between two bishops regarding the appointment of the above-mentioned Treasurer is quite amusing as well as revealing, but which, unfortunately, came to my knowledge quite late: 'At the 1992 Synod meeting, you had vehemently opposed my proposal to make the appointment of General Secretary and Treasurer as "term appointments" so that undue power did not concentrate on these offices. It was a good opportunity to introduce the change as both the posts were vacant. But vested interests opposed it. When the Treasurer was appointed, totally disregarding the unanimous resolution of the Synod, which had laid down the qualification of the Treasurer, and which Bombay diocese and another diocese were asked to publish in leading newspapers. During your long tenure as the General Secretary, you developed the culture and practice of the office bearers making all decisions concerning the Church and using the Executive Committee as a thumb impression to approve the minutes. In this practice it has become so evident that whoever amongst the office bearers is strong has his way! The appointment of Synod Treasurer w.e.f. 1st May 1995, was done despite the reasonable objection by the bishop, not having the proper qualification. Such culture has become cancerous in our church but it appears that all have become either helpless or silent observers'.

It is not uncommon to find the ideologies, moralities, and even anecdotes of the Bible recurring time and time again. Jesus tells Peter the story of a servant and a king. The servant owes the king ten thousand bags of gold, a clearly un-payable debt. Since the servant cannot ever hope to repay the debt, the king orders him and his family sold into slavery. The servant begs for time and patience. The king, being merciful, agrees and cancels the entirety of the servant's debt. At this point, the servant leaves and encounters a man who owes him a hundred silver coins, a much smaller amount. This man cannot pay, so the unforgiving servant chokes him, demands payment, and has him thrown in the debtor's prison. The king then calls the unforgiving servant back, labels him as wicked, and asks him why he didn't show the same mercy that was given to him. The servant is then thrown in prison to be tortured in order to pay off his original debt (Matthew18:23-35).

The leadership legacy in the church violates the servanthood model. Shifting from one post to another in order to retain power, is assumed to be a part of church administration. A similar story occurred in my own diocese of Cuttack when I was working as a Presbyter. I found the same people continuing as office bearers when the rule was that one cannot stay for more than two terms. I was informed that the best way to perpetuate this cycle was to change the designation from secretary to treasurer or vice-versa thus circumventing the constitutional mandate and ensuring that the office bearers remained the same for eternity! Once there was a seminar at CNI Bhavan and in one of the presentations, the former Principal of Bishop's College humorously said, 'The only culture that our CNI General Secretary knows is "Agriculture"'. This was because he had experience in that branch of the discipline. Nevertheless, thankfully, he developed a culture in the CNI that respected the vocation of a bishop. Whenever anyone entered his office, he would politely offer them a chair right in front of his desk where one could have a pleasant conversation. However, after his tenure, the two successive General Secretaries removed those chairs and expected visitors to either stand before them after entering or sit in a corner of the room on a sofa while they spoke from their desk. Definitely, both of them left a legacy that should not be nurtured in the CNI as people expressed anguish and some never visited that office again.

Joining the NCCI as General Secretary was not a haphazard decision but after careful discussion with the then Moderator of the CNI and the consent of the CNI Synod authority, with a resolution by the CNI Executive that I would continue to be a CNI bishop but not be invited to attend the Synod. The irony is that my name never appeared as a former CNI bishop in the diary of the CNI for reasons best known to the then General Secretary. It may sound trivial, but it reflects the decay that is within. The treatment of the former bishops of the CNI is part of a saga that is indescribable. Once you retire you become persona non grata, even in your former diocese; which is why now some stave off retirement by inserting a safety clause regarding extension of retirement age. Some people asked me why I left the diocese to join the NCCI. One reason was that in some dioceses, the bishop is merely a pawn in the hands of one or two persons who are known as 'non-consecrated bishops' and are involved in the diocesan property business. After my departure from the Diocese of Eastern Himalayas in 2000, no one was elected as bishop except one for a short period, and another who was transferred from another diocese but is not accepted by the people of the hill areas.

Amartya Sen in his speech while accepting the German Book Trade's annual Peace Prize on 18th October 2020, said that the 'world is facing a pandemic of authoritarianism'. Sen emphasised the importance of freedom of expression and debate as prerequisites for freedom, peace, and progress, noting that these values were facing increasing threats today. He asserted that books played an important role in fostering a democratic culture of discussion and argument: 'Reading books and talking about them, can entertain, amuse, excite, and engage us in every kind of involvement. Books also help us to argue with each other. And nothing, I believe, is as important as the opportunity to argue about matters on which we can possibly disagree'. I hope the present memoir will be no exception and addresses the pandemic of authoritarianism, fascism, land mafia under the cover of development, and, not least, the lifestyle of the so-called leaders of the church and ecumenical organisations.

The people in any diocese are loving and respectful. I am amazed at the faith and witness of people at the grassroot level in my diocese and the way most of the pastors work and struggle in the villages is a matter of praise and needs the support of prayer. There is a phenomenal yearning for spirituality being manifested through our local congregations challenging the formality, structure, and prerogatives of our historic churches. These outbursts are not sporadic and cannot be ignored. People are searching for answers to complex questions in a rapidly changing world. Spiritual formation is an integral part of the Christian life. The core issue lies in the realisation of the presence of God. The word in the Bible that is used to denote God's presence – *panim,* is the same word for a human face. The relationship between these two meanings can be found in the story of Jacob's encounter with God at Penuel. Jacob is forced to return to the land of the brother he cheated out of his inheritance. When he hears that Esau is coming to meet him with 400 men, his guilty conscience implies the worst, so he devises a scheme wherein at least some of his family and possessions survive. In the extremity of his distress on this occasion, Jacob wrestles in prayer and sees God 'face to face' (Genesis 32:30). The next morning as Esau runs to meet his brother and falls weeping on his neck, Jacob cries, 'For to see your face is like seeing the face of God, now that you have received me favourably' (Genesis 33:10). To focus on this encounter is not to reduce the divinity of God but to sensitise the presence that requires wrestling and listening in silence to the voice of God. Dietrich Bonhoeffer had called the church to a period of public silence in the 1940s. It demanded self-discipline that would give time to listen penitently to others and wait for God to renew the language of proclamation. Truth is an integral part of listening and rooted in innocence but not in ignorance.

The story of the removal of two CNI bishops is another episode that has been discussed and debated but will remain incomplete without the inside story. One day I received a call from one of my students inviting me to the consecration service of a bishop at Believer's Church and to give the consecration sermon. My only advice was that it was a matter of the church's faith and order and had to be done in consultation with the CNI as it involved the unification of ministry. Two of my colleagues, for reasons best known to them, decided to participate in the consecration despite advice to the contrary by the then Moderator. On the day of the consecration, I was at the same venue attending a Serampore Senate meeting, when the President of the Senate, a CSI bishop, cleverly adjourned the meeting in the morning so that he could go and participate in the consecration service.

The issue was sent to me as the Chairman of the CNI Theological Commission, to give my opinion regarding the participation of the two CNI bishops in the consecration service. The CNI Theological Commission met and said what needed to be said, citing the constitution and the unification of ministry. However, the drama continued to unfold and politics and bureaucracy took over despite my attempt to bring up the issue at a bishop's meeting in Calcutta which the Moderator circumvented. It must be noted that the issue was and is not administrative but theological. Laying hands during the consecration service of a bishop of another church is not in agreement with the CNI; it is a faith and order issue and definitely a question of ministry of unification. For 40 years, from the beginning of the union, we had negotiated to have ministry unification, debated its issues, and took a historic and unanimous decision that could not be set aside so lightly.

The church must face the ways in which globalisation and postmodernity are affecting the life of the church and its capacity to bear witness to the gospel of Christ. Mission and ecumenism function within economically competitive environments. The so-called uncontrolled 'free' market dictates how persons are valued. In our ever-increasing individualised societies, communities have given way to the power of the individual. Churches too are caught in the trap of seeing people primarily as individual customers and the Christian faith has become a product to be marketed. Today's phenomenon expresses itself in the form of an unholy alliance between evangelism and consumerism. In the marketplace of religious ideas and persuasion, an unfettered and rampant competition is flourishing. The quest for an increased market share is the key motive for the understanding of mission.

India is undergoing a transformation from within that is slowly resulting in the loss of intimate social relationships, autonomy, and care. Money and debt have become the bottom line. Some say that the stereotype of rural communities as being 'friendly and family-centred' where everyone knows each other and where uncles, aunts, and grandparents live together, may become romantic nostalgia of the 'good old days'. However, historically, rural communities have been rooted and stable with the people bonded to the community. Changes in values have perhaps not permeated as quickly through the rural environment yet change is inevitable. The rural congregations have an agricultural-oriented lifestyle. There is a growing realisation that the rural church needs to become more local if it is to survive. Its survival will depend in large measure on how the church is understood. If by the church we mean a community of believers, there is every reason to expect the rural churches to be with us for a very long time. If, on the other hand, we view churches as institutions within the local community, the question of their survival in the rural communities is less certain.

Our understanding of God, who He is, and what He has done in history for each of us, needs to be lived out in the uniqueness of the local situation. Thus, spirituality presupposes a way of life and to live in a certain way. Spirituality is thus the way one sees relationships with God, the world, the people, and with material things. It concerns lifestyle, values, and a way of life. The search for spirituality is in essence a call to a transformed daily life where faith and everyday life become integrated. It is a journey of discovery. Life in a rural setting has the potential to create transformed communities, which by their very 'being' and 'active witness' could be signs of hope and repositories of truth and living. The opportunity is there: it needs commitment to enter into a process and a journey. The proposal is for thousands of micro-communities to take the initiative to listen to God's voice.

Ecumenical Bankruptcy

It is very difficult to forget that day in January 2005, when I discovered, to my utter dismay, the chaos that I had inherited from my predecessor in the NCCI as the General Secretary. There were sleepless nights, agony, inquiries, debates, discussions, clarifications, questions and answers, evaluations, restructuring, resolutions, and, not least, the humiliation that we had to face as a premier ecumenical body in India. I was sitting in front of the guest house in Nagpur as our quarters was being prepared for occupancy in the NCCI Campus when two people came up to me and said that they were from the Electricity Department and had come to cut the electric line for non-payment of bills. The following day in the office, when I tried to make a call, I found that the telephone line had been disconnected. Slowly pandora's box opened; it is all now part of the print, perhaps part of history but not forgotten. At that point, the question facing me was whether I should leave the NCCI and return to the diocese or not. I decided to accept the challenge and build a respected organisation. It took almost three years.

As the General Secretary of the NCCI, I had the opportunity to attend the 9th Assembly of the WCC at Porto Alegre, Brazil in February 2006. It was the first assembly of WCC to be conducted in Latin America. The then Moderator of the WCC His Holiness Aram I, Catholicos of Cilicia, Antelias, Lebanon, in his inaugural address to the 9th Assembly reminded us that for several years ecumenical stakeholders and actors had been limited to churches and their hierarchies but now they included donor agencies and specialised ministries. New ways of 'being' ecumenical and 'doing' ecumenism were enfolding; networking was replacing institutions; advocacy was substituting the program; membership-based ecumenism was losing its importance and ecumenism of partnership and alliance was gaining ground.

On the other hand, the then General Secretary of WCC, Dr Samuel Kobia extended an invitation to all to consider the spiritual base of the ecumenical movement as the *festa de vida* – the feast of life. The invitation to the feast comes from God and all are welcome. This feast comes to us as grace. The wonder of grace is that it is an undeserved gift. The *festa de vida* invites all into the household of God to experience the pain and suffering of others, and to feel part of the fragile and imperfect community of humanity. I was fascinated by the two addresses that were so different in tone and asked myself why we could not grasp the thread of ecumenism from here to overcome the stereotype. If one reads the detailed report of the Moderator, one cannot miss its prophetic tone. Certain excerpts are very profound and meaningful.

'Mainstream Christianity is ageing and falling in number, and Christianity is re-emerging with new faces and forms. The formation of non-denominational congregations, para-church and mega-church organisations has dramatically changed the Christian panorama. Major changes are taking place also inside the churches: the institutional church is losing much of its strength and impact on society; tensions and divisions in many churches on ethical, social, and pastoral issues are creating confusion and estrangement; the divide between "belonging" and "believing" is growing; and we hear more and more in the mass media about the church in "confusion", the "polarised" church, and the "silent" church.'

***

A Pedagogical Process

The core vision of ecumenism is evangelical awakening and it ought to be so. The very breadth of the present ecumenical movement is to engage with grassroots movements and indicate the need for discussion on new models for ecumenical understanding, worship, service, and work at local, regional, and national levels. *Diakonia* is an essential part of being a church. One powerful point in the pedagogical process is building trust. The gospel is at the centre of the Christian mission. The values of spirituality, fellowship, and participation are at the core of the mission. New ecumenism should continue to stress service and complete cooperation among all partners; the principles of solidarity and subsidiary are expected to prevail over-privileged relationships among members of particular fellowships. The principle of mutual accountability remains a core value that ensures trusted relationships and long-term commitments. Vision demands a programme to articulate itself, a movement requires structure to survive, and a fellowship needs a framework to grow. What is therefore needed in our discussion is a holistic, balanced, and interactive approach that will preserve ecumenism. The question is not merely one of coherence and collaboration between actors and actions but oneness in our understanding of ecumenism.

Bishop Lesslie Newbigin states that the 'only possible hermeneutic of the gospel is a "congregation" which believes it' (1989:232). He declares that the gospel will challenge the public life of our society only 'as when "local congregations" renounce an introverted concern for their own lives and recognise that they exist for the sake of those who are not members, as a sign, instrument, and foretaste of God's redeeming grace for the whole life of society' (1989:233). The Bible is not that we examine it from the outside, but that we indwell it and from within it seek to understand and cope with what is out there. In other words, the Bible furnishes us with our plausibility structure. The structure is in the form of a story. It is a 'realistic narrative'. Newbigin explains: 'Consider what it means to get to know a person. One can read an account of a person's character and career such as might be embodied in an obituary notice. But in order to know the person one must see how one meets situations, relates to other people, acts in times of crisis and in times of peace. It is in the narrative that character is revealed, and there is no substitute for this' (1988:98-99).

The story of the ecumenical movement is the story of a Christian family comprising two billion of the world's population. It is estimated that half of the Christian population is Roman Catholic. The WCC is a representative body bringing together another 550 million people who belong to 342 member churches or denominations in 120 countries. The remaining quarter comprises a group of churches belonging to a confessional family such as the Lutheran World Federation (LWF), Baptist World Alliance, World Evangelical Alliance (WEA), Disciples Ecumenical Consultative Council, Anglican Communion, and World Alliance of Reformed Churches (WARC) or churches belonging to the Pentecostal confession. The LWF, Anglican Communion, and WARC each represent about 65-75 million Christians whereas the Church of the Brethren has less than 500,000 members. The

WEA has its roots in the mid-19th century and is a network of seven regional and 123 National Evangelical Alliances and over 100 special ministries. The WEA aims to foster unity and provide a worldwide identity and voice to evangelical churches and Christians.

The centre of global Christianity has shifted away from the West towards the East and South. The contemporary mission context is producing new churches primarily from the South with a worldview shaped by the religious right, a political ideology shaped by a manifest destiny doctrine. The missionary movements of thousands of Koreans, Nigerians, and other nationalities of the South are changing the equation of mission understanding and practice in the contemporary era. The 'ready to go' brand of spirituality supported by individual, financially endowed, missionary congregations is changing the face of missions in many urban centres. The paradox of 'success' is to live in disobedience to the call of the gospel which is to live in unity with one another. The primary role of being a Christian is implied in these endeavours not to be ecumenical and not to carry an active concern for the unity of the body of Christ, the Church. Some of the major ecumenical consensuses in mission relationships have been thrown overboard and missions by any means possible is carried out even if it betrays the gospel call to reconciliation and unity.

In my report as the General Secretary of the NCCI to the XXVI Quadrennial Assembly, hosted by the Presbyterian Church of India from 30th – 5th April 2008 in Shillong, Meghalaya, I attempted to paint a vision of the NCCI after struggling relentlessly for three years. However, I was betrayed by my friends and colleagues, especially my fellow bishop who was the President, whom I had trusted the most. That is now history but I remember it as a nightmare. The Open Session of the NCCI Assembly was a fascinating sight in the stadium in Shillong with approximately 100,000 people squatting and standing with umbrellas on a rainy day to hear the message. It was my vision to include a full session inviting members of local churches. The response was overwhelming and I was told was the first of its kind in the history of the NCCI.

The guest speaker was Rev Robert Cunville whose story is interesting. Robert went to hear 'a barefoot evangelist' who was preaching from the porch of a house. He could not escape the powerful conviction of sin. When the evangelist gave the invitation, he repented and committed his life to Jesus Christ. Robert's parents supported him in his choice to pursue full-time ministry. Years later, he served as secretary of the North East India Christian Council when Billy Graham held a crusade in Kohima, Nagaland. Robert was the crusade coordinator, and he and Mr Graham became close friends. They remained in contact and in 1977, Mr Graham asked Robert to join his team. For almost 35 years, Robert had served as an Associate Evangelist for the Billy Graham Evangelistic Association.

Applause after the success of the NCCI Assembly in the following NCCI Executive Committee meeting still echoes in my mind but I am unable to forget the hypocrisy and conspiracy that crept in merely a year later. After setting the house in order, cleaning out the mismanagement and corruption, bringing back financial stability through effective stewardship of our resources, and presenting a detailed report in the Assembly, the Chairperson, who happened to be a bishop, conspired to dispense with me for reasons only known to him. Unfortunately, he did not live long in the world after my departure from the NCCI, and his dreams to scale the ecumenical ladder remained unfulfilled.

Once, during a walk in Geneva at the WCC Executive Committee, he shared his vision of us working together in the NCCI. On another occasion in Bangkok, he shared his frustration after a meeting saying, 'Bishop Sahu, by giving a grant of $10,000 how can an employee of an ecumenical organisation dictate terms? How can we tolerate it?' Alas! After one year, that same person became the close confidant of the President of the NCCI, with obvious assurances and meticulous planning regarding the ecumenical chair. Later, while sharing my memories, one of the colleagues of the former President of the NCCI, shared his distress and told me that the bishop had done the same in their church. To my shock, I discovered that the NCCI President had conspired to not give me a second term, whereas in his own office in Bangalore, he had assured me of his full support and discussed enlarging the vision. Even when the executive committee in Bangalore decided to appraise my work, he confidently told me at the dining table in the ecumenical centre in Whitefield, 'Bishop, do not worry at all. This is just a cloud that will soon pass'. History is witness to the fact that I had unearthed the mismanagement within the NCCI, aided its recovery from bankruptcy, instituted an enquiry committee comprising professional and respected church leaders, and experienced the pain of heading a mismanaged organisation as General Secretary. Yet, when the house was in order and supposed to celebrate its centenary year, I was given an appreciation letter for only my first tenure of five years.

The letter of the former General Secretary of the CNI, dated 10th December 2009 addressed to the four elected CNI representatives in the NCCI speaks volumes. 'Role and leadership provided by the present incumbent (referring to me) at a time, when NCCI was going down in all areas and some of you are not aware of those ugly incidents. The evaluation report which was conveniently kept in cold storage will speak volumes about the activities of some people who are playing a key role today in humiliating the present General Secretary'. In addition to this, three heads of churches: the Metropolitan of Mar Thoma Church, Moderator of CNI, and Moderator of CSI also wrote a letter to the then President of the NCCI, dated 16th September 2009, that 'we direct the President and Executive to stall all the proceedings towards the appointment of a new General Secretary. We need in-depth consultation and right procedure'. Yet the President turned a deaf ear.

Perhaps one lesson that I did not learn as an administrator was to be ruthless and rude. I remember once when a couple of senior and experienced members of the NCCI executive committee told me to ensure that a particular executive secretary should not be given a second term. However, on second thought, I felt it would not be ethically correct given that person's young family and future leadership potential. Too late I realised that the advice had been excellent. That same person was instrumental in my not being offered a second term at the NCCI. My prayer, even if it is sometimes painful, is that God would bless him.

The bitter experience reminded me of the words of Professor John S Mbiti of Kenya, way back in 1979. He referred to a group called 'self-made theological advisors, whether they be African or foreigner, who have little or nothing to produce beyond their generous advice; and others want to play the role of theological engineers, who meticulously sabotage spontaneous theological output by African Christians' (Mbiti 1979). Similarly, in the NCCI, I encountered a small group of 'Indians and select Indian diaspora' who are not only vocal and articulate but also know actual ecumenical politics, which I did not dare to learn. They are 'self-made/migrant ecumenists' whose main object was and is to plan and hold on to power within ecumenical bodies in order to move to greener pastures in Geneva, Bangkok, USA, or UK. They obviously settle down or attempt to remain for as long as possible in the comforts of the West. Once someone from that group told me, 'Bishop Sahu, statesmanship in the ecumenical world demands diplomacy and political manoeuvres, which you do not have'. Thank God, I have never prayed for such a gift nor do I aspire to possess it now. I have not been able to fathom these mysteries and advice. However, that same person forgot that gratitude is not in his vocabulary of ecumenism. In the 2007-2008 quarterly newsletter, the then Director Emeritus wrote that 'The interesting part is, for reasons unknown to me, he turned against even myself… As one grows up in knowledge and power, you try to undermine your patron'. It is a reminder that politics makes strange bedfellows, implying that political alliances for a common cause may bring together those holding widely differing views. The Church and Christian Institutions are no exceptions. However, everyone cannot be tarred with the same brush; there are role models that we can and should cherish. One of them was Timothy Gorringe. I had the opportunity to attend some of his lectures in Oxford while I was doing research. Way back in 1983, he had succinctly stated, 'To be indigenous means to have existed in a place, in a climate, in a situation, for generations, to have adapted to that situation and also to have adapted the situation'.

***

Global Christian Forum

The idea of a forum of Christian churches goes back to the suggestion made by Rev Dr Konrad Raiser—the then General Secretary of the WCC—in the mid-1990s. It emerged in the context of a process of reflection on the common understanding and vision of the WCC, wherein there was recognition that neither the Roman Catholic Church nor the overwhelming majority of Evangelical and Pentecostal churches were part of the WCC and that a broader and more inclusive pattern of relationships was called for. The concept was adopted and given its present form of a Global Christian Forum at a meeting with Evangelical and Pentecostal representatives at Fuller Theological Seminary in September 2000.

The aim of the process since 1998 has been to create an open space wherein representatives from a broad range of Christian churches and inter-church organisations, which confess the triune God and Jesus Christ as perfect in His divinity and humanity, can gather to foster mutual respect, explore, and address common challenges together. Forum meetings attempt to bring the widest possible spectrum of Christian traditions around the table: Anglican, Baptist, Catholic, Disciples, Evangelical, Friends (Quakers), Holiness, Independent, Lutheran, Mennonite, Methodist, Moravian, Old-Catholic, Orthodox (Eastern and Oriental), Pentecostal, Reformed, Salvation Army, Seventh-day Adventist, African Instituted Churches, united and uniting churches.

I had the privilege of attending the Global Christian Forum at Limuru, Nairobi, Kenya from 6th – 9th November 2007. It was a culmination of consultations in four major regions of the world (Asia, Africa, Europe, and Latin America) from 2004 to 2006. The Forum, as a global initiative, reflects many initiatives in local situations that are independent of the Global Forum. One example from India is the National United Christian Forum consisting of the NCCI, the Evangelical Fellowship of India, and the Catholic Bishops Conference of India. The Forum is a space to engage, a space where trust can grow and new relationships can be established. A crucial element in all the meetings has been the exercise of sharing faith journeys and stories of faith communities. It has proven to be a powerful means of discovering the faith convictions that are commonly held by Christians from different traditions.

Our NCCI Council consists of 30 member churches, seven related agencies, 17 Regional Christian Councils, 17 All India Christian Organisations, and three autonomous bodies. The strength of the council lies in our constituencies and one ought to be proud of them. A senior ecumenical leader once said that the strength of the council lay in the potential within, but unfortunately the understanding of resources has been confined to 'grants' from overseas. One classic example of resources within is the local initiative of the women of the Mizoram Presbyterian Synod of the Presbyterian Church of India. Statistics from 2007 say that the amount generated through the collection of a 'handful of rice' from the families came to ₹5,75,94,831/-. Perhaps one of the greatest weaknesses of our journey is not being able to identify and share the potentials within.

One of the worst natural disasters in living memory devastated vast areas of South Asia on 26th December 2004. A huge earthquake off the western coast of Sumatra, Indonesia, triggered a massive tsunami that swept away coastal villages and seaside resorts around the Indian Ocean. It was a challenging experience personally as I had just assumed responsibility as the General Secretary. I made an extensive visit to the people of the affected areas with the Director of CASA. The scale of the disaster was matched only by the phenomenal sense of 'togetherness' experienced during the crisis. We are thankful for the support extended by the worldwide family. Support for the relief effort was coordinated by a marvellous communication system.

***

Institutional Conundrum

The commemoration service on Serampore Senate's Convocation Day was a momentous occasion as the members of the Senate and the graduating students gathered in solemn worship to remember the Serampore Trio. I had the privilege of giving the commemoration address on 7th February 2009 at the Tamil Nadu Theological Seminary. It was an occasion to remember the story of the Serampore Trio: William Carey, Joshua Marshman, and William Ward especially to 'indwell the story' which meant not only inhabiting it but also enacting it in our ministerial formations. I cherish the 18 years of my association, excluding my student days, with the Theology Department of Serampore College and the privilege of living in Carey House.

Association with the Senate of Serampore continued for 25 years and it ceased when I joined the Sam Higginbottom University of Agriculture, Technology and Sciences (SHUATS) in 2012. The story of my 18 years of association and struggle in Serampore College is one where the faculty of Theology, despite being in one college and under one administration with a legacy of egalitarianism enshrined in the foundations laid by William Carey, Joshua Marshman, and William Ward, were treated as second class citizens. It was not merely a question of salary but of not being a part of the autonomous theology faculty under the Serampore Senate.

A story is told about Menno Simons, one of the founders of the Mennonite tradition. He was often pursued by the authorities who wanted to judge him for heresy and burn him. Once while he was traveling by coach on the roof because all the seats inside were occupied, it was halted by armed men on horseback. 'Is Menno Simons in there?' They shouted. Menno looked inside and asked, 'Is Menno Simons in there?' The passengers said no. So, he turned to the armed men and said, 'They say he is not in there'. The armed men rode off and Menno Simons survived. The Mennonite Confession of faith today reads that 'We commit ourselves to tell the truth, to give a simple yes or no'.

How can we comprehend a cobbler called William Carey having heard a call to come to India to preach the gospel to heathens? The call to serve in India has a tale. Timothy Gorringe, a former lecturer of Theology at the Tamil Nadu Theological Seminary, in his book *Redeeming Time* says, 'To do theology in India is not to do theology at 120°F, as it has been romantically described, but to take part in a struggle between death and life' (Deut.30:19).

Memoirs of the Serampore Trio are worth narrating. A wretched disaster occurred on 25th March 1812. It was the Serampore fire. 'The immense printing office, 200 feet long and 50 feet broad, reduced to a mere shell. The yard was covered with burnt quires of paper, the loss was immense. Carey walked over to the smoking ruins. The tears stood in his eyes. "In one short evening," said he, "the labours of years are consumed. How unsearchable are the ways of God! I had lately brought some things to the utmost perfection of which they seemed capable and contemplated the missionary establishment with perhaps too much self-congratulation. The Lord has laid me low, that I may look more simply to Him"'.

Carey had grossly underestimated what it would cost to come to India. His early years were miserable and he was forced to move his family repeatedly as he sought employment that could sustain them. Illness struck the family, and loneliness and regret set it: 'I am in a strange land', he wrote, 'no Christian friend, a large family, and nothing to supply their wants'. Yet he retained hope: 'Well, I have God, and His word is sure'. He learned Bengali with the help of a pundit, and in a few weeks began translating the Bible into Bengali and preaching to small gatherings. When Carey himself contracted malaria, and then his five-year-old son Peter died of dysentery, it became too much for his wife, Dorothy, whose mental capabilities rapidly deteriorated and she suffered delusions, even threatening him with a knife. She eventually had to be confined to a room and physically restrained.

In October 1799, things finally turned when he was invited to relocate to Serampore, a Danish settlement near Calcutta. He then came under the protection of the Danes, who permitted him to preach legally whereas, in the British-controlled areas of India all of Carey's missionary work had been illegal. Carey was joined by William Ward, a printer, and Joshua and Hanna Marshman, teachers. Mission finances improved as Ward began securing government printing contracts, the Marshmans opened schools for children, and Carey began teaching at Fort William College in Calcutta. In December 1800, after seven years of missionary labour, Carey baptised his first convert, Krishna Pal, and two months later, he published his first Bengali New Testament. Carey and his pundits over the next 28 years translated the entire Bible into India's major languages: Bengali, Odia, Marathi, Hindi, Assamese, and Sanskrit and parts of other languages and dialects. He also sought social reform in India, including the abolition of infanticide, widow burning (*sati*), and assisted suicide. By the time Carey died, he had spent 40 years in India and his mission could count only some 700 converts in a nation of millions. According to our modern-day church growth theory, his mission was a total failure but we are proof that that failure ultimately laid an impressive foundation for Bible translations, education, and social reform.

The relationship between the Home Committee with their supporters on the one hand and the Serampore group on the other was ideal until the arrival of John Dyer as the Society's secretary from 1817-54. His letters were described by Carey as 'commercial letters' and the missionaries felt themselves to be ranked simply as 'paid agents'. The story is unpleasant but very much part of the Serampore mission memoir. It was perhaps inevitable that the ageing group of missionaries with properties they had planned, built, and paid for, the chain of mission stations, and last but not least a close-knit community with its very special financial basis of arrangements should have presented a difficult set of problems to a committee far away in London. The question of property and trusteeship, matters of authority and control were elevated above grateful recognition of unparalleled services, sacrifices, and the saintliness of the trio whose place in history will remain secure.[2]

The history of Protestant missions is in many ways an extended commentary on the phrase 'Expect great things from God and attempt great things for God' based on the text: 'Enlarge the place of your tent, stretch your tent curtains wide, do not hold back; lengthen your cords, strengthen your stakes' (Isaiah 54:2). It is not a question of how fast we can go, how fast our numbers can increase, and how fast we can work. Sometimes we are like the person on a horse galloping swiftly down the road, who is asked by an old farmer standing in the field: 'Where are you going?' The rider turns around and shouts back, 'Do not ask me. Ask my horse'.

Doing theology means following the footprints of Jesus of Nazareth with non-negotiable values. 20th January 2009 was a historic day when the first black person stepped into the White House. It symbolised a genuine revolution in a country where African Americans were bought and sold as slaves, segregated, and where, some 40 years earlier, the Baptist minister and civil rights leader Martin Luther King Jr in his famous speech said, 'I have a dream that my four little children will one day live in a nation where they will not be judged by the colour of their skins but by the content of their character'. A successor of that dream, President Barack Hussein Obama in his inaugural address said, 'Our challenges may be new. The instruments with which we meet them may be new. But those values upon which our success depends—honesty and hard work, courage and fair play, tolerance, and curiosity, loyalty, and patriotism—these things are old. These things are true. They have been the quiet force of progress throughout our history'. Basic values are timeless like the legacy of the Serampore Trio, which was to shape the minds of thousands who passed through our esteemed institutions of learning.

Commitment would require taking risks although some advice avoiding risks. 'Not to take a risk when it is time to take a risk is the biggest risk of all'. What prevents us from making a decision is the fear of change. Fear of change implies loss of control and power that results in resistance to change. Thus, insights into wider commitments beyond boundaries in the mission of God are both inspiring and educative. Can anything good come out of Chand Pur Bela locality in Patna? The Math wizard Anand Kumar from Patna used to hawk papad (Indian wafers) to earn a living. His father, who used to work in the postal department, died prematurely, so his mother would prepare papad for Anand to sell. Along with IPS officer Abhayanand, he began a noble initiative called Super 30 to coach 30 underprivileged students for the Indian Institutes of Technology-Joint Entrance Examination (IIT-JEE) free of cost for seven months. The result was that 18 of his students passed in 2003, 22 in 2004, 26 in 2005, 28 in 2006, and 30 in 2007.

The story of the Cobbler-Weaver-Printer despite its humble beginnings is the grand narrative of the modern protestant mission in India. However, there could have been no Serampore without Tranquebar and the work of Bartholomäus Zeigenbalg. After reading an appeal for help from a Danish soldier's widow in Tranquebar, the king of Denmark, Frederick the Fourth, decided to send two German missionaries, one of whom was Ziegenbalg. Eventually another missionary called Schwartz came to Tranquebar, whose life and work greatly influenced Colonel Ole Bie, previously an official there. Ole Bie went on to become the Governor of the Danish settlement in Serampore and he welcomed the missionaries who had been denied permission by the East India Company, to settle in Serampore. Thus, Tranquebar paved the way for Serampore.

The Serampore narrative has a definite providential dimension. William Carey was educated in a village school and thereafter learned the trade of a shoemaker. It was during this period that he underwent a religious experience that was to shape his future life. Subsequently, he became a village schoolmaster and a country minister. Joshua Marshman was educated in a village school and worked as a weaver. He was appointed as a master of a school in Bristol and there he met Mr Ryland, one of the founders of the mission who helped to turn his thoughts towards missions. After completing his school education, William Ward was apprenticed to a printer where his interest in literary work and journalism grew. He met Carey once, who suggested that he use his gifts and experience in the service of God in India. Such were the famous Trio of Serampore who were remembered and celebrated 200 years later in 2018.

In 1818, the missionaries decided to build a college. The Danish Governor's colleague Major Wickedie planned the iconic noble building which is one of the finest edifices of its kind in Asia. The prospectus on 15th July 1818 of Serampore College states, 'A College for the instruction of Asiatic Christian and other youth in Eastern Literature and European Science'. Thus, the Serampore College was established in 1818 and empowered to grant degrees by the incorporation of the Royal Charter of the King of Denmark in 1826. The hope was that the College would be considered 'pre-eminently a divinity school, where Christian youth of personal piety and aptitude for the work of an evangelist should go through a complete course of instruction in Christian Theology'. At the same time, it was made imperative that the College should be open to all without distinction of caste or creed, 'with the understanding that the instruction is divested of everything of sectarian character'. In 1845, after being a Danish colony for 90 years from 1755, Denmark sold her possessions in India to the British Government. Thus, Tranquebar in the south and Serampore in the north—the two cradles of Christianity in India—passed into British hands on 11th October 1845 and Serampore College became affiliated to Calcutta University.

The interesting part of the story is that although the College itself had the authority to award university degrees and diplomas, it was never implemented probably because the struggle for its very existence had occupied the founders in the early years. Rev W H Denham thought that Serampore could be of greater service if it was affiliated to an existing university rather than being independent. So, the association was established in 1857 and Serampore was one of the first colleges to affiliate with Calcutta University. Alongside Calcutta University's syllabus, which aimed at training students for Government service, Serampore had its own syllabus that aimed to train Christian youth for the service of the church and missions. Eventually, it was observed that the College had deviated from the original object with which it was founded, which is the training of Christian ministers. Hence, in 1883 it was decided to shut down the Arts department and the High School and revert the College to a purely theological institution.

Rev George Howells is gratefully remembered as the second founder of the College. He visited Serampore and was filled with depression, 'I felt glad that the authorities in London decided to send me to backward Orissa rather than to Serampore with its dead hopes. A young man sees more hope in an uncultivated wilderness than in a graveyard filled with monuments of the mighty dead'. In 1910, the Higher Theological Department was opened and in 1911, the Arts department was again affiliated with Calcutta University. Serampore conferred the degree of Bachelor of Divinity on the first three theological graduates of the College in full exercise of the rights under the Charter of 1827 for the first time on 14th December 1915. Dr Howell became a member of the Bengal Legislative Council in 1918 and revived the Charter under the Bengal Act of 1918. The Serampore College Bill was passed on 28th March 1918 and subsequently received the assent of the Governor-General and was gazetted on 1st May 1918. The privileges under the Charter and Statutes remained untouched under the Act except that if degrees were to be granted in any other branch of knowledge or Science apart from Theology, they must satisfy the Government that they were equipped for the purpose.

The dictum – 'Expect great things from God. Attempt great things for God', provides the important criteria to evaluate the works of the Serampore Trio. They seem to have operated on two models: the primitive, i.e. to carry out public relations in Britain and North America as faith missionaries, and the professional, symbolised by the creation of Serampore College, which began to look like a 'white elephant' leading to the subsequent dispute with the Baptist Missionary Society (BMS) and Carey's appointment as Professor at the Governor General's prestigious Fort William College in Calcutta. One major task in reading popular biographies is to isolate imaginary idealisation, distorted representation, and unverifiable interpretations of the past. In the words of Stephen Neil, the task of a responsible mission historian involves concealing nothing that s/he believes to be the truth and refusing to accommodate the errors of mythology. The Serampore

Trio need to be seen as players on a multi-cultural playing field at a very unusual moment in history.

One may ask now whether it is valid to view Carey's 'Enquiry'—published in 1792—as a paradigm for his and his colleagues' missionary career. This work contained careful and accurate statistical information about the various races of the world, as well as a powerful plea for the cause so dear to his heart, and its publication did much to arouse a wider interest. On 2nd October 1792, a decisive step was taken by 12 ministers of the Northamptonshire Association of Baptist Churches to found a Society called 'The Particular (Calvinistic) Baptist Society for Propagating the Gospel among the Heathen', which later became the BMS. It is very difficult to respond in the affirmative now. The Baptists' missional polarity between Calcutta and Serampore was born out of political and financial expediency in the early 19th century. Working simultaneously in those two centres was apparently crucial to the survival of their mission in British Bengal. Carey was engaged in Fort William College, Calcutta, a colonial service, and the Trio established a college of their own in a Danish Colony at Serampore.

Under the patronage of the most noble Marquis of Hastings, Governor-General of India, Serampore College was founded in August 1818 'for the instruction of Asiatic[,] Christian, and other Youth'. It was deliberately established as a liberal arts and science college for both 'Christian and heathen' students, rather than a strictly theological seminary for missionary students, native or East Indian. The mere absence of a comma between 'Asiatic' and 'Christian' in the College's second Report (August 1821) could have led the British evangelical public to believe that the student body was much more 'Christian' in composition than ever was the case. John C Marshman rectified this 30 years later when he cited the prospectus issued on 15th July 1818 and inserted a comma. Christopher Smith makes a very good observation that the college had two rather different personae by which it appealed to contrasting constituencies. In India, it functioned as an Arts and Science College, while to missions' supporters in the western world it was portrayed as a school designated 'to train Indians to replace Europeans completely as missionaries, and so to create a truly indigenous church'. That ambiguity was already apparent to Britain's BMS leadership by 1825, with the result that they firmly refused to yield to the Trio's appeal for its support.[3]

The Bengal Act of 1918, which revived the Charter of Serampore, clearly states that 'if at any time, the Council shall intend to grant degrees in any branch or branches of knowledge and science other than theology, such degrees shall be confined to students who shall have received regular instruction at the Serampore College'. However, such authority has not been implemented till today. Serampore College is an affiliate college of Calcutta University as far as Arts-Science-Commerce degrees are concerned, but functions as a university offering theology degrees with affiliated theological colleges across the country, not found in any 'State or Central Act of the University of India'. It is this anomaly as well as two functional identities of Serampore College under one administration that has been a major concern which has not been addressed by the leaders.

The former Registrar of Serampore College made a valid point: 'One must note that the Serampore College Act - 1918 is not a University Act; Serampore College was not made a university by this Act, Serampore College is a university by its Charter, granted by His Danish Majesty, King Frederick the Sixth, in 1827. The Act is restrictive in nature, on the one hand, and expansive, on the other. Legally, its jurisdiction is not clear, more so after 1947. There are a number of legal issues related to the College, the Senate, the Council, and affiliated colleges, which are not attended to for a long time, and if they are left unattended for long, the repeal of the Act may be a real threat'.

Serampore belongs to us. In fact, it is a gift belonging to Indian churches, therefore belongs to no one specific body. The need of the hour is to address the future of Serampore. Many would be willing to engage in such a conversation. There are excellent reasons to do so that are specific to Serampore, ranging from the jurisdiction of the Act of 1918, governance structure, funding, and, not least, Serampore's place in the larger compass of higher education in India under the University Grants Commission (UGC) and now more likely to be under the Higher Education Commission of India Act, 2018. Perhaps the most disturbing thing is, how little fundamental collaborative intellectual effort has been made to understand and respond to them. It is, of course, nobody's field, and all of us want to get on with 'our own work'. Yet, outside influence and pressure will continue and perhaps intensify, which can be good as well as bad. However, if they meet with a virtual vacuum where there ought to be thinking, conversations, advocacy, and action then we will be accountable to future generations for failing to nurture a precious inheritance.

Sometimes I wonder about the calling to ministry and rendering service in Serampore. Because, the College although unique in having Arts, Science, and Theology under one roof with one Principal, never recognises the qualifications and teaching experience of a theologian working in the same college while appointing its principal. Such is the irony and anomaly that continues to prevail without being addressed. After the transfer of the Council to India in 1948, no serious effort was made to develop satisfactory administrative and executive structures. In the 1960s, under new bye-laws, the Council recognised, and organised the College into two departments, two committees, two rectors/vice-principals under the existing faculty and a unified principal, the counterpart of the Senate for internal management. The Council has so far closed its eyes and failed in its stewardship of the Trio's Institution.

The case of the Department of Theology is one of neglect, hegemony, suppression, and exploitation. In the past, it was the jewel of the sciences but now has lost its pristine glory and honour. So also, as its staff and students. The salaries of the staff of the Theology Department are much less than their counterparts in other departments. The Charter has been given to the Council which is the Trustee of the College. The University now functions through the Department of Theology for which the Senate was created by the Serampore College Act of 1918. The Department of Theology currently does not function as the teaching department of the University and this serious lacuna needs to be addressed by the Council and all the stakeholders. The Council needs to rethink its own structure, composition, and membership for making itself relevant in the witness and service of the College. The College needs to be restructured as per the dictates and demands of universities in India.

Building the Kingdom of God

The story of Ida Scudder, the founder of Christian Medical College (CMC), is one about the establishment of an institution with a different note. She was a 14-year-old student when she was asked, 'What will you do when you get out of here?' 'I know one thing I will not do', she told her friends emphatically, 'I will not be a missionary in India like my parents'. Later she received a cable saying, 'Come immediately, your mother is ill and needs you'. So, Ida came to India for a short visit. One day, there was a knock on the door. A young Indian stood there, tall, grave, and dignified. 'I desperately need your help. My wife is dying in childbirth'. 'It is my father you want', she replied. 'No, I cannot take a man'. The same scene was repeated two more times that evening. In the morning she sent a servant to find out what had happened and learnt that all three young women had died. Troubled but resolute, she wrote a letter to her friend saying she was returning to America to study to be a doctor. In 1899 she graduated and after raising funds to build a hospital, she returned to India and began with a small clinic where she treated women.

The following statement by Ida Scudder is not only profoundly astounding but also very true: 'Not building a Medical College but the Kingdom of God'. Celebrating 103 years of medical education from 1918-2021 is a milestone of the church's healing ministry. However, there is a need to hear the prophetic voice. In the words of Pauline Jeffrey: 'Organised welfare work is, of course, necessary; but the gaps in it must be filled by personal services, performed with loving-kindness. A charitable organisation is a complex affair like an automobile; it needs a broad highway to run on. It cannot penetrate the little bypaths; those are for men and women to walk through, with open eyes and hearts full of comprehension. It is often these little bypaths that you can find "Aunt Ida" now'.[4] Can we find 'Aunt Ida' in the little bypaths of India today? There was no prophet to predict that 9th December 1870, the day baby Ida arrived, was to become the Founder's and College Day for several hundred medical school graduates and friends, half a century later.

In 2005, after joining the NCCI, I attended the CMC Council Meeting and for the first time entered its campus. When I completed my tenure of five years in the NCCI and conveyed to the then Director of CMC that I would not be attending the council as the NCCI representative, to my surprise I was told that my relationship with CMC would continue. Now it is a story of my association with CMC for a total of 15 years that includes being a member of the Council, Executive Committee, Staff-selection Committee, Admission Committee, Nomination Committee, Ad-hoc Nomination Committee to appoint Associate Directors, Principal and not least, the Director. Such a spread of warm memories is overwhelming and I am grateful to God for such an experience in an esteemed institution.

CMC was the first Medical College that was established by a woman, staffed by women, and run for women only, until men knocked at the door so persistently that it had to be opened as a co-educational college. Often the sequence has been the opposite in the West where many a time a Men's Medical College has had to open its doors to women. Yet, for this, Ida Scudder was accused of being disloyal by a few of her old friends on the American Committee. Today CMC Vellore is a 2700 bed, teaching, referral, and multi-specialty medical college, training 100 undergraduates and 178 postgraduates every year and 9000 patients knock on the door of the outpatient department every day.

The vision statement of CMC Vellore – to be a witness to the healing ministry of Christ through excellence in education, service, and research has remained undiluted because of the commitment of the generations of faculty and staff of the institution. In 2018, CMC Vellore was deemed the best Private Hospital in India as per a survey and came second in 2020. It was also rated the best COVID-19 hospital in India in 2020. The CMC students of medicine receive almost a free education. At CMC, an MBBS student pays just ₹3000/- per year for tuition fees while a post-graduate pays ₹4000/-. This has been the same since 1978 and the fees have not been revised in the last 25 years. This has created a social environment for medical education that benefits all people instead of a commercial environment where healthcare is becoming an industry for profit. A medical student who is a beneficiary of this low fee privilege realises that some poor patient has a role to play in their education. He completes his education and begins his career with a deep sense of obligation to those unknown patients whose mite has been part of his resources.

In the words of my elder son, 'Entering the campus of CMC Vellore, one is confronted with the magnitude of malaise in the world and the faith of the multitudes in the CMC medical fraternity. At the same time, to the uninitiated, the world of CMC Vellore can be a labyrinth of procedures and confluence of communities and possibly confusion. It is unlike any other private medical institution in India with a sea of humanity pouring in through the gates of CMC Vellore. At this point, it is pertinent to applaud and appreciate the institution for the services rendered to the patients over the years even when the ground reality is that they are expected to cater to far more than they can handle'. Having read that I must add my experience. I wanted to obtain the advantage of the facility during one of my visits to CMC with my wife, and the Director generously provided a staff member to accompany us from department to department, one lab to another, and until finally, we met the consultant in the afternoon who was very polite and kind. Their humility overwhelmed me. On another occasion, I decided to be one of the 9000 outpatients without wearing a cross. The experience was devastating and I told my wife I would never go to CMC again for treatment. However, there are very good people also. One of them was the Public Relations Officer, who has always been very helpful to some of our pastors when they have required access to medical care.

'The concept of time and space takes on new dimensions within the campus as does the harsh reality of one's own mortality. Time slows down with every step of appointments, moving from test to test, the interminable wait in between, and the confrontation of one's own thoughts. It is the perfect ground for the collision of hopes and dreams, researching the internet for news/views/contradictions, and snatching at snippets of succour. An experience in CMC Vellore demands your patience and mindfulness'.[5]

The environment within the A-Block can be summed up in one word – hope! I will never forget the day when I entered the block with Prof Dr Raju Chacko, when my daughter-in-law was diagnosed with Stage 4 lung cancer. He was as quiet as a pastor as we went to her room with my son. Then he revealed the truth in a manner that was hopeful that we would be able to overcome the battle. The doctors and the staff have an ever-present smile on their faces that is both reassuring and hopeful. The level of patience and commitment to service is unparalleled in the medical fraternity. I have often heard words of encouragement ranging from: 'I'll be praying for you' to 'Don't worry, have faith and trust God'. During the most trying of times, these few words can provide a layer of comfort for those who are hurting. Their attention to detail from the cleanliness of the bedsheets, the pain threshold of the patient, lighting, meal timings and just popping in to smile and engage in small talk is meticulous. Being far away from home, CMC Vellore can become a lonely place with the whole world buzzing around and visitors few and far between. During such times, these interactions become a lifeline to the world outside and break the temptation to dive into a rabbit hole of despair.

Celebrating a hundred years of its existence is a milestone in the life of any institution. It was indeed special for me to celebrate 100 years of medical education in CMC Vellore in 2018 as the Acting Chair of CMC, a privilege granted to me when the then Chairman played hide and seek for a couple of months and subsequently resigned. The 4th of May 2018 was indeed a historic day when CMC, Vellore was honoured to have Shri Ram Nath Kovind, the Hon'ble President of India to inaugurate its centenary year. In his address, he said, 'The medical education programme here combines professional expertise with social relevance and ethical practice. I understand clinical training in your hospital is complemented by placements in villages and underserved areas. This is commendable. Please keep it up. Doctors need a sharp mind – but much more than that, they need a warm heart. And CMC Vellore must continue to train doctors and nurses with warm hearts'.

When I presented a memento to the Hon'ble President of India on the stage, I said, 'We are honoured by your presence'. Instantly, he responded, 'Bishop, I am honoured by your presence'. Such was his humility and respect, surely not to me as a person, but to a servant of God in the attire of a bishop. In retrospect, his words were a contrast to the disrespect I experienced as the Acting Chairman on the last day of the Council in June 2018 when the Director whispered to me, 'We need an IAS officer in the chair position of CMC'. Normally the incumbent vice-chairman is nominated to continue in the office as I had completed only one year as Acting Chairman, but was told that I must leave to make way for an IAS officer. I had no words to react to that and had to compose myself. Afterward, I silently prayed, 'May God help CMC, if that is the new vision and mission of building the Kingdom of God'. If IAS officers were now needed in the Chair, then eventually clinicians, selected in a strange five-year-musical chair game from among the CMC faculty, may not be needed as the Director.

I continued as a member of the Council for one more year after the ignominy accorded to me as a clergyman unsuitable for CMC's Council chairmanship. Some fellow Council members expressed that I must raise this and other visible governance issues on the floor. However, I posited this question to them - where was their voice when the Director appointed the chairman in absentia, someone who had no experience of CMC's governance. He had been a member of the Ad hoc-Nomination Committee that chose the current Director controversially and was appointed chairman to defend the position of the Director from the contradictions that were unfolding. I followed the words of wisdom I knew: 'Do not waste words on people who deserve your silence. Sometimes the most powerful thing you can say is nothing at all'. If they have a conscience and are genuinely prayerful people, then vindication will come.

I have been part of the governance structure of CMC Vellore for about 15 years. The experience has been both enriching and mystifying. Governance is the process of decision-making and its efficient implementation. In simple terms, governance is the act of governing. This act is performed by a governing body, in our case, the Council. Governance is the creation of policies that define the identity of an institution through debate and discussion. In our institution, the Council members deliberate on the direction to propel the organisation forward. The administration is concerned with the implementation of the decisions of governance. The identity of the Council is shaped by its 52 varieties of stakeholders who play or ought to play a decisive role in governance. In his autobiography called A Life and its Lessons,[6] Samuel Paul, the former Vice-Chairman of the CMC Council and former director of the Indian Institute of Management (IIM), Ahmedabad narrates the story of CMC in one chapter. He states, 'CMC has received numerous accolades and is widely perceived as a great success story'. The credit goes to generations of committed faculty and staff who have imbibed the story in their life and work. The oversight mechanism is a major contributor to its success and longevity, not least because CMC is a healthcare provider.

CMC Vellore's model of administration where the CEO and higher hierarchical positions are filled by the homegrown, in-house medical faculty, goes against established healthcare management paradigms. Paul makes a cautious observation, 'There is, of course, no guarantee that CMC's reputation and survival is assured forever just because it has outlived its first century. Failure to induct competent and experienced persons to guide and oversee non-medical management functions at senior levels is likely to hurt the institution's effectiveness and credibility'. Perhaps, CMC may need IIM graduates with corporate experience or, as in St Johns Medical College, Bangalore, ordained priests with leadership skills, but definitely not the homegrown clinicians in the position of Director or Vice-Chairperson. Unfortunately, they bring their memories of student-hood and professional rivalry into the administration. The members in the Council are given a sermon by some retired senior staff, that the Director must be comfortable with the selection of his colleagues. The discomfort arises when classmates are selected to the position of unequal status, or to stretch it further when a retired faculty sits as a chairman with a younger colleague as director, which could result in narratives like, 'four years and five seasons vis-à-vis five years and four seasons'. The former was a 35-page document comprising 9,349 words by the former Chairman submitted on 30th December 2017 to the Council Secretary as a closing reflection and sent to selected Council members without marking a copy to me as the acting Chairman. The latter was a 61-page document comprising 19,981 words by the former Director submitted on 31st May 2018 to the Enquiry Committee of Kanigapuram Campus. The copies were made available to me as acting chairman only after these were in circulation and the report of the enquiry committee was complete.

'Four Years and Five Seasons', the narrative of the Ex-Chairman was referred on the Council floor by one of the members and it was decided that his resignation be investigated by the same members of the 2nd Audit Committee of the Kanigapuram Housing Project. Unfortunately, the enlightened and competent members of the Enquiry Committee including two respectable, retired IAS officers did not have the courage to expose the issues raised by both the former Chairperson and former Director, which have larger implications as a Christian institution in India and in the world. Instead, one of the members of the Enquiry Committee was rewarded with the offer of chairmanship of the CMC Council.

Reading the two documents, one is not only perplexed but also concerned about the issues raised if we are 'not building a hospital but the kingdom of God'. In our journey from Chennai to Bangalore by road and over a cup of coffee in his home in Bangalore, Dr Samuel Paul expressed several times that the line between governance and management is blurred in the Council. Interestingly, he also underlined 'the silence of good people', especially the 'silence of the stakeholders in the governance process in the Council', which may become a deterrent to the growth of an esteemed institution. During a stormy council meeting in 2018, which I was chairing, one bishop quietly told me, 'Bishop, this is diabolical', referring to the behaviour of a senior former Director who was controlling the entire thought process of the Council without allowing anyone's point of view. Many expressed and wished that I would bell the cat. It must be known that earlier, in the executive committee in September 2017, a decision had been made that the council membership of former directors be limited to a couple of years, unlike the present practice of 'till death do us part' and be tabled in the January 2018 Council. Unfortunately, that numbered EC resolution was neatly removed and never saw the light of day for reasons known to all. When I questioned the omission, I was told, 'Try and see the outcome'.

The story of CMC will be incomplete if I do not pick up the threads from the two narratives - 'Four Years and Five Seasons' and 'Five Years and Four Seasons' for the sake of posterity and propriety of building the Kingdom of God. Let me dissect them as the officiating Chairman during that period.

Being the acting Chairman in 2017-18, I cannot absolve myself from the unpleasant part I was forced to deal with regarding the: 1) the second audit of Kanigapuram Housing Project, 2) the appointment of Director and Associate Director, 3) appointment and unceremonious removal of the Council Secretary, 4) extension of incumbent council secretary, and

5) resignation of the Council Chairman. They may now be part of history but cannot be swept under the carpet.

The most controversial and unpleasant issue that I had to handle and, in the end, paid a price for, was the second audit of the Kanigapuram Housing Project. The rights under Article 30(1) as a Christian minority institution do not give us the license to avoid auditing our own governance structure. As the Acting Chairperson, I had agreed to call for an arbitrary audit—a second one—in the January Council of 2018 with a view to clear the air. I did not think it right to succumb to the pressure, both implied and spoken, directed at me by a powerful few to shame the outgoing Director and his team and subvert the controversial appointment of the new incumbent. While instituting the audit, towards the end of the second day, a council member mentioned that an audit had already been conducted on 28th October 2016. I remarked that it would then be easier to expedite the second audit and permitted the same. I had seen and participated in the lengthy discussions and decisions about the Kanigapuram Campus in several Council meetings over the previous four years. The clarifications given by the former director on the floor and in the executive committee received applause in both. He was honoured with a silver plaque on 22nd September 2017 for exemplary leadership. Therefore, since I was sceptical about the allegation of corruption, I thought the second audit would clear things up. Unfortunately, it turned out to be malicious and vindictive by a small group of individuals whose intent, now I think, was questionable. After a marathon discussion and debate extending till midnight after dinner on the first day of the Council in June 2018, the report was presented and decisively resolved by the Council. The Council resolution itself was self-explanatory – an executive decision was taken under a specific situation which was clearly clarified by the then Director and accepted by the Council. One interesting part of the report and recommendation of the inquiry committee was 'that ensuring adherence to the constitutional provisions is the collective responsibility of the Executive Committee and the Council'. Yet, even after the closure of the second audit and the recommendation of the enquiry committee and approval by the Council, I was told by an irate veteran council member, 'You did not indict the former Director and did not dismiss the General Superintendent after the hard work done by the enquiry committee'. Another senior council member who was part of the group that schemed the various controversies in 2017-18 said, 'He had never seen corruption of such magnitude'. I did not respond to this malice verbally because of what Jesus said in the Gospels, 'Cast not your pearls before swine' (Matthew 7:6).

Institutions, in general, are facing identity crises all over the world. The ethics of governance is in question. Christian institutions like CMC need to be particularly conscious of the disruptive trends globally. Honesty, ethics, and transparency in governance must be prized above trivial concerns, and it is the Council's responsibility to insulate the institution from anything that could derail the vision and mission. The crucial question that the Council must ask continuously is, 'Will we pass a test of credibility if conducted by an external agency?' Samuel Paul's concern, which comes as the worldview of a renowned management guru, holds much water.

There are examples of the vacillating indecisiveness of CMC's management. First, was the issue of not increasing the retirement age from 60 to 65 years with the argument that the junior faculty needed to be allowed in the decision-making process – 'for them and by them'. I failed to understand this because in the medical profession at the age of 60, most clinicians are at the peak of their efficiency and corporate sectors were looking to recruit them unless they volunteer to render service in a mission hospital in a rural area. The second was the second CMC Campus in Chittoor when the land was given by the then Chief Minister of Andhra Pradesh. I remember several visits to the site, the discussions, and finally, the decision to land there. Third, was 'chasing the chimera', as a former executive and finance committee member described the Institute of National Importance. I recall that on the day of the meeting since the Chairman could not come, I was requested by the Director to chair the meeting as a member of the Executive. Much sound and fury ended in nothing because we were scared to lose our rights rather than gain privileges.

Peter Greer and Chris Horst share their journey of discovery as they address a pivotal question in Mission Drift, a book given to me by the Council Secretary elected after the CMC Executive Committee meeting in September 2017. Unfortunately, this new Council Secretary was, in an unscrupulous and unchristian way, removed by a clever misrepresentation of an archaic resolution passed 20 years earlier in the Council. God surely works in mysterious ways but I have failed to understand human nature playing hide and seek not only among ourselves but also with God. Mission Drift draws attention to the fact that faith-based organisations inevitably drift from their foundational mission. The stories cited in the book are fascinating as well as alarming. Slowly and silently organisations routinely drift from their original purpose. It has happened repeatedly throughout history. While reading these stories with wider implications, I recognised the similar parallels in CMC. I had initiated a process of reconciliation in the January 2018 Council but did not know that there was a conspiracy behind it. After the audit, my sudden departure from CMC in the following Council did not diminish the fulfilment of my 15-year association with it since 2005. It was only marred by that undignified exit towards the end of 2018. Perhaps my expectations of CMC were too high, believing that its ethics were above the CNI and the NCCI.

I must describe my leadership selection experience at CMC. My first experience as a member of the Ad-hoc-Nomination Committee to select the Principal/Associate Directors/Director was amazing and I often cited the model at other institutions with whom I was associated. It is a process where the candidate never applies for a post but is nominated by colleagues. The nominators are the ones who are interviewed to short-list the candidates. Eventually, only short-listed candidates are called for interviews. It is a lengthy process but very meaningful. Unfortunately though, as I participated and was part of the decision-making process, I slowly discovered that human weakness is prevalent here as well. CMC is no exception. I was reminded of my experience as a diocesan bishop while chairing and interviewing candidates, and at the end of the whole process, of being told quietly to approve a specific candidate as recommended by a political party leader or the district school authority before finalising the list.

The process of appointing the CMC Director includes lengthy deliberations, discussions, and, not least, hammering out differences before bringing it to the floor of the Council. However, this was not the case that we witnessed in the June 2017 Council. The candidature of the present incumbent was uncertain and even I, as a council member was requested to extend my support despite a shortfall of the required eligibility clause. Several bishops were contacted via phone the day before, to extend their support for the candidature of the incumbent despite the glaring ineligibilities. Canvassing is banned in CMC but a covert form of canvassing is custom under the guise of ethnicity. Allegations of canvassing can be used to disqualify a candidate. In fact, once such allegation of canvassing was planted by the then Director against a candidate during the selection of the principal in 2011. I remember, one of my teachers in Oxford remarking lightly, 'What you call nepotism in India, we in the UK say to "put in a good word"'.

One member of the Director's Ad-hoc-nomination Committee of June 2017 later told me that the eligibility issue was debated extensively, but although the chairman had assured that it would be settled on the floor of the Council, neither did the Chair settle it nor did the same member raise the issue. In the Five Years and Four Seasons narrative of the former Director, he made a serious allegation that 'on 11th May 2017, two months prior to the selections, he was verbally asked by the council secretary to come for a post-dinner meeting to Room 1 in the Big Bungalow with the Chairman and Vice-Chairman. The agenda was to unconstitutionally reset the eligibility criteria of the candidature of the new Director to suit one individual'. It is not a minor charge and the way the Vice-Chairman read the eligibility clause through his laptop without appending the document to the council minutes does not convey transparency. Even on my way from the Council meeting, I received a call from a senior Council member advising me to be prepared to file a caveat as the Chairman was shirking his responsibility.

The Nomination Committee recommends the names for the post of Chairperson and Vice-Chairperson, which, in my experience, has never been put to vote in the last 15 years. I had complete faith in the process, but after reading the two documents, I asked myself what sort of system had we inherited. The Director, who is an employee of the Council has not only a say but also a strong position in proposing the names. A former chairman wrote, 'The director had proposed new persons for the positions of the Chairman and the Vice-Chairman. However, such changes to the Vice-Chairman and the Chairman are not done during a transition time of the leadership, when a new Director is about to take charge. The former Chairman and a former Director insisted that it was inconsistent with earlier traditions. I was requested by them and the Director designate to stay on. My question is about the logic and justification of such a tradition. It is merely an excuse to hold on to power. The truth is that the Chairman, who must be a favourite of the Director, must do the mid-term evaluation of the Director. It is just giving a conventional affirmative recommendation to the Executive Committee for the Director to complete his full term'. Therefore, the issue is whether the Chairperson can be neutral and objective when the Director has a role to play either in recommending or ditching him.

The selection of the Associate Director for Kanigapuram in Sept 2017 was done with the usual formal spectacle of prayer, the ceremonious opening of the sealed ballot box, providing pencil and paper to write the number of nominations received, and interviewing the nominees. With the precedence of what had occurred in June 2017, I told the Chairman that if we had a pre-selected candidate then we should call him/her and interview them rather than perform this show. May I quote from the reflections of a former Chairman: 'While going through the nomination letters received from the faculty members, it was found that one candidate had forced others to nominate him. A statement to this effect by one staff was allegedly kept sealed in the council secretary's office for the record'. I think we lack the courage to face such unscrupulous statements. It is like, in our judicial system, giving something in a 'sealed cover'. It turned out to be an outright lie. Ultimately, the same candidate, who had, to his credit, handled the project well and which was quarter-way through, received the highest nominations without any sealed cover pressures. The Chairman conveyed his disapproval saying that the 'Director designate must be comfortable with our choice'. I had no issues with that score but my concern was why go through such a lengthy process? The Chairman absented himself from the EC the following day. Even when I presented the majority decision to the EC on the next day with my remark that 'The Director designate was not comfortable with the decision', the executive decided to accept the majority decision. One of the distinguished members of the Executive Committee remarked, 'In the civil service the leader has to work with a team and not necessarily pick-up each member of the team'. That remark cost him his membership in the Council the following year. When I chaired the subsequent Council in January 2018, one senior Council member and former Director had the audacity to tell me, 'You did not support our preferred candidate for Associate Director of Kanigapuram'.

One regrettable and unethical decision of mine as the Vice-Chairman was to give tacit approval to the actions of the Chairman in the matter of the newly appointed Council Secretary in 2017. The Council Secretary-designate was appointed in and by the Council in June 2017, introduced, and welcomed in the following Executive Committee in September 2017 where he was asked to take down the minutes. A note of farewell appreciation was given to the outgoing Council Secretary. The outgoing Director and outgoing Council Secretary were expected to hand over the charge to the Director designate and Council Secretary-designate in September 2017. The appointment of the new Council Secretary had been notified on the intranet. However, the tenure of the outgoing Council Secretary was extended for one year by an office order by the new Director immediately after taking over the charge without the approval of the Executive and Council. When I questioned this, the Chairman told me over the phone, that he had advised against it but had been told to obtain the approval by the next Council in January 2018. It is not only the propriety of the advice in question but the unethical act of humiliating a professor. 'The Secretary may be honorary or salaried officers of the association, whose election or appointment, removal or suspension shall be made by the council or its executive committee'. The Council Secretary's one year extension was based on the sudden discovery of the 1997 Council Minutes where the Council Secretary's term was for four years. The interpretation of such is beyond my limited understanding because, since 1997, seven Council Secretaries had been appointed on three-year terms only, highlighting the accepted tenure as three years, not four. A Trustee removing another Trustee is illegal as per the bye-laws. The matter was brought to the January 2018 Council, by which time the Chairman had resigned and was unavailable. As usual, the moral guardians of the Council, who normally conduct an unconstitutional pre-Council meeting in the Alumni House the earlier day to set the agenda, defended the violation with calculated falsehood. The Council remains oblivious of the details till today. My conscience pricks me even today as I wonder, 'Did I play the role of Pilate in washing my hands off the matter since both the outgoing and incoming Council Secretaries were good friends of mine'. The former Chairman wrote, 'I had suggested to the new Director that he consult the Executive Committee and get its endorsement to allow the Council Secretary to complete his full four-year term and postpone the regularisation of the appointment of the new Council Secretary, who was already appointed by the Council in June 2017. Instead, the new Director through executive order allowed the Council Secretary to continue and kept in abeyance the appointment of the Council Secretary-designate appointed by the Council earlier'. I was hopeful of a reconciliation between the Director and the Council Secretary-designate by reinstating him after the incumbent's completion of four years, but it was an unrealised dream.

The larger issue is who makes the decisions and what is the process? CMC carries on because of established routines. Senior medical professionals are expected to provide expertise in areas of management. In my observation of chairing the Finance Committee, I have noticed that it functions meticulously, and the Finance office staff members are knowledgeable and expert while the Finance committee members give their valuable service out of love for the institution. I take the liberty of repeating the words of a former member of the Executive and Finance Committee: 'Life was simple when CMC was a 30-crore operation with supporting funds from abroad. Those who paid the piper had a representative(s) here at Vellore or there were regular visitors who called the tune. The entire spectrum of supply and demand for medical services has changed. CMC's method of working had to change but no alternative management procedure was developed or laid out'.

I must say that the governance and management style of CMC Vellore needs restructuring. In fact, I initiated a process for discussion and decision but in my ignorance and naïveté, I never realised that I would be denied such a privilege despite supporting the administration with the intention of not rocking the boat during the transition period. However, the solace is that CMC history does not lack precedence. The suggestion that CMC style of governance and management needs to be restructured in the light of changing circumstances was first made by Mr Thomas Abraham, former Ambassador, when he was the Chairman of the CMC Council. It was made in a well-explained letter and addressed to the Director, and is now safely buried in the archives of the directorate.

Historically, the entire process of selection of leadership in CMC Vellore is based on the tenets of truth and transparency. Honesty, in letter and spirit, has been the basis of governance in this institution. I am sorry to have witnessed a serious deviation from that commitment to truth. I saw constitutional violations being applauded by former directors. I saw frank dishonesty in speech and documentation. If the events of 2017 go unchecked by the stakeholders of the institution, the mission drift described by Peter Greer will become a sad reality in CMC Vellore. It has already commenced. My prayer is that the stakeholders in the Association and Council will take stock of this and institute corrective measures.

The nomination process at CMC is sacrosanct, unique, elaborative, and sometimes exhaustive but how do we make good and ethical use of such a legacy which is grounded on truth and honesty. The Kanigapuram Project has become an enigma. The project was initiated in full length by the outgoing Director, presented, discussed, and scrutinised threadbare at least 14 times in the Council. At the end of the day, we must face God not humans. I am a clergyman and anointed by 'His grace only'. I had to pay the price for not succumbing to the unethical demands of a handful who had disruptive and divisive agendas.

I presided as acting Chairman over the aftermath of the June 2017 turbulence. My fellow bishops as well as very committed and senior staff of CMC faculty were deeply grieved over the developments that were uncalled for. I am not questioning the integrity of the person selected as the Director but the people involved in the process. It is the intent of a few to interpret the CMC constitution with a parochial view and not consider the opinion of the law of the land under the pretext of being a minority institution. It surpasses my understanding as a citizen of India.

All good things come to an end, but may lead on to another

Long before the rest of India figured out how to select candidates suitable to be trained as future doctors for the healthcare-strapped nation, CMC Vellore had formulated its well-thought methodology. The underlying principle of selection was to find overall suitability for this difficult journey of learning and practice. The admission process evolved over the years through a collective appraisal by its staff and college administration, year after year. To train doctors and nurses for the huge needs of the country in the spirit of service remained the non-negotiable value guiding the education at Vellore. One cannot fathom the depths of thinking and fine-tuning that goes onto this process unless you are part and parcel of the exercise. I was privileged to be involved peripherally as a Council member initially, and later as the Acting Chairman, compelled by circumstances in 2017 to be it the apex team from the institution to the Supreme Court when the admission process was sub-judice.

Sponsorship of students by churches, denominations, and healthcare-linked organisations has been a CMC tradition and policy for nearly 70 years now. The vision was to create a model of medical care resources that would render services in specific areas and to particular people that churches and healthcare-related organisations served through their hospitals. The 52 stakeholders of CMC Vellore range from Eastern Orthodox Churches to the dioceses of the CSI, CNI, Lutherans, Baptists, Presbyterians, Evangelicals, and Pentecostals. On completing their studies, students return to their respective regions to fulfill their service obligations. Their services are not only exemplary but quite humbling. The practice ensures that mission hospitals and marginalised regions receive a constant flow of well-trained young doctors but for a short period of the bond. Only a few stay on and spend a lifetime serving in CMC or in the mission hospitals in remote areas.

CMC developed a unique selection system that evolved from the belief that the practice of medicine was a calling, not a career. Attitude along with aptitude is a non-negotiable prerequisite for the formation of a complete doctor. CMC's dual yardstick of 'merit and suitability is not opposed to merit but to the notion of the 'exclusivity of merit' as it goes beyond numbers and ranking. However, with the introduction of the National Eligibility cum Entrance Test (NEET) this has been difficult to practice. Legal battles have been intriguing, costly, and time-consuming. I had first-hand experience on a few occasions meeting our lawyers in Delhi prior to hearings in the Supreme Court. It was quite interesting to stand in the courtroom of the then Chief Justice of India and later in Courtroom No 10 to hear the arguments of our lawyers including Mr Harish Salve, Mr Shyam Divan, and Mr Mukul Rohatgi. I remember when we entered the chambers of Mr Mukul Rohatgi, he stood up and greeted me saying it was a privilege to have a bishop in a lawyer's chamber.

The question often asked by the judiciary is not about CMC's minority status as 'a Christian Institution' but rather multiple stakeholders maintaining 'minority within a minority' status to claim a seat in the College. When we were told to fall in line with NEET and admit students from that list, we were a little nervous in 2017. I received a call from the principal one night and assured her that God would be with her as she planned to meet the state officials in Chennai. It reminded me of the story of Esther and I told her to go in faith believing that God would honour our prayer. The miracle happened and she rang me saying that the counseling had gone smoothly through the NEET process and we could admit students as per our sponsorship criterion except for the long tradition of CMC's entrance test and interview.

I feel sad writing this, as I helplessly watch a time-tested system undone. The process of selecting students in a fair, non-discriminatory, and equitable manner has been challenged in the highest courts of the nation. The honorable judiciary in its wisdom had always judged CMC's enviable record of excellence in a contextual manner, which helped the institution to produce batches after batches of doctors committed to serving for long periods of time in India. It is 2022 as I pen this chapter, and those long-held rights of selection have been extinguished. While, the new regulations will allow minority students from the state to be trained in CMC Vellore. the purpose of CMC's education towards equipping remote mission hospitals under the Churches stands disabled. As a clergyman associated with several faith-based organizations, this move is a blow to the backbone of the Christian health network. The predictions of our legal counsel in 2017 have come true. He fought hard but kept telling me that our rights would go eventually. He was right.

Saddened as I am at the end of my association with CMC Vellore over this closing chapter of CMC's admissions, I must also record my unhappiness at the resistance of the CMC administration in seeking my non-legal advice. The council secretary dealing with CMC's case was terminated unconstitutionally, disrupting the continuum of legal paperwork. My voice as a clergyman with administrative experience in Serampore, CNI, and NCCI was not heeded in several matters of governance. I remained skeptical about the roles that certain council members played in the legal discussions in New Delhi. They were clearly unacceptable as warned by the legal luminaries. As Acting Chairman, my discomfort over the way the Council was being usurped by a handful of members remained unheard. Gentle dissent from my side was put down. Instead, I was made to leave the Council with some expensive teardrops in both my eyes. I should have said a prayer to the God of justice, not to hold anything against the institution. I did not. But now I do. 'Father forgive them for they know not what they do.' I pray that CMC Vellore will be blessed with the privileges of admissions that empowered the institution towards its vision, for so many decades.

While it is all over, as some say, history will speak for itself. While it may not be worth lamenting as we wait, I stand by the premise that the truth will prevail. Building the Kingdom may now be a relic of CMC's past as we have made a mockery of this esteemed institution in front of the faculty and the world. All that we stand for—Prayer, Process, Intent, Collegiality—have taken a beating, but that should not deter us from the vision of the founder that we are 'not building an institution but the kingdom of God'. CMC needs God's grace in plenty, a touch of inner healing, and reconciliation for the fountain of mercy to flow again. God is looking forward to continue abiding in and with us. However, that will only happen if we collectively bend our knees and ask God to forgive us our failures of omission and commission. Institutional drift may sometimes be fundamentally unintentional, but it calls for institutional humility and accountability. My attention was drawn to an article on 23rd March 2020 that referred to the following quotation by the Chief Justice of the Supreme Court of the USA:[7]

"'President Reagan used to speak of the Soviet constitution, and he noted that it purported to grant wonderful rights of all sorts to people. But those rights were empty promises because that system did not have an independent judiciary to uphold the rule of law and enforce those rights" (John G. Roberts, Chief Justice, US Supreme Court). The extent of independence of the judiciary is directly proportionate to the degree of mistrust between the executive and the judiciary of the nation. Put conversely, it is inverse to the extent of bonhomie prevalent between these two pillars'.

'The celebrated case of Marbury against Madison, where Chief Justice Marshall gave the US's Supreme Court the constitutional weapon of 'judicial review', was also born out of this mistrust. At its founding stages, the battle for the soul of the new nation was being fought between two conflicting ideas. One won a presidency and tried to nullify appointment warrants issued by the other's president, just before he demitted office. The warrant had been signed but not delivered. Marbury, who had been appointed by the outgoing regime, invoked a law passed by Congress to directly take his cause to the highest court. Chief Justice Marshall had no sympathy for the new president. However, he did not want to rock the boat either. If the court ruled in favour of Marbury, there was no telling how the penny would fall. It is then that genius struck him. He ruled that the very law which allowed Marbury to directly come to the Supreme Court could not have been enacted by Congress. The court asserted the right to judicially review laws passed by Congress and yet seemingly ruled in favour of the president. A classic case of operation unsuccessful but the patient (in this case, the rule of law) alive'.

***

Former Vis-À-Vis Latter

The twin paradigm of the former and latter is the impressive narrative of a Christian University. The former paradigm is of the founder of the Agriculture Institute: 'Serve the Land and Feed the Hungry' based on a wholistic theology of the 'Gospel and Plough' that connects the gospel with agriculture and technology. Sam Higginbottom said, 'I was accused of having lost my first love and of having grown cold, of having become a materialist, and of having lost my aspirations, of being indifferent to spiritual and eternal things'.[8] He draws attention to the commands of Jesus,

'His commands to His disciples and His commendation of those who feed the hungry, clothe the naked and give drink to the thirsty all call for more than preaching. They call for the practical application of that which gives meaning and content to the oral presentation of God's truth.'[9]

The latter paradigm is SHUATS' appropriation of a verse from the prophet Haggai: 'The latter glory of this house shall be greater than the former, says the Lord of hosts' (2:9). A visitor to the main campus can hardly miss the words of Haggai written on the wall and echoing in different forums in sermons and discussions. Haggai was a post-exile returnee to the land of Israel, whose primary ministry was to encourage the people to rebuild the temple in Jerusalem and to let them know that God was with them and would help them. Zerubbabel, the governor of Judah, and Joshua, the high priest, responded to Haggai's call to rebuild. Haggai prophesied that the glory of the future temple would surpass that of the previous one. His prophecy began with the Lord asking the returning remnant two questions: i) Who is left among you who saw this temple in its former glory? ii) How do you see it now? Those who had seen the grandeur of the former structure and remembered the majestic glory of Solomon's temple must have wept. Even though the rebuilt temple would be less magnificent than its earlier counterpart, God promised that the final glory of the Lord's house would eclipse its former glory, which must have seemed impossible to those lamenting elders. Not only was its glory to outstrip the former temple, but the Lord also promised to bring peace to the temple court and the city of Jerusalem. Today the full and final fulfilment of this glorious prophecy regarding lasting peace in the holy land including the temple, is still futuristic.

There is a story of a person who visited Holland once and the Dutch host took him to a neighbouring dairy farm. The farmer was not in the barn, but the host helped himself to some milk, and then paid for it by depositing money in the basket beside the milk tank and searching for the appropriate change in the basket. The guest was stunned by what he saw, knowing that most Indians would have walked out with the milk and the money, since no one was looking. The guest later explained the cost of corruption succinctly:

'If this were India and I walked out with the money and the milk, the dairy owner would need to hire a cashier. Who would pay for the cashier? I, the consumer, would; and the price of milk would go up. But if the consumer were corrupt, why should the dairy owner be honest? He would add water to the milk to make more money. I would then be paying more for adulterated milk. I would complain, "The milk is adulterated; the government must appoint inspectors." Who would pay for the inspectors? I, the taxpayer, would. But if the consumer, producer, and supplier were corrupt, why should the inspectors be honest? They would extract bribes from the supplier. If he did not bribe them, the inspectors would delay the supply and ensure that the milk curdled before it got to me. Who would pay for the bribe? Again, I, the consumer, would pay the additional cost. By the time I paid for the milk, cashier, the water, inspector, and the bribe, I would have a little money left to buy chocolate for the milk – so my children would not drink the milk and would be weaker than the Dutch children. Having spent extra money on the milk, I would not be able to take my children out for ice cream. The cashier, water, bribe, and inspector add no value to the milk. The ice cream industry does. My corruption keeps me from patronizing a value-adding business. That reduces our economy's capacity to create jobs'.[10]

Today, in SHUATS, the story of milk is no different. If you go early in the morning to get fresh milk, you will find a small and a large container. If you ask for milk from the small container, the reply will be, 'No sir. The large one is for you'. And if you get milk from that, you must pray for a miracle to get pure milk. The irony would not have been lost on Sam Higginbottom, who must be laughing listening to this decades long narrative of milk in the college he founded. He writes, 'I went forth there and then to buy a cow. After about an hour's hunt, I was directed to the home of an elderly Anglo-Indian lady who had been making her living by running a dairy… she would let me have one of the best for 25 dollars. I brought her home and fed her myself. The cow was then giving about six quarts a day of good rich milk and in about two weeks that cow was giving twelve quarts a day'.[11]

Sam Higginbottom was born on 27th October 1874 in Manchester, a city in England to a modest family. He grew up in poverty, leaving school early and working in different capacities as a butcher's boy, cab driver, and milkman. He attended Mount Hermon School from 1894 to 1899 and continued his education at Amherst College and Princeton University in the United States till 1902. The will of God guided him to India in 1903, supported ably by the Presbyterian Board of Foreign Missions in New York. He lived in India for several years before retiring. On 11th June 1958, Dr Sam Higginbottom left for his heavenly abode.

The history of SHUATS is a story of the struggle and identity of an institution. From 1980, the story began moving swiftly downwards and remained unchecked over the next 17 years, with eight individuals either briefly occupying the principal's chair or acting temporarily for short periods. The chaotic condition of the men's hostels and mess became alarming.[12] However, from 1992 onwards, the scene changed with the appointment of a director who restored discipline, and later became the Vice-Chancellor of the Deemed to be University. Credit goes to him for initiating the process and taking bold decisions to restore the institution's image and forge forward with a vision. Due to his untiring efforts, on the 15th of March 2000, the Indian government's Ministry of Human Resource Development, gave its approval to the recommendations of the UGC and awarded them the status of Deemed to be University. Thereafter, on 29th December 2016, the same institution was established as a State University by the Uttar Pradesh government. We observed how he struggled but persisted in faith in God to obtain the State University status in 2016. Historically, in 1932, the Institute had been formally affiliated with the University of Allahabad and in the same year, its Bachelor of Science degree in Agriculture was recognised by the State Government. Sam Higginbottom once said, 'I am anxious, to see the day when India shall take her proper place as one of the great self-governing people of the world ... India's future can be richer than India's past. I am always brooding over ways and means of avoiding this fearful waste of human life, of transforming it into a positive asset to enrich the world'. He was delighted when the Indian Government gave top priority to agricultural development in its first Five-Year Plan.

Education, in general, is a very big business and only increasing. Theological education is such a tiny drop in the ever-expanding pool and beset with so many challenges that it is easy to forget how other forms of education are flourishing. The real question is not 'What is education?' But rather 'What is education for?' When translated into the area of theological education, this becomes a vocational question. Enormity and growth are typically modern virtues. In sorting out the priorities in our expanding educational development we are confronted with the decisive question about the chief purpose behind what we are doing.

The National Education Policy (NEP) in India was framed in 1986 and modified in 1992. Thus, NEP 2020 is built on the foundational pillars of access, equity, quality, affordability, and accountability. It envisages broad-based, multi-disciplinary, holistic undergraduate education with flexible curricula, creative combinations of subjects, integration of vocational education, and multiple entry and exit points with appropriate certifications. Undergraduate education can be for three or four years with multiple exit options: Certificate after one year, Advanced Diploma after two years, Bachelor's Degree after three years, and Bachelor's with Research after four years.[13]

The policy seeks to restructure school curricula and pedagogy in a new '5+3+3+4' design, where there is the flexibility of two-year Master's programs for those who have completed a three-year undergraduate program, one-year for students who have completed a four-year undergraduate program, or five-year integrated Bachelor's and Master's programs. It envisages that the Higher Education Commission of India (HECI) will be set up as a single overarching umbrella body for all higher education, excluding medical and legal education. HECI would have four independent verticals, National Higher Education Regulatory Council (NHERC) for regulation, General Education Council (GEC) for standard-setting, Higher Education Grants Council (HEGC) for funding, and National Accreditation Council (NAC) for accreditation. HECI will function through faceless intervention through technology and will be authorised to penalise those not conforming to norms and standards. Public and private higher education institutions will be governed by the same set of norms for regulation, accreditation, and academic standards.

The faculty of Theology at SHUATS had a humble beginning in 2002 in a small classroom with seven students. In 2003, the foundation of the Gospel and Plough Institute of Theology (GPIT) was laid with a ground-breaking ceremony and consolidated in 2008. Theological education today derives its academic norms from university education based on ability, quality, excellence, and maturity. The inevitable corollary of upward academic mobility is increasing selectivity based on predetermined standardised tests. If ability, excellence, and quality education are linked directly with high cognitive performance, then the best education must practice restrictive admission policies. Only so, it is argued, can the incompetent be excluded for the high achievers to progress at their own pace. If general education perpetuates the social conventions, could it not be argued that seminaries contribute to the rigidities of institutionalised religion?

Before NEP 2020, the faculty of Theology had initiated to study theology from interdisciplinary perspectives and within the framework of general education. This was implemented in 2017. The vision is to equip and produce servant leaders, who know God's word, engage in God's world, and discern God's will for His entire oikoumene (inhabited world) in keeping with the legacy of the Founder: 'Feed the Hungry and Serve the Land'. An undergraduate student is expected to take Core, Discipline Specific Elective, and Generic Elective from an unrelated discipline/subject, including Ability Enhancement Courses (AEC) and Skill Enhancement Courses (SEC). The Practicum is a supervised practical application of concurrently studied theory. The postgraduate student irrespective of their specific branch must take common core courses in the first semester before opting for discipline-specific.

It is understood that the various branches of theology require an overarching standard of the Bible as it is the source of truth. Theology is the natural standard by which other scholarships must abide. One's view of God and the Bible affects every other area of life. Theology is the foundation of one's worldview and shapes the study of philosophy and other fields. Therefore, theology, is the 'queen of the sciences'; essentially, God's Word is the majestic source of knowledge that informs all other knowledge. Then the question arises: is it possible or desirable for a theologian to criticise a scientific idea theologically? Is it possible or desirable for scientists to criticise a theological idea scientifically?

The greatest challenge today is to express the Gospel with its spiritual power in terms of the best science, art, philosophy, and critical reflections. There is also an implied concern about the cost of education including theological education, employability, and competition. It is imperative to understand the prophetic dynamic in the context of global culture. It demands reflection on the meaning and relevance of the globalisation of education which influences lives both directly and indirectly. Theological education occurs in many settings, not all of them institutional. Theological seminaries differ based on geographical location in cities, suburbs, rural areas, in size, in wealth, means of securing wealth through endowments, denominational support, local church support, tuition fees, as well as overseas' grants for the growth of bible schools like management schools. These variations legitimately affect what theological education should mean in different contexts.

I accepted the invitation to join the faculty of Theology at SHUATS a little reluctantly and needed two friends to persuade me. Initially, I accepted the offer for one year but on the date of joining, was asked to commit to at least five years. The decision to join SHUATS was against the advice of some of my well-wishers. I remember the remark of the late Metropolitan of Mar Thoma Church who had come to attend a consecration service on 4th November 2012, just a month after I joined SHUATS. He knew me very well but was surprised by my decision. During our conversation, in his own style, he quietly but humorously told me, 'Bishop, anything can happen here and one may even become the Chancellor'. It reminds me of a similar conversation that I had with the former late Chancellor while chatting with him at Allahabad Airport. He shared his frustrations about being a Chancellor, a post that is purely ornamental but extended cooperation to avoid confrontations. The post, which is honorary in theory, now carries a very good honorarium and offers several privileges. If appointed once, it is possible to continue on; then there is no need to seek employment elsewhere to earn a livelihood with hard work. However, one must be ready to compromise with one's conscience. My joining SHUATS also cost me the severance of my long-standing association and membership with the Senate of Serampore. The then President of the Senate had warned me saying that he was aware of the inside story and said, 'It is not as it appears to be'. My wife had told me to consider carefully before joining and several times repeated her request that I leave as it was becoming suffocating and humiliating to work under autocratic authority that can best be described as 'absolute dictatorship' and 'hero worship'.

The chasm between the haves and have-nots cannot be more apparent than at SHUATS. Nepotism runs deep within its corridors. Some, including the higher administrators, are on the government payroll. However, the majority are on the society payroll in two categories: one group under a proper pay scale and the other on a contractual, negligible consolidated amount. The people on the society's payroll live with the uncertainty of irregular salary payments and some have not been paid for five months at a stretch. The appointments in society are intermittent and humorous. One should not be surprised to find people appointed with pay according to the whims of a single person. They are on the payroll even without working, no job description, or even appropriate qualification, which is unheard of in any organisation that I have worked and managed.

It was very painful and humiliating to hear from the podium in the presence of distinguished guests, such an immature statement like, 'You have jobs here because of my father'. We could not but laugh and wondered who benefits the most. Yet, no reprimand was made. Whereas, once when I made a statement that, 'The latter glory of this house shall be greater than the former', I was reprimanded in public, 'Bishop, you should have joined us earlier to witness the latter glory', and again privately at the altar, 'Bishop, I am very angry with you'. I could only ask him, 'Why should you be angry at all?' My statement was not unfounded because we have been told on multiple occasions: 'A vision of forty thousand students in SHUATS, another Immanuel university at Raebareli, and a medical college and hospital'. Everybody knows that the present facility for 10,000 students is appalling and we are unable to commence any new construction due to legal restrictions and given the severe financial constraints.

The faculty of Theology is considered a parasite and several times we were told, 'Let us close down the theology department'. The reason is the huge investments with no expected return of producing Spirit-filled students to go and evangelise the nation. It is insulting and abusive to hear words like – 'Door is open, pack your things and go', said to the Theology faculty and students at the University Chapel in the presence of an overseas guest. The reason was because none had been present at a seminar, although in our defence, no notice had been given to us. When repeated, again and again, I made the mistake of clarifying the same from the floor. Unfortunately, that was an unpardonable sin because nobody ever dared to oppose the Vice-Chancellor! Often, we had to suspend Theology classes to listen the visitors from abroad tell us what is the Gospel and the meaning of persecution. The most appropriate course for SHUATS is to have a good Bible school that offers three months of training to produce only evangelists. However, that is also not viable because the expectation of the Bible School students is to obtain employment after the completion of the short training, which we cannot provide.

The Theology students and staff truly value being stewards during worship, counselling the sick, and regularly serving food on weekends but they do not like to be passive onlookers, always expected to surrender their lives to Christ at the end of each service, and cast out demons. A forgotten fact is that demon-possessed persons only come to *Yeshu Darbar* but not to the church. As soon as the special prayer is offered towards the end of the service, immediately those who are demon-possessed start dancing in a rhythmic way and shrieking. One cannot help but wonder why primarily only ladies happen to be possessed by the devil. The students often asked me, 'How many times during our course of study shall we stand and surrender our lives to Christ and be anointed with the prayer – "Receive the Holy Spirit"'? My calculation is a minimum of 378 times (3 times in a week × 42 weeks × 3 years). Most of us in the Theology department do not speak in tongues in public. As St Paul said, 'I thank God that I speak in tongues more than all of you. Nevertheless, in church, I would rather speak five words with my mind in order to instruct others, than ten thousand words in a tongue' (1 Corinthians 14:18-19).

We get exhausted, repeatedly listening to the lessons on commitment, sacrifice, ethics, morality, greed, and courage with fabricated stories. Imagine for a moment, someone is granted study leave for five years to go abroad to pursue a second doctorate, and eventually, completes the degree in perfect time, being a brilliant research scholar with an excellent academic track record. However, he/she forgets to return to India after five years. Signs of dementia at such an early age, perhaps? No, but what follows is a story of revelation and God's call to 'Go back to India as India needs you'. The issue is not the calling to obey but the constant beating of a drum about the sacrifice made in leaving a good job, excellent salary, and the privileges of the West as if we are all naïve and do not know the reality.

The actual story of commitment and sacrifice which must be acclaimed and retold time and again to the younger generation is that of the founder of Agriculture Institute. It is not only commendable but also exemplary. Sam Higginbottom was a Princeton graduate in 1902, who came to India and taught economics at a Christian college now called Ewing Christian College in Prayagraj, formerly Allahabad. At that point, he discovered that despite its naturally rich and fertile soil, India's agriculture production was among the lowest in the world and he felt the desire to do something to improve agricultural productivity in the country. With a vision to 'Serve the Land and Feed the Hungry', he decided to establish an agricultural school. 'But it was a drastic decision. I was 35 years old and had already spent many valuable years in education. I was married and responsible for a family. Was I to change the entire direction of my activities in response to an idea, convincing indeed to me but new to others than myself? How would it work out? And what about the attitude of my colleagues? We rented an apartment in Columbia near Ohio State University. In the College of Agriculture, where I had to start as a freshman…I was able to complete the requirements for a degree in two years. At Ohio State University, I crossed my Rubicon'.[14] Subsequently, he returned to India to translate the vision into reality.

Most of us in the faculty of Theology failed to comprehend the Biblical interpretations that were often made, but we could not question or initiate a debate because every word that was uttered was considered a direct revelation and immediately recorded. For example, once suddenly, we all became 'gods'. What an amazing revelation! The declaration was based on Psalm 82:6: 'I said, "You are gods"'. The point that was never acknowledged was that 'You are gods' is a title, conferred as an appellation that indicates a greater closeness to God than any other bestowed on men – an appellation that implies we are God's representatives on earth and that any decision we make, in a sense, is to be regarded as His. Even Psalm 82:1 and 6 were quoted by Constantine at the opening of the Council of Nicæa in 325 AD, to remind the bishops that their high office should raise them above jealousy and petty feelings. Therefore, all of us are children of the Highest – sons of God. We occupy a rank that makes it proper that we should be considered His sons. On another occasion, we were told in a sermon, 'Do not adopt family planning' and have as many children as possible, referencing the biblical passage, 'Be fruitful and multiply' (Genesis 1:28). Obviously, for some of the listeners, it was too late to adopt family planning. Again, one morning there was another revelation, 'The campus will be a 70-kilometer radius of the crime-free zone in Allahabad'. In the space of a few hours, the computer design had been made, printed, circulated, and placed on the altar and in the prayer room. Prayer for a crime-free zone was offered religiously every time, but we never prayed for an 'insecurity and trust deficit-free zone' on the campus.

The University functions on three holy days each week: Friday, Saturday, and Sunday. Christian staff and students are expected to attend worship at Yeshu Darbar. Attending three days of worship without fail is the yardstick to measure the spirituality of the Theology students and staff. The first is the Friday evening service at 5:30 pm, after working at the university from Monday to Friday from 8:30 am to 5:20 pm. The wardens herd the students from the hostels and everybody is forced to listen to the one-hour sermon in Hindi, which is never translated into English for the audience. They are also required to watch how demons are cast out and prayer is offered for the sick. Some theology students can repeat the entire sermon verbatim because if you've heard it once you've heard it forever. Saturday is the Sabbath as per the ten commandments and is observed as holy to obtain blessings. Two services are held, one in the morning and another in the evening along with Holy Communion. Sunday is obviously the holy day and the morning worship—*Mahasabha*—is held at *Yeshu Darbar.*

One visiting professor asked me when theology students and staff have a weekend if they work Monday to Friday and then all the way through till Sunday! Unfortunately, if anyone dares to ask that question then it is considered a sign of lack of spirituality and not being born again. Life here can be compared to NDTV: 24×7. Young theologians barely have time for their families and often burn out. Even during the Covid-19 pandemic, the Theology students were expected to stay back on the campus like frontline soldiers to pray at *Yeshu Darbar*. Fortunately, they had the courage not to oblige us and stay on the campus, but left for home.

The basic issue is a lack of understanding of the meaning of worship and prayer. Worship has become ritualistic and the altar has become a stage for performing. 'When ministry becomes performance, then the sanctuary becomes a theatre, the congregation becomes an audience, worship becomes entertainment, and man's applause and approval become the measure of success. But when ministry is for the glory of God, His presence moves into the sanctuary. Even the unsaved visitor will fall down on his face, worship God, and confess that God is among us (1 Corinthians 14:25)'.[15] The Sunday evening service at the University chapel as well as the different regional and linguistic fellowship groups are vibrant, full of activities, and fulfill the spiritual needs of the students. The students love to attend them as they are not compulsory and are under the directorate of chaplaincy, barely figuring on the official spiritual map of the authority.

The faculty of Theology at SHUATS is the first of its kind in an Indian university. Academic integrity and spirituality are inseparable and cannot be subverted. Theology is the queen of sciences but unfortunately has been displaced. A university is a place where people think, and instruction and research are judged based on the intellectual content and efforts they demand. Academic engagement aims to cultivate theology as a wisdom-seeking inquiry and to hold to the truth of Scripture as the Word of God. A Christian university like SHUATS is responsible to the academy, the church, and to the wider society. The Word of God is always true but our interpretation of it is not necessarily true. Interpretation of Scripture requires the gift of the Holy Spirit, insight, understanding of faith and experience, and a life lived in the light of divine revelation. The faculty of Theology at SHUATS is expected to maintain academic integrity, and spiritual discipline, and prepare people for ministry in church and society but they are completely denied freedom. Any deviation from the main is questionable. For example: 'The decision was taken by the experts, namely, the UGC and the Delhi University, to the effect that the respondent No. 5 possesses essential qualifications, for the post of Principal of St Stephen's College, is a decision which in my view ought to be left to experts rather than to courts' (High Court of Delhi, Date of decision: 3rd July 2012 + WP(C) 12422/2009). The decision was in our favour that the PhD in Theology offered by SHIATS was a valid degree. We value the decision of the court. Yet, the question that was raised and is still debated without any aspersion on the person concerned, is that if someone teaches English for 30 years, possesses an excellent academic record, integrity, and definite Christian commitment, but has never pursued a PhD in English instead has chosen to obtain a PhD in Theology from a faculty that is still nascent, is that valid? While PhD in Theology has been declared a valid degree, the Under Graduate and Post Graduate Theology degrees offered by SHUATS are still not listed under the degrees of the UGC. Although we appealed this with rational and relevant documents when the Vice-Chancellor became the President of the Association of Indian Universities (2013-14), it has yet to see the light of day.

The words of the late Metropolitan of Mar Thoma Church that 'anything can happen in SHUATS' is almost prophetic because, even a Professor in Agriculture/Soil science without having any theological qualifications, can become the only supervisor for PhD Theology research scholars at SHUATS, something that is unheard of, or a Professor of Animal Genetics and Breeding can become the Dean of the Faculty of Theology. A Department of Graduate studies offering PhD in Christian Studies can be established only by visiting Professors from India and abroad. While the commitment of the visiting faculty is not in question, the only issue is that, as per regulations, a doctoral program under the UGC cannot be offered by visiting faculty alone. To circumvent the situation, GPIT faculty members, who are resident faculty, are assigned as co-supervisors in Christian Studies in addition to guiding PhD Theology students registered there. However, their real role is not to guide but to sign the documents required for administrative purposes. Amazingly, one visiting faculty member from the USA, an Indian-American, even became the honorary head of the same department. The Indian-Americans are more American than Indian. One wonders why they do not take leave for a period or resign from a secure job to work and stay on campus, attend *Yeshu Darbar* from Friday to Sunday, and teach Theology at 120°Fahrenheit with regular, unannounced power cuts for hours throughout the year. Easier said than done.

No action is taken against liars and gossip mongers. They are like vacuum cleaners who collect the gossip, manicure and pedicure it, and then spread it. They are retained by grace to feed the rumours that will be used at the right moment if necessary. The voice of dissent, academic freedom, integrity, issues of justice, discipline, governance, and transparency are silenced in very subtle ways either through termination, if contractual, or through humiliation. Yet I have one close associate and confidant. He is a very good friend of mine and once, was kind enough to warn me, 'Bishop, be careful in sharing sensitive issues with the Chancellor if asked because it will boomerang'. How true were his advice and I wish I had heeded it. On another occasion, he was very restless and expressed his anxiety, 'Bishop, we are moving towards becoming a cult at *Yeshu Darbar*'. I could only express my helplessness that the culture that was being nurtured in the university and at Yeshu Darbar was very hard to break. I remembered the prophet, Amos. 'Amaziah said to Amos, "O seer, go, flee away to the land of Judah, and eat bread there, and prophesy there, but never again prophesy at Bethel, for it is the King's sanctuary, and it is a temple of the kingdom"'(Amos 7:12, ESV).

Fear and suspicion rule the campus. One spiritual mentor who is well-respected and admired in the university, on a visit to the campus after several years, met me while walking on the campus. I asked him the difference between the former and the latter. He said, 'Bishop, there is a "fear psychosis and trust deficit" which is alarming. There is no more social life and collegiality'. A close friend of SHUATS in his email dated 16th November 2017 wrote to me saying, 'You will find the following discussion painful. Writing it was very difficult for me. Since deep down in my heart, I believe that neither of them took any unjust money from SHUATS. However, it will be naïve to rule out the possibility that they did create a slush fund and used it to bribe others in the interest of the university. If so – that evil has now caught up with the university. Therefore, may I suggest that Gospel and Plough School of Theology should organise a seminar, at least for SHUATS staff, open to other seminaries, on the question of bribery'. I did not dare to organise it because, as an employee, my head would have been on a platter like John the Baptist. There was never any initiative by the authorities to deal with this demon, which had become chronic and cancerous despite praying for a 70-kilometre radius crime-free zone.

The Vice-Chancellors are senior Professors and normally hold the post for tenure. They function within the system and are accountable to the management. Similarly, the bishops are elected from the collegiality of priests who have gone through theological studies, and ministerial formation, served congregations for years, and are selected through a screening process of the church. Commitment and dedication of the bishops should not only be exemplary but their lifestyle should be Christ-like and a model for younger generations. The slogan that is oft-repeated is 'Persecuted for preaching the Gospel'. One wonders whether one is ever told not to preach the gospel. We are in a democratic country and are privileged to be Indian-Christians. The real issue is that one can either be the Vice-Chancellor or a Bishop of Yeshu Darbar but not hold on to both the posts. Both are endowed with authority, power, salary, perks, flamboyant lifestyle, a plethora of security guards, sometimes bouncers, and a coterie. The coterie we create, mirrors who we are. While pretending to be a shield around us, it in fact imprisons us. Unless we are happy to be thus walled in, why should we erect such a wall? Whether a coterie renders advice—good or bad—, or functions as sycophants, or runs the administration by proxy, depends on the administrator concerned. The issue is not that the administrator should not consult colleagues or heed their advice but it becomes a liability if it ends in flattery. Perhaps, the latter glory of SHUATS will be free from the present governance structure which is not conducive for a Christian minority institution. Life membership of one family and offering life membership to a select few to give tacit approval to their decisions is a perpetuation of a legacy of nepotism, corruption, and greed.

Christian institutions must be built with a vision grounded in the Bible and biblical principles of management structure based on ethics and justice. Appropriating the Word of God for self-propagation and shrewdly building a 'family dynasty' in the name of building the kingdom of God is nothing but deviation from the path. There is always the temptation for power, greed, nepotism, and, not least, becoming a dictator without realising it. The family is so insecure that when they stay at home, have evening walks, attend office, teach, go for a walk, go to school, and even while praying and preaching the Word of God, they need to be escorted by security guards. One prominent theologian during a visit advised me to change the motto from 'Gospel and Plough' to 'Gospel and Gun'. He bluntly asked, 'Why is a man of God, who preaches the Gospel of salvation, so afraid of his life as well as of his family? Will it not be better if such people, who feel so insecure, do something other than making a mockery of our Lord and Saviour Jesus Christ'?

The excerpts below are an eye-opener, from when the Germans bid farewell to Angela Merkel, now former Chancellor of Germany, the largest economy in Europe. 'With six minutes of warm applause, on the streets, balconies, windows, the whole country applauded for six minutes – a spectacular example of leadership ...The Germans elected her to lead them, and she led 80 million Germans for 18 years with competence, skill, dedication, and sincerity ... During these 18 years of her leadership of the authority in her country, no transgressions were recorded against her. She did not assign any of her relatives to a government post. She did not claim that she was the maker of glories ... A standing ovation nationwide ... [She] was not tempted by the fashion or the lights and did not buy real estate, cars, yachts, and private planes, knowing that she is from former East Germany ... She left and her relatives did not claim advantage'.[16]

Someone asked me to sum up the challenges that I faced in SHUATS. The constant struggle during my tenure was, 'To Question or Not to Question'? That is the Question. That is what remains unresolved in my association with that esteemed institution. Of course, the above quote is not mine but Romila Thapar's, the prominent historian and Professor Emeritus at Jawahar Lal University (JNU), who emphasised the right to question authority.[17]She explained, how personalities—both in European and Indian history—laid the foundations of the present by asking questions. Public intellectuals are not absent in Indian society, nor are they alien imports. 'But where there should be voices, there is now often silence. Are we all being co-opted too easily by the comforts of conforming? Are we fearful of the retribution that questioning may and often does bring?'[18] A university cannot function where one is not permitted to ask questions both academic and spiritual. The constant struggle was when to take a call to leave. It was also not easy because we were implied to be cowardly, if we decided not to stand in solidarity with the authorities or leave the institution during a period of crisis. I was invited to build a faculty from the quandary, and brought some discipline and academic integrity after a struggle. However, I could neither bite the hand that was feeding me nor touch their feet, touching feet is a unique culture at SHUATS done in public which is nauseating.

We must pray and ask God's forgiveness. SHUATS is a God-given institution based on a profound legacy of sacrifice and the theology of 'feed the hungry and serve the land'. The words we preach, are the words of God and our life must be the living letters of Christ. We need to be honest before God who knows our intentions and actions, both hidden and displayed. It is a futile exercise to play the game of 'hide and seek' before God. It will be most unfortunate to hear the words, 'And if anyone will not receive you or listen to your words, shake off the dust from your feet, when you leave that house or town' (Matthew 10:14). We need to change ourselves, something which we often do not do.

'I used to believe that prayer changes things, but now I know that prayer changes us, and we change things' – Mother Teresa

Endnotes

[1] Sahu, D. K., United and Uniting, I.S.P.C.K., 2001, & Ian S. Markham et al eds., Church of North India, Willey-Blackwell Companion to the Anglican Communion, 2013, pp 319-328.

[2] Middlebrook, J. B., William Carey, Kingsgate: London, 1961.

[3] Smith, Christopher, The Serampore Mission Enterprise, Centre for Contemporary Christianity, Bangalore, 2006, p 138.

[4] Jeffrey, P., Ida S. Scudder, Word of Christ, Chennai, India, 2014, p 227.

[5] Sahu, Bibhudutta, The Caregiver's Cross, In: Sahu D. K. Eds Conversation on Health Healing, ISPCK, 2018, p 277-90.

[6] Paul, Samuel, A Life and Its Lessons: Memoirs, Public Affairs Centre, Bangalore 2012.

[7] https://thewire.in/law/court-government-bonhomie-ranjan-gogoi

[8] Higginbottom, Sam, The Gospel and the Plow, Nivedita Good Books, 2014, p 107

[9] Ibid, p 120

[10] Mangalwadi, Vishal, The Book That Made Your World: How the Bible Created the Soul of Western Civilization, Thomas Nelson, 2011, p 250

[11] Higginbottom, Sam, Farmer: An Autobiography, New York, Charles Scribner's Sons, 1949, p 88

[12] Shepherd, Henry, The Institute and its Servant Leader, In: Footprints of Faith, University Publication, SHUATS, 2016, p 33-48

[13] http://front.player.fm/series/2928109

[14] Higginbottom, Sam, Farmer: An Autobiography, New York, Charles Scribner's Sons, 1949, p 103

[15] Wiersbe, Warren W. and Wiersbe, David W., 10 Power Principles for Christian Service, Baker Books, 2010

[16] https://johnmenadue.com/this-is-leadership-germany-bids-farewell-to-angela-merkel/

[17] Thapar, Romila, Perspectives: To Question or Not to Question? That Is the Question, In: Economics & Political Weekly, Vol. 49, Issue No. 50, 13 Dec, 2014

[18] Ibid.

■■■

1975
Beginning of a Journey

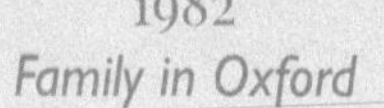

1982
Family in Oxford

1992
Manju with Mother Teresa

2010
with Natashia-Tia-Kyra

2017
with Rosy-Tia-Kyra-Nora

2017
Three Angels

2018
with Hon'ble President of India Shri Ram Nath Kovind

6

Identity

In 1979, the Professor of United Theological College, Bangalore, and later the director of Commission on World Mission and Evangelism (CWME), World Council of Churches (WCC), Christopher Duraisingh[1], published the article 'Indian Hyphenated Christians and Theological Reflections' where he argued that the emergence of indigenous theology in India must be viewed as a process of critical self-awareness by Indian-Christians. He further noted that the shaping of the Indian Christian ethos was doubly determined by a confluence of Judeo-Christian traditions on one hand and Pan-Indian traditions on the other. He further maintained that these two traditions were single and complete wholes, best designated by a hyphen, laying emphasis on the hyphenated character of Indian-Christian identity. This sparked a debate about the nature of Indian-Christian identity in the contemporary context. Earlier, Paulos Mar Gregorios had pointed out that the 'Indian' component is far more differentiated and complex than previously thought, especially in terms of the relationship between Jainism and Buddhism. James Massey had also noted that the Dalit element, which forms an indispensable part of any discourse on identity, has been systematically and deliberately left out of the discourse.

The debate regarding the issue of identity by J Jayakiran Sebastian, Sathianathan Clarke,[2] and Sebastian C H Kim has raised the complexity of the question. Clarke makes a conscious and much-needed break from mainstream Indian Christian Theology by asserting that its Indianness not only fosters the hegemonic ideology of upper castes but also refuses to engage with the collective religious resources of the Dalits.[3] Whereas Kim extends the discourse to another level. In the book review, Corinne Dempsey narrates the meticulously researched story on the many-angled history of conversion debates in India and the problem of conversion on theological rather than practical grounds.[4] The answer relates to shifting and conflicting socio-economic, cultural, and political realities. It is an attempt to respond to the criticisms of the Niyogi Report. The Protestant debates during the 1960s and 1970s repudiated forced or coerced conversion yet disagreed over the proposition developed primarily by M M Thomas and Kaj Baago – that Hindus and Christians alike were called not to separate communities but to a common, Christ-centred, secular fellowship. Kim finds this position unrealistic and particularly problematic for Dalit converts. Since Dalits do not typically identify with Hinduism to begin with, denying them a sense of community would be to deny them the religious identity they finally gain through Christianity. On the Catholic front, conversion debates during the 1980s spawned inculturation and liberation approaches that, Kim notes, are often at cross purposes. Inculturationists who integrate Sanskritic practices into liturgy accuse liberationists of being insensitive to Hindu traditions; the latter accuse the former of elitism and insensitivity to caste inequity. Kim presents the writings of Arun Shourie as thoughtfully representative of Hindu nationalist views and notes that although he may have unfairly criticised diversity within Christianity as a sign of weakness, he offered an opportunity for honest debate that Christians missed. They failed to convince Shourie and others of Christianity's new humility. Without acknowledging Shourie's theological reservations, Christians responded to the connections he drew between Christianity and imperialism. To deny links between Christianity and the empire is to drive a false wedge between the past and present. Kim proposes a Christian theology of conversion developed through open scrutiny by peolpe of other faiths. He suggests Christians assess the entanglement of foreign missionaries as well as the processes of colonialism, post-colonialism, and globalisation yet take into account converts' testimonies of transformation. Christians must work from the Golden Rule, offering the same respect for the Hindu faith and identity that they would wish in return. In other words, Christian evangelism would be justified only to the extent that Christians are willing to listen to and learn from Hindus.

Grace Ji-Sun Kim in an interesting study proposed an identity called Hybridity[5]. Kim defines Chi as 'the Eastern term for life force energy, which manifests the idea of wind and Spirit…Chi is essential, as it is what makes one alive and is the life force that makes one a living being. Every living thing has Chi; it is the central, animating element of our overall energy system, giving power and strength'. She puts the concept of Chi in conversation with the Christian concept of the Holy Spirit on primarily three fronts: 1) through comparing Chi's characteristics to those of ruach in the Christian Old Testament and *pneuma* in the New Testament, 2) through criticism of Western dualistic thinking, and 3) through an exploration of Western Christianity's diminishment of the Holy Spirit's standing and role in the Trinity. It helps to negotiate a deeper and fuller understanding of the Divine that draws on various religious and cultural contexts by developing a more inclusive understanding of Spirit. In the midst of postcolonial studies striving for liberation, postcolonialism recognises a plurality of oppressions that exist today. There is no homogenous category, but rather multiple identities based on class, sexual orientation, ethnicity, race, and gender. Within the complexity of perceiving the Other, postcolonialism is concerned with acquiring a new identity. One legacy of colonialism is an intermingling of people and cultures and the result of a hybridised identity. Hybridity has become an important category that paves the way to openness and new ways of thinking, which has positive implications for theological discourse.

Postcolonial studies suggest a 'Hybridity identity' in constructing local or contextual theologies. The argument in general is based on their refusal to press for a particular religious stance as final and ultimate. It opens the door to interreligious dialogue and openness to other expressions of faith and the divine. She writes, 'We can no longer take it for granted that the centre will always remain the centre as we are in a constant flux. In other words, theological discourse also needs to be decentred, disconnected from its European centre and welcomed into the faith discussions of those who have been marginalised. Black, Asian, African, Latin American, feminist theology, among other theologies, were understood to be insignificant and irrelevant to theological discourse. However, these theologies can add richness and diversity to the traditional forms of theology. We need to ask why white Euro-theology is at the centre'?[6]

She continues that in many ways we are all mixtures of different cultures, ethnicities, and religious identities. Hybridity and Fusion Hybridisation involves fusion, the creation of a new form, which can then be set against the old form of which it is partly made up. It is like an evolutionary process that moulds and changes individuals and societies. It combines with other ideas, concepts, and beliefs, to come up with a new and different understanding of self, context, and the world. Hybridisation is constantly occurring, which implies that new concepts and forms are always emerging. We do not live in homogenous communities but in mixed cultures with inculturation continually taking place.[7]

The renowned missionary and historian Andrew F Walls, Professor Emeritus of Edinburgh University, and founder of the Centre for the Study of Christianity in the Non-Western World, in his book *The Missionary Movement in Christian History: Studies in the Transmission of Faith* brings together lectures and articles and examines the many aspects that have characterised mission, indigenous Christianity, and colonialism in modern Africa. The Missionary Movement in Christian History has a far broader reach. Walls states that 'Church history has always been a tension between two principles of "indigenizing" and "pilgrim" but both have origin in the Gospel itself'.[8] The essence of the Gospel is that God accepts us as we are, on the basis of Christ's work alone, not on the basis of what we have become or are trying to become. However, 'as we are implying that He does not take us in isolation because we are conditioned by a particular time and place, by our family, group, society culture, "If any man is in Christ, he is a new creation" does not mean that one starts life in a vacuum. But there is also the "pilgrim principle" of Christianity. God in Christ accepts us as we are but accepts in order to transform into what He wants to be. The Christian inherits the pilgrim principle, that we have no abiding city. While the indigenizing principle, associates Christians with the *particulars* of one's culture, the pilgrim principle, equally of the Gospel, brings a dimension of transformation with no abiding city. The paradoxes of the Christian movement as a whole from different primitive Mediterranean Christianity have been from early Catholicism, from Celtic monasticism, from Reformation Protestantism, and from Nigerian Spirit Christianity. Andrew Walls shows how the central question for Christianity has always been one of identity in many different forms, a phenomenon revealed at each stage of its history by the missionary movement. The interesting point is the "Indigenizing Principle" and "Pilgrim Principle".

Pilgrims are simply men and women who are travelling through a country in order to get somewhere else. They are not residents of the country where they are present, rather, they consider themselves citizens of their homeland. The 'Pilgrim Principle' has to do with what makes us Christian. Paul tells us, 'Do not be conformed to the pattern of this world' (Romans 12:2) and Scripture reaffirms this teaching that we must not squeeze ourselves into the mould of the world/culture around us. Rather, we must proclaim Christ Jesus and obey the Lord. Christians should be different from everyone else. If you are a Christian and people can't tell there's anything different between you and your non-Christian neighbour, then there's a problem.

Indigenous means that everything relates to the culture in which it is found. One example is folktales: every culture has its own folktales that are well-known by the people of that culture, although they make no sense to those outside. The 'Indigenizing Principle' teaches that there are aspects of culture that are entirely appropriate for Christians and the Church to embrace. Jesus prayed, 'I do not ask that you take them out of the world, but that you keep them free from the evil one' (John 17:15). Ultimately, God Himself embraced this principle by sending His Son to take on flesh, to live in our world in order to redeem it. 'Emmanuel' means 'God with us'.

In my published doctoral dissertation, I had suggested that the three categories of ecclesiology – story, doctrine, and institution need to be interrelated in a coherent whole. The presupposition behind the argument is that a community cannot exist as a recognizable, distinctive, and collective entity unless it has some practice by which it can be identified. One activity of the community which is vital for interrelating the above three categories is the *koinonia* (fellowship) of the people of God – worship. The importance of worship lies in its being that activity that seeks to invoke the fundamentals and induct the worshipper into the heart of the Creator. Stephen Sykes suggests that the phenomenon of Christian worship makes a vital difference to the conditions under which vigorous arguments of a radical kind may be regarded as a constructive contribution to the performance of Christian identity. The centrality of worship has been more evidently emphasised in recent theological discussions irrespective of different traditions. At the heart of Christian worship is the recognition of the story of the triune God, established in the act of thanksgiving. Daniel Hardy and David Ford draw attention to praise as a central act of Christian life. All creation is a work of God's love and Jesus Christ is God's giving of Himself in love to restore and fulfil all creation. The Holy Spirit is the pouring out of this love in endless fresh creativity. Their thesis is that such a category opens a new vision of the other because it is an activity related to God and to other people in the context of creation. Worship is central to the life where the identity of God is witnessed by a people in praise, confession, repentance, hearing the Word, and breaking bread.[9]

***

Indian Christian Theology

The trajectory of Indian Christian Theology is multi-layered and multifaceted. There is no contention in my view that in our history of Christianity, Christian theology emerged and developed within the Greco-Roman cultural context and takes the categories of its philosophy. There are external influences that have definitely impacted the formulation of theology. The debate of the coloniser and the colonised has dominated the discourse in developing contextual theologies and not least, the East-West dichotomy in the discourse of Indian Christian historiography and Indian Christian theologies. However, it has reached a saturation point. It is appropriate to narrate the historical debate first, without losing sight of the broader spectrum of the Bible and Christian tradition.

Contextualisation may be defined as the articulation of the biblical message with the language and thought-forms of a particular culture or ethnic group. Contextualisation is not merely an academic matter, but an existential necessity for effective evangelism, Bible translation, church planting, Christian social action, and pastoral ministry. The need for contextualisation in theology arises as the church engages in missions.

It is not a modern idea being imposed on the Bible from without, but is required in the very fabric of biblical revelation itself. The ideal way is neither 'Christ above culture' nor 'Christ of culture' but rather 'Christ transforming culture'. Contextualisation is rooted at the heart of incarnation but caution must be underlined regarding inappropriate contextualisation if any, and the need to guard ourselves against the danger of the absolutisation of contextualisation. Any basic consideration must include the importance of clarifying the underlying epistemological foundation of contextualisation.

Indian Christian Theology is conducted at two levels. One, obviously, is the academic theology taught in seminaries/universities by Indians, being in India, even though some of them are educated in the West. The other is a minority who make every effort to migrate to the West to discuss and do theology in the comforts of the West. This minority group receives all the benefits of the empire but speaks theological jargon against the empire. It makes for interesting reading but is far removed from the ground reality in India. The theology, practiced by the majority of those in India also has two segments: the minority urban elite and the majority rural poor. The majority of rural poor perceive the Holy Spirit as illuminating what is needed to be a faithful follower of Christ today. I am not altogether certain whether they consciously articulate theology or need to do so but consider the question pragmatically – this definitely includes a theologising but not one that bears sustained reflection. However, it demands a call for more conscious theological engagement with the Bible and overabundance of wider sources as well as voices that demand to seriously listen to stories of people, context, and history.

One of the interesting pursuits of Indian Christian hermeneutics has been to search for the authentic Indian or a quest for how to make Christian theology, Indian. Some scholars argue that true Indian theology is to be found only in the speech of an adivasi, a tribal, a common man, an illiterate villager, in a few folk forms, and to some extent in the writings of rural and Dalit writers. One of the dominant features of Indian Christianity has been the tendency to be retrospective or ironic. There is a lingering backward glance to look again for the prime sites of ancient India and to look to its texts, architecture, art, painting, and poetry for inspiration and new direction.

Kristeen Kim in the review of the book *Beyond Captivity* by Robin Boyd gives an excellent summary of Boyd and his work.[10] 'Boyd has done remarkable service in ministry, mission, and theological education in England, India, Australia, Ireland, and Scotland since he was ordained in the Irish Presbyterian Church in 1951. He left India in 1974 and his legacy is cherished in India because the book is used in teaching Indian Christian Theology. It has been produced by the Centre for Contemporary Christianity as Volume 24 of the 'Studies in Gospel Interface with Indian Context' series edited by Siga Arles. The book includes a useful index and a bibliography of Boyd's work.'[11]

'In India, Boyd's best-known monograph is probably An Introduction to Indian Christian Theology. This illustration of how Indian Christians had expressed the gospel in their own languages and symbols was one of the first in the field. It was followed by a monograph with Cambridge University Press in 1974, *India and the Latin Captivity of the Church: The Cultural Context of the Gospel*, which questioned the universal use of Latin categories and styles for doing theology even in the West and advanced alternatives inspired by Indian insights. Some of the explorations of Indian thought which led to these now-classic works are included in this edited collection along with candid reflections written since the turn of this century. At this distance, Boyd wonders whether there is such a thing given the diversity of its expression. Moreover, he recognises the challenge of subaltern and Dalit theologians who complain that it expresses Christian theology using the language and categories of the elite Hinduism that oppresses Dalits, and consequently it pays no attention to their struggle. Boyd concludes that 'Indian Christian theology' nevertheless has value among other theological approaches in India.'[12]

Boyd also asks a question, '"Is there a truly Indian expression of theological thought?" The church in India has a long reputation for appearing and sounding foreign. Often those who join an established church are taught using foreign resources with terminology and thought patterns originating in the West. To answer his question about a truly Indian theology, Boyd surveys the work of several Indian Christian theologians from the last two hundred years. Through this theological survey, Boyd attempts to show how these Indian theologians sought to work out their apologetic and systematic theology using the Hindu terms and thought patterns of their heritage. The goal of this book is that Indian followers of Christ will further the work begun by these early theologians in expressing biblical revelation from the Indian heart'.[13]

Boyd's survey included Brahmabandhab Upadhyaya, A J Appasamy, P Chenchiah, V Chakkarai, Sadhu Sundar Singh, R Pannikar, and Dhanjibhai Fakirbhai. 'These are the men who contributed the most to uniquely Indian theological categories. The first strength in Boyd's analysis is his relation of each theologian to specific Indian philosophical streams of thought. In order to understand the contributions these theologians have made to Indian Christian theology, it is helpful to see from which particular Indian stream of philosophy the theologian operated. At the risk of oversimplification, three major streams of Indian philosophy emerge from these theologians: *advaita* (non-dualism), *bhakti* (loving devotion), and *shakti* (power).

Brahmabandhab is the strongest proponent of advaita. The bhakti theologians were Appasamy, Dhanjibhai, and Tilak. Chenchiah taught in relation to the shakti tradition. Then there were Sundar Singh and Chakkarai who fell somewhere in between. Boyd does well in showing how each theologian's philosophical heritage affects their Christian theological work. Boyd even relates this to how Greek philosophy, linguistics, and geographical issues influenced the creedal formulations of the early church. Moving from the broad philosophical schools that influenced each theologian, Boyd excels in presenting the specifics of each theologian's uniquely Indian contributions to Christian theology. The most significant categories include the Trinity, Christology, and the new life in Christ. Brahmabandhab's work on the Trinity, expressed as *saccidananda,* is very insightful. For an *advaitic* Hindu, the Trinity can be very difficult. Brahmabandhab's relation of these aspects of the Godhead to a familiar idea in this Hindu tradition provides a possible bridge to teaching biblical truth. In Christology, several of these theologians expressed how the Hindu mind is perhaps more prepared than most to understand the incarnation of Christ because of the Sanskrit word *avatar*.

Finally, in the doctrine of the Christian life, Chenchiah and Sundar Singh are unique in their use of the idea of *anubhav* (experience) in expressing how the believer is to know the risen Christ. All these Indian terms and styles reveal exciting new insights into how the Hindu mind can bring fresh theological expressions of biblical truth. However, all these concepts bring difficulties and dangers. Boyd reveals both the difficulties and the exciting potential that each theologian presents. *Saccidananda* verges on the heresy of a monistic theology. *Avatar* can wrongly equate the eternal Son and his unique incarnation with that of Krishna or Ram. Another major difficulty for the Indian mind is the concept of penal substitution from Christ's work on the cross. The laws of *karma*, while it may be consciously rejected by the new believer, can still influence an Indian believer's conception of the work of Christ. Despite these difficulties, Boyd makes clear that there is exciting potential in the use of Hindu philosophical thought for developing a truly Indian Christian theology. A weakness in Boyd's analysis is that he rarely mentions how each theologian interprets passages of Scripture to express their theology. While biblical concepts are mentioned in each theologian's work, Boyd doesn't often present a theologian's interpretation and use of specific texts of Scripture. This would have been helpful especially when writing on the Indian concept of *sruti* (Scripture) as being the supreme authority in a believer's life. Also, Boyd seems ambiguous on how the Indian church should relate to early church creeds such as the Apostles and Nicene creeds. Should these be essentially ignored or must they be looked to as authoritative in accordance with Scripture? A balanced approach seems to be the best solution in developing an Indian theology. In conclusion, Boyd is successful in presenting how these Indian theologians think'.[14]

'From K M Banerjea in the colonial days to Amaladoss in post-independence time, Indian theologians have drawn on Hindu religious and theological heritage. Such an exercise has been seen as innovative in its implicit opposition to Western methodologies'.[15] Their efforts can be categorised as insiders' views of Indian philosophy. 'Raymond Panikkar was born in Spain in 1918. He is well known for his work called *The Unknown Christ in Hinduism*. In this book, he concludes that Christ is present in Hinduism. It has been an effective means of salvation and union with God. It is in Christianity however, that Christ is fully revealed and so the work of the Christian mission is that of unveiling the hidden Christ of Hinduism, and the relationship of Hinduism to Christianity can be spoken of as that of seed to fruit. It is true that many theologians have seen Christ as the link'.[16]

In the 20th century, D T Niles was a well-known ecumenist. His primary concern regarding theology was evangelism. The church was the centre of the activities pertaining to the beliefs and the mission of the church was to prepare for the coming of the kingdom. The church was not only an instrument of the gospel but also a part of the gospel itself. Niles' theology is in relation to the cultural and political setup. M M Thomas, born in 1916 in Kerala, advocated that theology must always be contextual, grappling with human problems in the midst of the socio-political and scientific-technological realities of the present day. His theology is characterised as the way of action and he is averse to any attempts at enculturation. Thomas believed that revolution is a partial fulfilment of the kingdom of God. He considered the church's call to socio-political engagement to be strong and not wrong in being faithful to Christian traditions. Additionally, all revolution was imbibed with Christian values and the spirit of Christ. His theology is action-oriented. He places orthopraxis before orthodoxy. He finds three resolutions in the world. The scientific and technological, revolt of oppressed groups, nations, classes, and races, demanding social and international justice, and finally breaking up the traditional integration between religion, society, and the state. Behind the revolutions, Thomas saw a revolution in the human spirit. He defined the image of God in man as the obligation to respond to the call for freedom as the core of his personalities, the basis of his eternal status as a person.[17]

In re-invoking spiritual aspects of our heritage, we have silenced and overlooked the rational and sceptical aspects of our past. The Indian traditions were not merely spiritual and devotional, there were also materialistic, such as the *Lokayata* and *Sankhya* schools, and there were atheistic religions such as Jainism and Buddhism. Interestingly, some of them looked unnecessarily to Marx, when a more local variety was available. In other words, we have been reinforcing the European image of India as the eternal spiritual home, an image concocted by European orientalists in the 18th century as the handmaiden of colonialism. In projecting the spirit of India as timeless and changeless, we fail to note the struggles and miseries of the present. Indigenization/inculturation and even the more recent contextualisation are evangelistic and apologetic in tone and content. They are concerned with injecting, translating, or interpreting a given text and gospel for a culture.

Chad M Bauman of Butler University in the review of the book *India and the Indianness of Christianity* a festschrift for Robert E Frykenberg summarises the history precisely.[18] Bauman states that Frykenberg matters to historians of Christianity because, beginning in the mid-1970s, he began to write about Indian Christians. When he did so, he adopted the same approach as in his earlier work, writing 'bottom-up' histories of Indian Christians focusing on how they mediated, translated, and altered the message to which they had been introduced by missionaries. What the possibility of applying similar methods to the study of imperial and Indian Christian history should make clear is articulated succinctly by Chandra Mallampalli, one of the volume's contributors: 'Debates that have preoccupied historians of the Raj—local versus central power, indigenous agency and resistance versus colonial power, cultural imperialism, and so forth—find many parallels within the history of Indian Christianity'.

'Frydenberg's methodological approach to Indian Christianity resembles that pioneered by Andrew Walls in the context of Africa. As Walls might put it, with agreement from Frykenberg, the Christianisation of India also entailed the Indianisation of Christianity. Christianity, therefore, regardless of what its critics might say, is an Indian religion. The very comparability of Walls, Sanneh, and Frykenberg is telling. Despite the fact that he worked for almost his entire career in the University of Madison's South Asian Studies program, Frykenberg has been more open to learning from self-consciously Christian scholars, and more candid about his own Christian commitments than is currently fashionable in the secular academy'.[19]

'There is no doubt that Frykenberg's influence has inspired a significant number of Western scholars working on Indian Christianity to shift their scholarly gaze away from missionaries—the traditional focus of Western histories of 'Indian Christianity'—and toward Indian Christians themselves. That influence is nowhere more obvious than in the Eerdmans series – *Studies in the History of Christian Missions,* edited by Frykenberg and Brian Stanley, which includes a number of important edited volumes and monographs on Indian Christianity. Frykenberg's method has appealed to many scholars precisely because it exposes the inadequacies of earlier histories of Indian Christianity, which were often just Eurocentric missions' histories masquerading as histories of Indian Christianity. Unfortunately, in the process of reacting against one inadequacy, scholars in the Frykenberg school risk introducing another. As Mallampalli puts it in this volume, "As much as such perspectives from below offer a corrective to Eurocentric interpretations of Indian Christianity, they run the risk of minimizing the very real impact of the foreign hand on the minds of converts and the direction of Christian movements". If Frykenberg's research and that of those who were influenced by him helped swing the pendulum of Indian Christian historiography away from missionaries and toward Indian Christians themselves (at times going a bit too far, perhaps), then research like that in Jeffrey Cox's Imperial Fault Lines, which provides a thoughtful and nuanced analysis of Western missionaries at work in British India, may swing it back again to a more fruitful equilibrium'.[20]

***

People of the Way

VARANASI

There are two emerging identities of God's people in Uttar Pradesh in India that has initiated two different kinds of discourse. Uttar Pradesh is a state located in North India. It was created on 1st April 1937 as the United Provinces and was renamed Uttar Pradesh in 1950. Lucknow is the capital and the largest city of Uttar Pradesh. On 9th November 2000, a new state, Uttarakhand, was carved out from the Himalayan hill region of Uttar Pradesh. The state is flanked by Rajasthan in the west, Haryana, and Delhi in the northwest, Uttarakhand and the country of Nepal in the north, Bihar in the east, Jharkhand in the southeast, Chhattisgarh in the south, and Madhya Pradesh in the southwest. It covers 243,290 square kilometres (93,933 square miles), equal to 6.88% of the total area of India, and is the fourth largest Indian state by area with over 200 million inhabitants as per the 2011 census. The two major rivers of the state, the Ganges and the Yamuna converge at Allahabad, now known as Prayagraj, and continue to flow on as the Ganges further east.

Situated on the northern bank of the Ganges, the city of Varanasi is historically and religiously important as it is located midway between Delhi and Kolkata. Varanasi is known as the religious and cultural capital of India where many heritages have their roots and people respect and come here in reverence. There are riverside cremation grounds at *Harishchandra* Ghat and *Manikarnika* Ghat recognized by the smoke that rises from the pyres of the dead. It is believed that if one dies here, one gains liberation from the earthly round of *samsara* (cycle of rebirth). Varanasi is India's mega pilgrim city and entry into the city itself will fill one with a sense of the religious. With the coming of our Prime Minister Mr Narendra Modi to the Varanasi constituency, this has become a centre of attraction. The holy shrine of Lord Kashi Vishwanath (an incarnation of Lord Shiva), makes Varanasi a place of great religious importance to the Hindus.

The first story of a 'people of the way' is of *Matri Dham* or the *Khrist Bhakta* (devotees of Christ) movement. It is an indigenous model that envisages a new form of identity, free from controversies, and offers no complaints neither about being persecuted for preaching the gospel nor following Christ as personal saviour as propagated in some circles. It emerged as a religio-cultural conciliation of subaltern people seeking to be liberated from their inherited bondage. I had the privilege of taking a group of theology students with three faculty members and an assistant Chaplain to visit the Ashram over a weekend to experience the life there just before the lockdown was declared on 24th March 2020. The people are known as *Khrist Bhaktas* because of their devotion to Christ, seeing him as '*Sat Guru*'. *Matri Dham* Ashram is situated on the outskirts of Varanasi, in the Sindhora area for over 55 years. The Ashram was established in 1954 with the support of the Roman Catholic mission, the Indian Missionary Society (IMS) which was founded by Father Gasper A. Pinto (1905-1972). It was his conviction that the sacred work of spreading the light of Christ in North India must begin with and from the religious capital of India, i.e. Varanasi, then known as Benares. Priests such as Father Pinto and others felt the need to develop an indigenous missionary community of the Roman Catholic Church in North India with its conscious effort to make the gospel relevant in the North Indian cultural context. The Lord fulfilled his dream by planting the Society in Varanasi itself.

Since 1995 Ashram has been under the leadership of Father Anil Dev, a gifted preacher and talented composer whose lifestyle is exemplary, very simple, and free from controversies. He has written 136 *bhajans* in the Hindi language, which have become popular among the people regularly visiting the Ashram. The place attracts thousands of Hindus among others to its prayer meetings that are held every Sunday and special healing services every second Saturday of the month. Even during the other days of the week, the Ashram is open to anyone who wishes to come there to pray and meditate. Today, the Ashram is a center of a mass spiritual movement of the devotees of Jesus Christ, especially the non-baptised followers of Jesus Christ who are called *Khrist Bhaktas*. At present more than 7000 people gather in the Ashram on all second Saturdays for the day-long *Satsang* for Gospel discourse and healing services. In my conversation with Fr Anil Dev, I found that they do not have any problem in preaching the gospel and he is not persecuted by the Government, despite being in the same state of Uttar Pradesh; rather he has a cordial relationship with the authority. The lifestyle of the Father and the leaders in the Ashram exemplifies the life of Christ. Prayer and simplicity rule their life and they do not have any security guards with guns to protect them. The worship is participatory and the crowds, though overwhelming in number, are very disciplined.

Fr Anil Dev prefers to call these believers *Khrist Bhaktas* or devotees of Christ, stating that they profess faith in Christ Jesus and are committed to Him as their saviour. He insists that they are not called Christians because very few of them have been baptised and have not entered a church. However, Fr Anil Dev continues, these devotees of Christ are the disciples of Christ, as they have entered the kingdom and made an option for the kingdom. However, there are some cases in which the believers themselves have asked for baptism. Thus, a small minority of devotees have been baptised, although they continue to live within their birth communities without joining the Roman Catholic Church. The local Roman Catholic churches in association with the Ashram encourage them to not disrupt living with their communities. These devotees identify themselves as Hindus for all practical purposes. *Khrist Bhaktas* are devotees of Christ, but not members of any mainline church. *Matri Dham* is a localised initiative to contextualise the gospel, which is related to self-identity and belongingness. It provides an opportunity for those who are on the margins to engage with theology. The movements indicate the freedom and openness that all who have a personal encounter with Christ can come and join the fellowship. It is a call for discipleship in the community within the community.

The story is a reminder of Dietrich Bonhoeffer (1906-1945), who advocated for religion-less Christianity, which affirmed the true Christian faith in the midst of an oppressive context. Bonhoeffer was trying to find a non-religious vocabulary so as to speak of a God who is found in the midst of the struggles of the world. He said that Christians today must learn to speak of God in a secular way and to live out Christianity in a way that is responsive to the context of injustice and oppression. Bonhoeffer's proposal was a 'Religion-less Christianity' – that we should see Jesus Christ as 'Lord of the religion-less'. It was not the religious act that made the Christian, but it was through partaking in the sufferings of God in the secular life. He said the experience of the absolute was found only in a new life for others, that is, by participating in the being of Jesus as one whose only concern was for others. We can never know God as an idea, but only in and through our tangible meeting with others in our life in this world. Thus, we are called to be Disciples of Christ, not members of a particular confessional church.

The church cannot exist by and for itself. Self-contained and self-centred existence is simply the end of a church. Under the imperative of Christ's command and in the power of the Holy Spirit, churches are called to transform their fear to hope by engaging with each other in a mutually enriching and strengthening fellowship on the way towards visible unity. Churches should not aim to expand the confessional boundaries but the boundaries of the kingdom of God. The church is challenged to promote the values and the imperatives of the kingdom. It exists for the kingdom of God. The proclamation of the gospel in the context of the brokenness and dehumanisation of the world is the essential task of the church.

The church is called to live out its faith and take the gospel to the world where people are struggling and looking for peace and stability. The church is not destined to remain immutable and untouchable as traditional churches usually are. Rooted in the life of society, the church is in constant interplay within the world. Thus, there is always an urge for the church to be relevant and to look for new and acceptable models within the given context. The being of the church is not static; it is conditioned by its becoming. In line with this, both the movements try to bring a change and present Christ in a form and model through which people can easily access Him and be transformed by Christ.

The concept of discipleship also varies from the traditional understanding of the term. The reality that traditional churches are facing is people being a disciple of Christ without being a member of the church. In the traditional church understanding, belonging to the church had always been controlled by baptism. Here, the criterion of belonging to this fellowship is a personal relationship and faith in Jesus Christ. In the *Satsang* of the *Matri Dham* of Varanasi, the Word of God is shared in the form discourse which is the decisive factor where all are welcomed without any distinction. Here people meet without any dichotomy of sacred and secular, which itself is a sign of the kingdom of God.

Rowan Williams developed the idea that, in biblical accounts, 'revelation' is an event that generates for a people or community new possibilities for human living, which they were not aware of before and which they attribute to an initiative on God's part. So, in the Exodus, God's action of liberation opens up for the freed community new possibilities for life in relationship with God. Likewise, the disciples of Jesus came to understand that the events they had witnessed had also disclosed new possibilities for human life. They came to believe that the possibilities generated were not for one community alone but were offered to all communities. The church, therefore, may be understood as the community that professes faith in God, who is the source of these possibilities and which, in response, witnesses to them and works to realise them both in its own life and in the wider world. The church is thus the people of the new creation. 'So to come to be "in Christ", to belong with Jesus, involves a far-reaching reconstruction of one's humanity... a new identity in a community of reciprocal love and complementary service, whose potential horizons are universal' (William 2000: 134).

Reconstructing the identity of a community in the postmodern condition is a theological task that ought to be pursued if the church is to be relevant. The postmodern condition is generally used to describe the economic or cultural state or condition of society that is said to exist after modernity. Some schools of thought hold that modernity ended in the late 20th century, in the 1980s or early 1990s, replaced by postmodernity, while others would extend modernity to cover the developments denoted by postmodernity. In most contexts, it should be distinguished from postmodernism, the adoption of postmodern philosophies in art, literature, culture, and society. Postmodern sociology can be said to focus on conditions of life that became increasingly prevalent in the late 20th century in most industrialised nations, including the ubiquity of mass media and mass production, the rise of a global economy, and a shift from manufacturing to service economies. David Harvey described it as consumerism, where manufacturing, distribution, and dissemination have become exceptionally inexpensive but social connectedness and community have become rarer. The sociological view of postmodernity ascribes it to more rapid transportation, wider communication, and the ability to abandon standardisation of mass production, leading to a system that values a wider range of capital than previously and allows value to be stored in a greater variety of forms.

Therefore, reconstructing the identity of the church in the changing scenario must adhere to the power of discernment. 'The purpose of this discernment is to learn and live out, in the power of the Spirit, those forms of Christian discipleship that arise out of, on the one hand, the church's fidelity to the Word and on the other, its understanding of the needs of the world' (Lonsdale 2011: 246).

PRAYAGRAJ

The city of Allahabad, now known as Prayagraj, is historically and religiously important. Allahabad is a city in north-central India, at the confluence of the Yamuna and Ganges rivers, east of Varanasi. It was built on the site of an ancient Indo-Aryan holy city and is still a pilgrimage site for millions of Hindus. Prayag, the place where three sacred rivers—Ganges, Yamuna, and the invisible Saraswati—converge, has since time immemorial been considered a holy place, where millions of people come every year to take a dip at the holy meeting place. It is famous for the *Kumbha Mela* (fair) which takes place every 12 years. Every year from January to February there is a *Magh Mela* where millions of pilgrims flock to this holy city from every corner of the world to take a dip.

The second story is of Yeshu Darbar which began humbly with weekly cottage meetings initially at the Director's bungalow in 1994. The venue then shifted from the residence to the University Chapel and eventually to the University Chapel lawns. For some time, it was held in an old Engineering Hall during the monsoon, but soon even that place was too small to accommodate the crowds, and eventually, it was moved to the football ground as it provided a comfortable place for the worshippers to sit. Most of the people who attended the prayer and healing crusades were from the nearby villages, cities, and neighbouring states. Thousands of people came to hear the gospel messages and receive healing from various diseases at *Yeshu Darbar*.

The former glory of *Yeshu Darbar* is a story, not only inspiring but also humbling. It charted a new course on being disciples of Christ without being a member of any church. The founder of this movement received the baptism of the Holy Spirit in 2000, during the visit of Dr Ulf Ekman, and was endowed with spiritual gifts particularly for preaching the Word of God and healing. Dr Ulf Eckman was a former charismatic pastor and the founder of the Word of Life organisation in Sweden, which brought the word of faith movement to that country, but who is now a Roman Catholic.

The latter part of *Yeshu Darbar's* story has a different tone. Given its close association with *Yeshu Darbar*, the University became famous all over India. The former late Chancellor of SHUATS consecrated the founder as the Bishop of *Yeshu Darbar*, along with 12 other believers, as pastors to help him.[21] Such a glorious and humbling story entered a theologically disputed undertaking when a decision was made on 18th July 2012 to consecrate and install 'the Bishop of Yeshu Darbar' on Sunday 4th November 2012. While across the denominational boundaries there is unease about episcopacy and *Yeshu Darbar* had charted a new course, surprisingly the decision did not take cognizance of the fact that the anointing of the Holy Spirit in 2000 was the abundant grace of God with the power of Holy Spirit to move forward. The act of consecration on 4th November 2012 was performed by a principal consecrator assisted by co-consecrators. The principal consecrator was a Roman Catholic bishop of very good standing and repute but assisted by bishops of protestant churches with no historic succession tradition.

Episcope is oversight and so 'episcopacy' was a second-generation requirement. The groups of Christ's immediate followers were small and nurtured by the apostles themselves. Kallistos Ware states it well. 'What is a bishop? All too easily we assume that the answer is obvious, yet in fact, the bishop's role has varied in different periods. Which is to be our model: the collegial episcopate of the New Testament times, with groups of presbyters -*episkopoi* in each local church? Or the so-called monarchical bishop of the second and third centuries, clearly distinguished from the presbyters, yet presiding over no more than a single congregation, the normal celebrant at the Sunday Eucharist? Or the bishop of the fourth century onwards, ruling over a diocese of not just one but dozens or even hundreds of different parishes?'[22]

The office of the bishop has all sorts of possibilities in the reformed tradition. For example, in Germany, continuity in the line of bishops was largely stopped through the Reformation, whereas the bishop's office in the Lutheran Church continued without interruption only in Scandinavia and the Evangelical Lutheran Church in Siebenburgen (Romania). In some protestant churches, the bishop is no more than the chairman of a church council who may be elected for life or for a certain number of years like in the United Evangelical Lutheran Churches in India. However, episcopal consecration is not conferred as a reward or to honour an individual. It is to fulfil a special service in the local community of believers within a diocese within the context of the universal church.

The consecration of the Bishop of *Yeshu Darbar* on 4th November 2012 had a sad conclusion because, on 31st January 2013, Pope Benedict XVI accepted the resignation of the Roman Catholic Bishop, the principal consecrator from the pastoral care of the Diocese of Allahabad. This was because according to Canon Law 401 § 2 of the Catholic Church, 'The bishop who, without a pontifical mandate, consecrates a person a bishop, and the one who receives the consecration from him, incur a *latae sententiae* ex-communication reserved to the Apostolic See. Can. 1382' (*latae sententiae* is a penalty that is inflicted *ipso facto*, automatically, by force of the law itself when a law is contravened). He knew very well that his act would call for ecclesiastical discipline that would invite papal censure. The founder of Yeshu Darbar, while often declaring in public that he did not subscribe to Churchianity or Christianity, embraced episcopacy of a kind that is uncommon in history. Even in practice, after ordaining so many presbyters and deacons of *Yeshu Darbar*, the Bishop cannot issue the ordination certificate. The people who come to attend the *Darbar* are followers of Christ and non-churchgoers. Their testimonies are worth hearing. Hundreds of people line up every Sunday morning to share their testimonies that range from healing from sickness as well as stories of their cattle giving birth as answers to prayer. They are believers with exemplary prayerful life.

However, the vision of *Yeshu Darbar* is now overshadowed by the concept of a Macro Darbar, following the trends of megachurches. The story of the megachurch has an interesting narrative that is worth reading. 'A fake shark – bathed in neon purples and blues – menaces the stage as pastor Ed Young, Jr, steps out to the standing ovation of his thousands of congregants. Church has started. Young, in his fifties with youthfully coiffed hair and tidy in a slick-grey suit, begins with a viral toddler song. He leads his audience in a call-and-response: "baby shark, bum bum bum bum bum, teenage shark, bum bum bum bum bum...." As he shakes his hips and moves his arms in a chopping motion, Young draws them in. The camera pans to the audience, all wiggling their hips and clapping their arms to follow. Young is an entertainer. He is also a social media personality, a rap-music satirist, and a man of God. The lead pastor of one of the largest megachurches in Dallas, Young has many fans. His primary congregation at Fellowship Church in Grapevine has an estimated Sunday attendance of 20,000, a figure that does not include the thousands of other members and visitors who frequent the seven satellite campuses or watch his sermon feeds on the "Fellowship Live" internet broadcast each week. On this particular Sunday in August of 2011, Young unveiled a sermon series called "Shark Weak". A puny reference to the Discovery Channel predator fish programme, the series spins popular television into spiritual self-help lessons so that congregants might navigate metaphorical 'sharks' in their lives'. [23]

The rise of megachurches may have begun in America, but it is no longer simply an American phenomenon. The form has taken on a life of its own and has been transplanted, with various modifications, to a wide array of socio-cultural environments. 'Megachurches are not an entirely new phenomenon', Scott Thumma and David Travis insist in *Beyond Megachurch Myths*. In this defining work for seminarians and pastors seeking to understand and perhaps replicate current trends, the authors place megachurches within the more recent history of the late-20th century. For several decades, congregations have experimented with the use of small groups, marketing, and personality-driven pastoring, all characteristics that have contributed to the rise of enormous congregations.[24]

The megachurch is concerned with people's various needs; representing a new experience of church and the Christian community. Donald Miller pointed out that large new paradigm churches design worship services which appeal to non-churchgoers, and in doing so significantly depart from conventional views on worship. The concept of 'seeker friendly' worship services is geared toward creating a non-threatening atmosphere. Indeed, the emphasis on being seeker-friendly has led many churches, despite their allegiances, to try to avoid being classified as 'Charismatic', 'Evangelical', 'Fundamentalist' or 'Pentecostal'. Rick Noack and Lazaro Gamio in their survey of megachurches in Korea, Brazil, and several African countries indicate that they are often much larger than their North American counterparts (averaging 60,000 in attendance). The world's largest churches are Yoido Full Gospel Church, Seoul, Korea (2,53,000); Works and Mission Baptists Church, Abidjan, Ivory Coast (1,50,000); Yotabeche Methodist Church, Santiago, Chile (1,50,000); Mision Carismatica Internacional, Bogotá, Colombia (1,50,000); Deeper Life Bible Church, Lagos, Nigeria (1,20,000); Elim Church, San Salvador, El Salvador (1,17,000); Nambu Full Gospel, Seoul, Korea (1,10,000); Assemblies of God Grace and Truth, Kyanggi-do, Korea (1,05,000); Kum Ran Methodist, Seoul, Korea (80,000); Vision de Futuro, Santa Fe, Argentina (70,000).

'Writing in *Christianity Today*, Lyle Schaller, a prominent evangelical spokesman for the megachurch movement, proclaimed, "The emergence of the "megachurch" is the most important development of modern Christian history. You can be sentimental about the small congregation, like the small corner grocery store or small drug store, but they simply can't meet the expectations that people carry with them today." This echoes the well-known marketing consultant Peter Drucker's claim that megachurches "are surely the most important social phenomenon in American society in the last 30 years." Critics of the megachurch follow a similar line. Gustav Niebuhr, grandson of the famous theologian H. Richard Niebuhr, and long-time religion writer for the *Wall Street Journal* and *New York Times*, summarises their emergence as follows, "A shift of power and influence is slowly, but profoundly, changing the way many of the nation's 80 million protestants worship. Since the 1980s, megachurches have gathered tens of thousands of worshipers into their folds and millions of dollars into their collection plates"'.[25]

The same story is unfolding in India today. Y A Sudhakar Reddy describes mega-churches in Andhra Pradesh, India, citing Calvary Temple in Hyderabad, Holy Ghost Fire Ministries in Vishakhapatnam, and Bible Mission in Gooty.[26] The Calvary Temple was founded by Dr Satish Kumar in 2005 with 25 members and the church membership has since grown to 3,30,000 people and 8 places of worship as of 2020. In 2012, the church began construction of an 18,000-seat indoor auditorium with galleries like an indoor stadium in Hyderabad, Telangana. It was built in 52 days and the venue was opened on 1st January 2013. Two more extension auditoriums were built to accommodate 50,000 members in one service in 2020. The Church of Signs and Wonders is a church in Punjab, pastored by Ankur Yoseph Narula. It began with three people in 2008 which grew to 500 members in 2009, 2000 members in 2010, 4000 members in 2011, 8000 members in 2012, 13000 members in 2013, 18000 members in 2014, 25000 members in 2015, 35000 members in 2016, 60000 members in 2017, and now a congregation of more than 2,00,000 people every week. New Life Assembly of God is an evangelical church affiliated with the Assemblies of God in Chennai India, which was founded in 1973 by Pastor David Mohan. In 1999, the church added a service in English, led by his son Pastor Chadwick Mohan. By 2004, attendance reached 30,000 people and as of 2020, the attendance is 40,000.

Megachurches should not be confused with crusades that are conducted with the aim to reach people with the gospel. The most famous pastor on television in the 1950s, Billy Graham became the face of the 'revival of revivalism', joining with other conservative forces to hold massive youth rallies and promote multi-city crusades. One of these early revival tours covered sacred evangelical ground. His four-week big tent revival in 1949 drew in celebrity admirers in Los Angeles, home of Aimee Semple McPherson's Angelus Temple. Later that year Graham appeared in Charles Grandison Finney's 'burned-over district' of New York and in the summer of 1950 his campaign 'reached a climax' on Boston Common, where George Whitefield had spread the revival spirit in 1740. Quickly becoming the most popular evangelical preacher in the world, Graham honed his preaching skills by listening to and learning from radio announcers, 'merging their timing and timeliness with his own passion to save lost souls'. His continued national success resulted from his ability to translate traditional evangelical teachings for a television audience. Leading the way for fellow revivalists, Graham served as a 'role model' for the shift to television broadcasting when, in 1950, he organised a revival in a 'specially constructed tabernacle' in Portland, Oregon, with equipment to film his sermons and documentary films.

The initial crowd of 20,000 at *Yeshu Darbar* has now reduced to a maximum of 4000 or a little less on a regular Sunday morning except Christmas, Good Friday, and Easter. The quantity occupies one major item of prayer to save millions of souls during the Friday night prayer. One pioneer member of the prayer movement shared, 'The Friday night prayer was the best time to sit together and pray but now it is changed'. The Friday night prayer has become a 'monologue' filled with criticism of the church, hero-worship, and barely any quality time of prayer except to fill the time from 10:00 pm to 2:00 am ritualistically with repetitive *bhajans* only of the founder of *Yeshu Darbar*, video recording of talks, and an air-conditioned room with no power cuts.

Nevertheless, the worship at *Yeshu Darbar* has some unique characteristics. The Friday evening service is the only one that begins on time as the Director of the campus ministry is always punctual with a choir that is well-prepared and rehearsed. During the worship on Saturdays and Sundays including special occasions, one must patiently wait for the arrival of the man of God. The order of worship is spontaneous and any meticulous planning with prior approval for special occasions of Consecration, Ordination, Annual Thanksgiving, and Foundation Days is hardly followed. The University Chaplain/Presbyter-in-Charge is paraded frequently before the altar to make changes. There is an unwritten order of service at *Yeshu Darbar*, which includes the coffee break for the speaker before the sermon. The coffee drinking is done just beside the 'High-Chair' on the altar, which is kept for Jesus where His presence is adorned. The theology of worship is that we are not expected to invoke God's presence to begin the worship but God must wait for us. Once, while listening to the sermon, a local professional photographer started taking photographs of the preacher on the stage from different angles. A visitor from abroad who was sitting beside me asked, 'Bishop, why are so many photographs being taken while preaching the word of God? Isn't it a distraction and quite annoying?'

***

Self-Understanding

The church is a reality. It is sent to the world to commit itself to *Missio Dei* which ought to be neither the reaction of the church to specific issues or situations nor a methodology related to the function of the church. It is essentially the dynamic action of the church by which the church perceives and fulfils its mission in the perspective of the kingdom of God. In his report, Aram I, the Catholicos of Cilicia proposed to the Harare Assembly in Zimbabwe in 1998 – 'A Church Beyond Its Walls'. He had asked: 'What kind of church do we project for the 21st century: a church confined to nation-states or ethnic groups and exclusively concerned with its self-perpetuation or a missionary church open to the world and ready to face the challenges of the world?' The emerging trends urge the church to go beyond its institutional boundaries, to transcend its traditional forms, and reach the people at the grassroots. In response to the changing environment, others are seeking new ways of 'being church'. The church can no longer stay inside the 'fortress' as a self-contained reality; it must interact with its environment. The church cannot transform the world from inside the walls; it must reach out. In a new world context 'being church' is, indeed, a great challenge with concrete implications. It means perceiving the church essentially as a missionary reality and not a frozen institution.

'A Church Beyond its Walls' is a response to the broken world wherein the church discovers its true being, fulfils its real vocation, affirms its authentic identity, and finds its *raison d'etre*. The being of the church is not static; it is conditioned by its 'becoming'. The church becomes truly a community of faith, the kingdom of God in anticipation, through its response to the concrete challenges and needs of the world with the vision of the Gospel. Is it not time, therefore, that ecclesiology turns its focus from the church *ad intra* (towards the inside) to the church ad extra (towards outside)? It is to describe the mission of God the Son and God the Holy Spirit. The Father sent the Son and the Spirit on a mission outside the inner life of the Trinity into the world. The Father lives in the Son, the Son, and the Spirit live in the Father. This is 'ad intra' (towards the inside) of the blessed Trinity. The 'ad extra' missions of the Son and the Spirit reveal to us the innermost life of the Trinity (life ad intra).

The initiatives to understand the church are quite informative. In 1889, 11 Oxford dons wrote a book called Lux Mundi (Light of the World). It is a collection of 12 essays edited by Charles Gore. The essays centre on the claim that the incarnation is the central tenet of Christianity. It informs and shapes all aspects of Christian thinking and life. The essays present an attempt at sympathetic engagement with contemporary thought, by presenting the Catholic faith as understood by Anglo-Catholics as thoroughly consistent with developments in science and politics. One of the essays is on the church by Walter Lock. He has tried to formulate the theological case for Catholic doctrines in a way that fits the situation. Similarly, to mark the centenary of Lux Mundi, a book called Keeping the Faith edited by Geoffrey Wainwright was published in 1989. The book contains an essay on 'church' by George Lindbeck, a member of the Evangelical Lutheran Church in America and a Professor at Yale University. He proposes a vision of the church as that of the messianic pilgrim people of God typologically shaped by Israel's story.

Lindbeck says that much has been said about the church but not what it is. The four *notae ecclesiae* spoken in the creeds are one, holy, catholic, and apostolic. The Reformation confessions added that the church is said to be *creatura verbi*: the creation of the word and a visible form of a *corpus mixtum* of the elect and the reprobate. However, these are attributes that can be predicated on other subjects like authentic preaching and sacraments, and of Israel. The three descriptions of the church: messianic pilgrim people of God, the sacrament of unity, and the institution of salvation were juxtaposed in the first three chapters of *Lumen Gentium*, the dogmatic constitution of the church. Bishop Newbigin's *Household of God* in 1953, under the rubric 'congregation of the faithful', attempted to integrate the 'people of God' motif with 'body of Christ' and community of the Holy Spirit into a Trinitarian framework. He suggests that the 'people of God' perspective has an advantage from an ecumenical perspective. In this chapter I have attempted to explore the imagery of the church as 'People of the Way' to be relevant in the present context.

***

Glimpses of Early Christianity

Christianity of the second and third centuries was a highly multicoloured phenomenon. It is difficult to imagine Christianity as a unified coherent movement. For example, the literature recovered at Nag Hammadi indicates that Gnostic Christianity didn't have the kind of clear hierarchy that other forms of Christianity had developed. They still clung to a charismatic leadership model. Perhaps the starkest contrast was among those who considered themselves Gnostic Christians, and those who considered themselves to be Pauline. On the one hand, Paul, and Pauline Christianity, placed all the emphasis on the saving power of Jesus' death and resurrection. Gnostic Christianity, on the other hand, placed its prime emphasis on the message, wisdom, and knowledge—the *gnosis*, the Greek word for knowledge—that Jesus transmits. So, while one would have faith in the saving event of Jesus' life, death and resurrection, the other would perceive knowledge as the great source of adherence to the Jesus movement.

In his *Apology*, Aristides, describes the early Christians as follows: 'They appeal to those who injure them, and try to win them as friends; they are eager to do good to their enemies; they are gentle and easy to be entreated; they abstain from all unlawful conversation and from all impurity; they despise not the widow, nor oppress the orphan; and he that has, gives ungrudgingly for the maintenance of him who has not. And when they see a stranger, they take him into their homes and rejoice over him as a very brother; for they do not call them brethren after the flesh, but brethren after the spirit and in God'.[27] The concern also extended to families of the dead, those who were persecuted or imprisoned, and of course, the poor. 'And whenever one of their poor passes from the world, each one of them according to his ability gives heed to him and carefully sees to his burial. And if they hear that one of their numbers is imprisoned or afflicted on account of the name of Christ, all of them anxiously minister to his necessity, and if it is possible to redeem him, they set him free. And if there is among them any that is poor and needy, and if they have no spare food, they fast two or three days in order to supply to the needy their lack of food'.[28]

Early Church historian J N D Kelly writes: 'As regards "Catholic", its original meaning was "universal" or "general" . . . in the latter half of the second century at latest, we find it conveying the suggestion that the Catholic is the true Church as distinct from heretical congregations (e.g. Muratorian Canon) . . . What these early Fathers were envisaging was almost always the empirical, visible society; they had little or no inkling of the distinction which was later to become important between a visible and an invisible Church'.[29]

In the letters of Ignatius at the beginning of the second century, the first surviving use of the term 'Catholic' is found in reference to the Church. At that time, or shortly thereafter, it was used to refer to a single, visible communion, separate from others. Ignatius of Antioch said: 'Let no one do anything of concern to the Church without the bishop. Let that be considered a valid Eucharist which is celebrated by the bishop or by one whom he ordains [a presbyter]. Wherever the bishop appears, let the people be there; just as wherever Jesus Christ is, there is the Catholic Church'.[30]

'And of the elect, he was one indeed, the wonderful martyr Polycarp, who in our days was an apostolic and prophetic teacher, bishop of the Catholic Church in Smyrna. For every word which came forth from his mouth was fulfilled and will be fulfilled'.[31]

Cyprian of Carthage said: 'They alone have remained outside [the Church] who, were they within, would have to be ejected. There [in John 6:68–69] speaks Peter, upon whom the Church would be built, teaching in the name of the Church and showing that even if a stubborn and proud multitude withdraws because it does not wish to obey, yet the Church does not withdraw from Christ. The people joined the priest, and the flock clinging to their shepherd in the Church. You ought to know, then, that the bishop is in the Church and the Church in the bishops; and if someone is not with the bishop, he is not in the Church. They vainly flatter themselves who creep up, not having peace with the priest of God, believing that they are secretly in communion with certain individuals. For the Church, which is one and catholic, is not split or divided, but is indeed united and joined by the cement of priests who adhere to one another'.[32]

The tent and temple occupied prominent space in the life of Israel. However, a march into the wilderness or a diaspora in favour of the absolute powerlessness of the Cross is not the obvious conclusion. If such would be then it would be theological naïveté. The Temple in Jerusalem was central in the life of Israel but it was also understood that God was by no means limited to the temple (I Kings 8:27-30), although His divine presence was to be found by those who sought God there. Isaiah in all probability experienced his call to ministry within the context of Temple worship (Isaiah 6:1-13). The penitent publican prayed in the Temple and went down to his home justified (Luke 18:9-14). When Jesus entered the Temple during Holy Week, it was to cleanse rather than to destroy (Matthew 21:12-14). Early Christians made regular use of Temple worship. However, the place of the Tent in the wilderness experience was characterised by innocence (Hosea 2:15). Yet Israel failed God in the wilderness as well as in the Promised Land. Paul reminds his readers in 1 Corinthians 10:1-5 that most of those who had been baptised into Moses through the Exodus had been overthrown in the wilderness for their failure to please God. Therefore, the answer is not either Tent or Temple with a march into some nostalgic wilderness or rebuilding a Temple, but the search for the presence of God.

***

Pilgrim's Way

In the Christian calendar, we mark the liturgical year by seasons: Advent, Christmas, Epiphany, Lent, Easter, and Pentecost. It may be said the Church Year is a spiritual pilgrimage, a sacred journey, where we travel by heart and soul to deepen our connection, our relationship, our understanding, our experience of God. However, this will only happen if we walk the 'pilgrim's way'. To walk the pilgrim's way is to experience healing and hurt, faith and doubt, grace and judgment, wholeness and brokenness. Life is a journey, a spiritual pilgrimage, in which we sometimes have to remove ourselves from ordinary routines and practices and create new ones in order to seek a closer connection with God and a better understanding of ourselves. This can be a demanding, even arduous, journey. History reveals that the pilgrim has often been prompted to perform acts of penance for forgiveness or engage in ascetic practices of deprivation and sacrifice to experience God in new and fresh ways.

In the 6th century, Irish Celtic monks added to the spiritual pilgrimage of the heart the physical pilgrimage of the body. In an imitation of Abraham whom God called to leave his own country and go in pilgrimage to the land which He had shown him—the promised land—Celtic monks developed the spiritual discipline of *peregrination,* which is a Latin word meaning 'going forth into strange countries'. This understanding of pilgrimage was different from what became the norm of Medieval pilgrimage, namely, a visit to a sacred site or shrine. The purpose of the Medieval pilgrimage was to arrive. The purpose of the Irish pilgrimage was not to visit a sacred shrine or to arrive at a certain destination but to seek out solitude, mystery, exile, growth, liberty and do this with complete abandonment to God. So crucial was this idea of total abandonment to God that Irish pilgrims often set out on their journey not knowing their destination, relying solely on the Spirit to guide them to the place God would have them go. The journey itself became the focus; the journey became the Promised Land for the Irish *peregrinatio*.

The Book of Acts records that there was a special event that occurred at Pentecost, which would have been the next pilgrimage festival after the Passover at which Jesus died. At that time the disciples of Jesus were gathered together in Jerusalem unsure of what their future would be, when all of a sudden, the Spirit took hold of them and enabled them to speak in tongues, and that speaking of tongues is understood by the author of the Book of Acts to mean speaking in all of the languages of the world. So, with the power of the Spirit behind them, the disciples of Jesus immediately began a journey that changed the face of the church. The followers of Jesus Christ were simply known as 'people of the Way' (Acts 9:2) in reference to their lifestyle, the way of life they lived. In other words, it was their lifestyle that identified them as being followers of Jesus Christ, not their words. They were called this because others recognised, and made it known, that they were always on a journey. Life for those early Christians was always a new beginning and a day full of hope. Belief in the resurrection had shattered their view that life came to a screeching halt with death. So, they did not fear death. They, in fact, befriended death. They could therefore expose themselves to the elements and the unknown without fear.

In the Gospel of Thomas, Jesus is reported to have taught: 'Become Passers-by' (Thomas 42). He also said in the Gospel of Luke: 'Foxes have holes and birds have nests, but the Son of Man has nowhere to lay His head' (Luke 9:58). Jesus was an itinerant; one who moved constantly from place to place. He and his disciples were pilgrims. The Bible is a collection of stories about people making journeys. Abraham and Sarah left their home in Ur of the Chaldeans and set out on a journey. Moses led the Jews on a journey out of Egypt to the Promise Land. Jesus sent His disciples out on journeys from town to town to share their faith. Saul was transformed into Paul as he journeyed on the road to Damascus. The disciples met Jesus as they journeyed on the road to Emmaus. We are all pilgrims for Christ. We are on a perpetual pilgrimage to the Promised Land. Each of us is unique. We make our own journey in life, but we are never alone in our pilgrimage. God is our constant companion.

T S Eliot beautifully expressed the Pilgrim spirit when he wrote: 'We shall not cease from exploration, and the end of all our exploring will be to arrive where we started and know the place for the first time'.[33] Everything is gained when we venture forth. The journey shapes us, and we shape those we meet on the way. The journey allows us to return to what we have left behind and know it for the first time. We are all pilgrims on a journey learning lessons about love and life, re-connecting with our true self, our inner self, with God and with our neighbour.

Endnotes

[1] Duraisingh, Christopher, 'Indian Hyphenated Christians and Theological Reflections: A New Expression of Identity', Religion and Society, Vol. XXVI, No. 4, 1979, pp. 95 - 101

[2] Sebastian, Jayakiran J., 'Pressure on the Hyphen: Aspects of the Search for Identity Today in Indian-Christian Theology', in Religion and Society, Vol. 44, No. 4, 1997, pp. 27 – 41

[3] Clarke, Sathianathan, Dalits and Christianity: Subaltern Religion and Liberation Theology in India, Oxford University Press, New Delhi, 1998, pp. 247

[4] Dempsey, Corinne, 'Book Review: In Search of Identity: Debates on Religious Conversion in India', Journal of Hindu-Christian Studies: Vol. 18, Article 16, 2005

[5] Kim, Grace Ji-Sun, Chapter 4: Chi, Self and Hybridity, In: The Holy Spirit, Chi, and the Other: A Model of Global and Intercultural Pneumatology, 2011

[6] Ibid. p 106

[7] Ibid, p 92

[8] Walls Andrew, The Missionary Movement in Christian History: Studies in Transmission of Faith, Mary Knoll, N.Y.: Orbis Books, 2001, pp. 7-9.

[9] Sahu, D. K., The Church of North India, Peter Lang, 1992, p 293-4

[10] Kirsteen Kim, Book Review of 'Beyond Captivity: Explorations in Indian Christian History and Theology' by Boyd, Robin, Studies in World Christianity, Vol. 22, Issue 2

[11] https://www.euppublishing.com/doi/full/10.3366/swc.2016.0151

[12] https://www.euppublishing.com/doi/full/10.3366/swc.2016.0151

[13] Boyd, Robin H. S. An Introduction to Indian Christian Theology, Madras: The Christian Literature Society, 1979. Reviewed by G. Ray Burbank II

[14] Boyd, Robin H. S. An Introduction to Indian Christian Theology, Madras: The Christian Literature Society, 1979. Reviewed by G. Ray Burbank II

[15] Sugirtharajah, R.S. 'Postcolonialism and Indian Christian Theology'. Studies in World Christianity 5. Part 2 (1999): 229-240.

[16] https://www.academia.edu/34070302/Contextualization_A_theology_of_Gospel_and_Culture

[17] https://www.academia.edu/34070302/Contextualization_A_theology_of_Gospel_and_Culture

[18] Young, Richard Fox, Ed., India and the Indianness of Christianity. Essays on Understanding: Historical, Theological, and Bibliographical—in Honor of Robert Eric Frykenberg. Grand Rapids: William B. Eerdmans Publishing Company, 2009

[19] Bauman, Chad M. 'Indian Christian Historiography from Below, from Above, and in Between'. Church History, vol. 80, no. 3, Cambridge University Press, 2011, pp. 622–29, http://www.jstor.org/stable/41240642

[20] Bauman, Chad M. 'Indian Christian Historiography from Below, from Above, and in Between'. Church History, vol. 80, no. 3, Cambridge University Press, 2011, pp. 622–29, http://www.jstor.org/stable/41240642

[21] Shepherd, Henry, The Institute and its Servant-Leader In: Footprints of Faith, p. 44

[22] Ware, Kallistos, Patterns of Episcopacy in the Early Church and Today an Orthodox View, In: Moore, Peter Ed. Bishops but What Kind? SPCK, London, 1982, p 1

[23] Rakestraw, Charity, Seeking Souls, Selling Salvation: A History of the Modern Megachurch In: Handbook of Megachurches Ed Stephen Hunt, Koninklijke Brill NV, Leiden, Netherlands, Vol.19, 2020, p 23

[24] Handbook of Megachurches Ed Stephen Hunt, Koninklijke Brill NV, Leiden, Netherlands, Vol.19, 2020

[25] Eagle, David E. 'Historicizing the Megachurch'. Journal of Social History, vol. 48, no. 3, Oxford University Press, 2015, pp. 589–604, http://www.jstor.org/stable/43919788

[26] Reddy, Sudhakar: Nurturing Globalized Faith Seekers, In: A Moving Faith Mega Churches Go South, Ed. James, D. Jonathan, Sage Publication, 2015, p 143

[27] Aristides, 'Apology', 2nd century

[28] Ibid.

[29] Kelly, J N D, 'Early Christian Doctrines', A&C Black, 2000, pp 190-1

[30] St Ignatius of Antioch, Letter to the Smyrnaeans, A.D. 110, 8:2

[31] Martyrdom of Polycarp, A.D. 155, 16:2

[32] Cyprian of Carthage, Letters, A.D. 253, 66[67]:8

[33] Eliot, T. S., from 'Little Gidding', Four Quartets, Gardners Books; Main edition, 2001.

■■■

7

An African Exploration

'Theology predominantly remains an intellectual exercise. It seems to have become a theology of theologians, by theologians, for theologians, instead of becoming a theology of the people, by the people, for the people'.

PROVIDENCE

Someone walks into my office in the faculty of Theology with his friends. He introduces himself as Rev Samuel Donkor from Ghana who is now settled in Toronto, Canada. His journey to Prayagraj (Allahabad) was quite humorous. They had been to Karunya Institute of Technology and Sciences, a private residential institute deemed to be a university in Coimbatore, India. It was founded by D G S Dhinakaran and his son Paul Dhinakaran. They were advised to travel to Prayagraj to meet me as he was exploring partnering the university he had founded in Ghana – All Nations University (ANU). It began with 37 students in October 2002 and currently has about 4000 students. It became an accredited university college in Ghana in October 2002 and in 2020 became a full-fledged University. They flew from Coimbatore to Kolkata and then boarded a taxi because the driver blithely advised them that the journey by road to Prayagraj would not be difficult or far. Not knowing the reality, they believed him and came by the well-known terrible road to Prayagraj and for their fortitude and endurance they deserved a medal! The MoU was signed with SHUATS and students were sent to study and do research in Engineering, Management, Agriculture as well as Theology.

Normally we understand the word Providence as referring to the rule of God over the events that make up the course of both nature and history. In the words of Karl Barth 'the lordship of God over all world-occurrence', or some using a more liberal term may say 'the purpose of God unfolding itself in the development of the cosmos and of human history'. Providence is, therefore, to be distinguished from *Heilsgeschichte*, or 'salvation history', in that it connotes the direct relation of God during the course of time not merely to those human creatures who are within the covenant but, as Barth says, to 'the creature as such and in general'. Providence in our life story is mysterious and we draw conclusions when looking back down memory lane, thus being grateful to God. The providential meeting with Samuel resulted in a friendship that inspired me to search for meaning and exploration in African theology.

***

Story Retold

The occasion was the evening ceremony at All Nations Full Gospel Church (ANFGC) in Toronto in 2016. The youth were re-enacting the story of the beginning of the ministry of Samuel Donkor and it really captivated me. Samuel Donkor was in the ministry as an evangelist in Ghana and was transitioning to include pastoral care into his itinerant ministry before he came to Canada. His fiancée, now Dr Rose Donkor, who also completed her doctoral research in the faculty of Theology at SHUATS in 2018, had emigrated to Canada in 1979. In his quest to further his education, Samuel had received an admission to pursue a Master of Divinity program at Reformed Theological Seminary in Jackson, Mississippi, USA. His intention was to finish the study first before he joined his fiancée in Canada. However, he decided to join his fiancée in Canada first and later pursue further studies. Rose sponsored him to join her in Canada and he arrived in Canada in May 1981 to begin a global ministry. He embarked on street evangelism to share his faith with everyone and anyone willing to accept Jesus Christ as Lord and Saviour.

His first cultural shock led him to modify his style of evangelism. In Africa, every time he was on a train or bus or where people were gathered, he would seize the opportunity to preach the Gospel to them. So, whenever he boarded public transportation in Canada the urge to preach to the passengers was almost irresistible, but this became an intense struggle within as he was unable to do so in Canada. The Toronto Transit Commission (TTC) Bye-Laws forbade solicitations and other forms of disturbances on public transit systems, such as preaching, distribution of literature, etc. How was he ever going to reach people in Canada? How could he do that without infringing on the bye-laws of TTC? So, he decided to do personal evangelism on a one-on-one basis to whoever would care to listen to him. Consequently, he always carried Gospel tracts to share with anyone who would accept them. Before he left the shores of Africa to North America, he had asked God to use him to reciprocate the 'white man' for their missionary efforts in Africa that had resulted in the deaths of many missionaries due to malaria and other causes. He saw his ministry as an opportunity to 'pay back' the debt of gratitude that African Christians owed to the white people in bringing the good news to Africa.

Eventually, he was able to start a small group in his apartment whom he started to disciple. This brought him great satisfaction but since the group only consisted of white people, he was ignoring his primary calling which was to the people in the diaspora. One day, he had a dream in which he was preaching in a big hall that was packed with people. In his dream, he saw people from many diverse backgrounds with only a sprinkling of white people in the congregation.

Samuel Donkor used both the personal and lifestyle evangelism methodology when he targeted people of colour in Toronto. He pursued them with all his heart and might with his wife Rose. If he saw a person of colour at a bus stop or walking by the road or street while driving, he would stop and ask if the person needed a ride, and would take the person to his destination. Then he would find the opportunity to invite him to church. He would even bring people who were stranded at airports or bus stops home to stay with them until they could be on their own. He would also pick refugees from the shelters and put them in apartments to establish them in the country. It was a common sight for his wife to see him coming home with a stranger who needed to be fed and accommodated.

One such story is of the treasurer of the church, Deacon Quame Boateng. Samuel Donkor gave him a ride home after an event in Hamilton. He did not tell him that he was a pastor but invited him to church the following day. Quame was, at that time, new in the country, so he agreed. Donkor picked him up the next morning and took him to church. How surprised he was to see Donkor, who had been so kind to him, in the pulpit when the service began. Quame continued to attend the church regularly and has been with ANFGC since 1987. With passion, dedication, commitment, and kindness he infused that spirit into everyone.

***

An Exploration

Reading an article by C B Peter, was not only interesting but also enlightening about the narrative of African Theology.[1] He had published an article in 1983 entitled, 'Israel and Her Neighbours: An Analogy to understand the Shaping of the Indian Christian Ethos', in which he sought to analyse the core values of Judeo-Christian and Pan-Indian traditions in a bid to understand what really has gone into the shaping of the Indian Christian ethos. Professor John S Mbiti of Kenya, way back in 1979, after surveying some 300 published papers and books on African theology, in preparation for his article, issued the following warning: 'Some of us are getting tired of seeing all sorts of articles and references under the big banner: African Theology or some similar African Hyphenated Christians wording. The substance of these articles often turns out to be advice on how African Theology should be done, where it should be done, who should do it, what it should say, *ad infinitum*. Some of these self-made theological advisors, whether they be African or foreign, have little or nothing to produce beyond their generous advice; and others want to play the role of theological engineers who meticulously sabotage spontaneous theological output by African Christians'. But following Duraisingh, C B Peter says that African Christian ethos like its Indian counterpart was also doubly determined by the confluence of two independent traditions – the Pan-African, if one may use this term here and the Judeo-Christian. In a slight departure from the conventional rules about the formats of citations, he goes on to quote the below two statements from Duraisingh which he has deliberately tampered with by replacing 'Indian' with 'African'. He concludes that the argument in the below statements runs so smoothly that it is difficult to see that they have, in any way, been tampered with. My own attempt tends to confirm the affirmation that the content of memory and imagination of hosts of African-Christians is doubly determined or co-constituted by the simultaneous operation of two traditions (Duraisingh 1979: 96). He goes on to argue:

'If, in fact, these two traditions are in a constitutive relationship in the formation of all that which is African-Christian then I propose that it is the term 'African Hyphenated Christians' that describes more accurately our self-identity. We are not simply Africans who also happen to be Christians; nor are we Christians who, by accident of birth, happen to be also Africans. We are African-Christians, hyphenated wholes wherein both the components of our complex heritage are in a holistic and coalescing relation' (Duraisingh 1979: 97).

What are some of the modes of theologising currently prevalent in Africa? Mbiti looks at African theology in three ways: written theology (academic), oral theology (grassroots), and symbolic theology (art forms) (Mbiti 1979: 84). Roughly corresponding to Mbiti's analysis are Father Charles Nyamiti's three 'schools' of African theology: the speculative school (systematic and philosophical), the socio-biblical school (dealing with sociological and ethnological questions), and the reactionary school (e.g. the South African type of Black theology) (Nyamiti 1973: 1). Obviously, the emphasis seems to be on the 'written theology' (Mbiti), or the 'speculative school' (Nyamiti). Africans and non-Africans are busily engaged in publishing articles and books on African theology but various contemporary approaches to African theology seem to revolve around the following basic concerns.

There is a battle of words to entitle African theology. Should it be called 'African theology', or 'African Christian theology', or 'Christian African theology', or 'Theologia Africana', or 'Theologizing in Africa', or some other fancy name (Mbiti 1979: 83; 1971: 195)? If African people can be seen as the true authors, doers, and subjects of their theology rather than the objects of theology done by theologians, then other implications will follow. First, the realisation will arise that common people are not trained in theological methodology, rather, they use their own. The theologian's task will, therefore, be to understand the people's methodology of doing theology within the vast homogenous African milieu (Sawyerr 1987: 25) as well as in various local heterogeneous contexts. Second, people do theology not only as a voluntary endeavour but also (and mostly) as a subconscious and spontaneous process.

Peter sums up an alternate model to understand African theology as a critical self-awareness by African Christians whose religious ethos as doubly determined by the confluence of the two co-constituent wholes of value-systems (African and Christian) is best designated by a hyphen. The theologian's task is not to 'do' theology or even to 'advice' on doing it but to understand theology as done by the African people. African theology should be done in close relation with African sociology, African anthropology, African traditional religion, African Independent Churches, and African socio-cultural change. Indigenization in Africa or in any context is not a finished product in any given time in history, but it is an ever-continuing process occurring subconsciously and spontaneously within the religious psyche of African Christians, currently involving a wedding between the 'given' – Christian dogma, and African tradition, and the 'becoming' – socio-cultural change through rapid modernisation. The following statement from the final communique of the Pan-African Conference of Third World Theologians seems fitting to sum up the discussion:

'We believe that African theology must be understood in the context of African life and culture and the creative attempt of African peoples to shape a new future that is different from the colonial past and the neo-colonial present. The African situation requires a new theological methodology that is different from the approaches of the dominant theologies of the West (*African Theology En Route*, p. 11)'. [italics mine]

'In 1971, John Gatu, General Secretary of the Presbyterian Church of East Africa, issued a famous moratorium on foreign missionaries and funds. The immediate reaction was strong and provoked a debate about the mission that continues to this day ... Gatu's motivation for such abrupt and controversial action and makes a case for considering the moratorium to be a milestone in mission history, marking the symbolic end of the colonial mission paradigm and the start of the postcolonial mission era'.[2] Michael Cassidy in the article 'The Call to Moratorium (Perspective on an Identity Crisis)' notes 'The first thing to say about the Moratorium issue is that it is complex, and the temptation to resolve it simplistically is to be resisted at all costs. Neither unqualified approval nor uncritical disapproval will do, and anyone resolving the issue along either of those lines is, to this writer, on the wrong track. Our second preliminary comment is to note that we dare not deny that the moratorium call has both manifested and created an identity crisis, not only for sending agencies and the missionaries they send, but also for receiving agencies, local churches, and "nationals", so-called, who man them. At stake in the debate is the true nature, calling, and mission of the church of Jesus Christ in our time' (p 265).

Rev John Gatu argued at the Mission Festival of the Reformed Church of America in Milwaukee in 1971 'that the time has come for the withdrawal of foreign missionaries from many parts of the Third World; that the churches of the Third World must be allowed to find their own identity; and that the continuation of the present missionary movement is a hindrance to the self-hood of the church'. Professor John Mbiti in his *Crisis of Mission in Africa* sounds the same note. Affirming 'that the age of foreign missions in Africa is now over', he goes on: 'We all agree that for too long the church here has depended on Canterbury, Rome, Athens and now Geneva, not just in financial matters but in its structures, its decisions, its outreach and the profession of the faith in Africa'.

***

Learning Process

My interest and learning process in African theology took a turn when the students from Ghana registered for doctoral research at SHUATS in different disciplines including Theology. I had the privilege of learning from two doctoral students from Ghana who are settled in Toronto. One of them was Samuel Donkor[3] and the other Cynthia Gyimah[4]. The story of the doctoral work of Samuel was interesting. After signing the MoU with our University and knowing his visionary ministry about establishing ANFGC and founding the ANU in Ghana, SHUATS decided to confer an honorary doctorate. But he came to me and said, 'Bishop, I do not want an honorary degree but want to earn a PhD in Theology'. I asked him if it would be possible for him to go through the process of a minimum of three years of research and attend the classes in GPIT to complete the course work. It would require him travelling from Toronto or Ghana to attend the classes during the first two semesters. His answer was in the affirmative.

Being a visionary in establishing the ANFGC and ANU in Ghana, one is fascinated by the story of his faith journey. Samuel Donkor was born in Koforidua, Ghana to a rich cocoa farmer. He was baptised and confirmed in the Methodist Church – Koforidua, but was later sent to Accra for his education and to live with his half-brothers. In Accra, he attended an Anglican church and studied mechanical engineering. He accepted Jesus Christ as his personal saviour in 1972 at a crusade and was nurtured in his spiritual growth through his involvement in Scripture Union. Samuel Donkor received his call to ministry through an eschatological revelation where he saw hell and people who were there because they had not been ready when the Lord returned. This vision changed the course of his life.

The story of obtaining the land to build the church in Canada is an encouragement in learning how God uses people to initiate something that appears to be difficult. The ANFGC in Toronto is situated on 4.4-acres of land that was purchased on a mortgage in 1991 at a massive cost of $4.3 million. The church moved into the 25,000 sq. ft building in 1992. Five years after purchasing this property, the Canadian economy went into a recession with high unemployment in the country. By faith, Samuel Donkor approached the vendor for a reduction in the mortgage despite owning the building for half a decade. On the very day of the re-negotiation, he was named 'African-Canadian Achiever'. The award was publicised by the media extensively on both television and print media in 1997. As the parties sat down to re-negotiate, the vendors slammed a copy of the Toronto Star article of his award on the board table and exclaimed, 'He is more popular than us, we can't fight him; how much will he pay?' That took Samuel by surprise as he struggled to name an amount. Then, they said to him, 'This is what we will do. We will re-appraise the property and you pay whatever the new appraised value would be'. The day the vendors sent the appraiser to value the church property, the Italian who had been working on the building walked in as if by design. Samuel told him, 'You know the building better than anyone else, so tell the appraiser the deficiencies in the building'. So he shared a litany of the problems with the building with the appraiser. After listening for a while, he confessed, 'This brings to mind a building my dad once purchased when I was young. He spent more money fixing the property than he paid for'. To his surprise, the new appraised value came in at $1.6 million. Indeed, that was the Lord's doing and it was marvellous in our eyes.

***

African Story by an African

We had invited Samuel Donkor, after the completion of his doctoral studies to deliver a lecture in the faculty of Theology. I have taken the liberty to insert the lecture to repeat the story[5] that African Christianity is simply the African expression of Christianity. It focuses on the influences of 'Africans' and 'African' ideas on mission enterprise, conversion, religious innovation, and church life. Every religion is influenced by local and regional cosmologies and traditions. Although a majority of Christians share a universal belief in the fundamental doctrines of the birth, death, and resurrection of Christ, however, there are differences in our perceptions and expressions of faith. Everything in the world is fluid, including Africa. Even Christianity is not cast in iron and stone. Rather, Christianity is cast in new forms and new understandings. While earlier studies of Christianity in Africa focused on the roles of European missions and missionaries in establishing Christianity there, historians now tend to stress the roles of African converts, pastors, translators, and evangelists in interpreting Christianity, spreading it to their neighbours, and establishing new Christian movements and churches that are as distinctly African as they are Christian.

In seeking to understand African Christianity, we need to understand its origins in the ancient church as well as the processes by which European missionaries and African converts of diverse religious hues have reinterpreted and reformed it to establish a varied and vibrant Christian religious presence today. The literature on African Christianity is huge and often characterised by diverse colonial and religious perspectives and biases, requiring one to read it critically. In his 2015 paper titled, 'Christianity in Africa: A Beacon of Hope for Christianity in Europe', Michael Fuseini Wandusim, stated that Christianity existed in Africa before the advent of the missionaries in the 19th century. One of the leading fathers of African Theology, John Mbiti, said that Christianity in Africa is so old that it can aptly be termed as an indigenous, traditional African religion. The origin of African Christianity has links to the church of Ethiopia. Ethiopia had contact with the Jews way before Jesus Christ was born. This contact is found in the encounter between King Solomon and the Queen of Sheba as recorded in 1 Kings chapter 10. When Jesus was born also, he sought asylum with his parents in Egypt to escape the plot of King Herod to kill him as a baby. The Coptic Church in Egypt values this event and argues that the good news came first to them through the preaching of the apostle Mark who is believed to have been martyred in Alexandria.

Moreover, the case of the Ethiopian eunuch (an African) who met the evangelist Philip is often considered in talking about the history of Christianity in Africa. This eunuch who was a high-ranking official in charge of the Ethiopian Queen's finance believed the gospel of Jesus Christ preached to him by Philip and was baptised by him (Luke 8:27-39). Wandusim, went on to say that Africans were present on the birthday of Christianity: the day of Pentecost as recorded in Acts 2 because mention was made of people from Egypt and Libya. He also indicates that Africans first preached the gospel to non-Jews before anyone because the account of Acts 11:19 talks about believers coming from Cyrene witnessing to Greeks in Antioch. He further posits that the great apostle Paul could have been ordained by persons including Africans in the church in Antioch as Acts 13 records it.

***

African Church Fathers

Africa's extra-canonical information is equally impressive. St Anthony the Great, the father of monasticism, was Egyptian. Several African church fathers defined the Christian faith for us as we understand it today: Athanasius, Clement of Alexandria, Origen, Cyprian, and Tertullian. Indeed, Athanasius was the leading theologian in the Trinitarian controversies as well as in the determination of the biblical canon. Athanasius's home city, Alexandria, was well known as the leading academic centre of the ancient world. Alexandria and Carthage (Tunisia) were pivotal in shaping the earliest medieval Western universities. One of the most important theologians in Christian history, Augustine (354-430), was an African Berber from Algeria.

Subsequently displaced by Islam in the 7th and 8th centuries, the ancient Coptic and Orthodox churches nevertheless remain active in Egypt, Ethiopia, and Eritrea today. Further south, Christianity was introduced later by European Christian missions, initially on the heels of Portuguese expansion into the Kingdom of the Kongo and Angola in the 16th century, the slave trade in the ensuing centuries, and the general expansion of European influence and colonialism in the 19th and 20th centuries in an explosive combination of 'Christianity, Commerce, and Civilization'. While conversion to Christianity increased with the extension of formal European colonial rule, Western education, and new economic opportunities, Africans interpreted the new faith in the light of their own religious concerns and concepts and made it their own. In the process, Western missionaries were slowly displaced by African evangelists, who helped translate the Bible, interpret it for themselves, and spread the faith far beyond the mission compounds. Consequently, African Christians struggled for control of the church and its messages, often emphasising charismatic prophecy and healing, founding thousands of new churches and popular movements within mission Protestantism and Catholicism, and playing prominent roles in contemporary African society and politics.

***

Explosion of Christianity

The explosion of Christianity in Africa in recent decades is phenomenal, both in relative and absolute numbers. Clearly, Africa has made a major contribution to the shift of the centre of gravity of Christianity to the global South taking place in the 20th and early 21st centuries. According to a recent report, in 1910 only 9% of Africa's population was Christian, which in 1970 had grown to 38.7% (143 million people) and by 2020 will have gone up to 49.3% (631 million people) (Centre for the Study of Global Christianity 2013: 22). Today, out of the 59 countries in continental Africa, 31 countries have Christianity as the dominant religion. Most Christians in Africa today are Protestants and Pentecostals/Charismatics while the Roman Catholic Church draws about a third of the Christian number in Africa. The ancient orthodox church which is found mainly in the Nile Valley constitutes a tenth of the Christian population in Africa. Christianity in Africa is now more vibrant and energetic than it is in Europe. Daughrity, citing from Terence Ranger, by 2030 there will be more Christians in Africa than there will be in Latin America.[6]

Different from a century ago, by far the majority of African Christians now live south of the Sahara, in the Western, Eastern, Central and Southern parts of the continent. Alongside this numerical growth, there has been a proliferation of many different churches, movements, and denominations. This increasing diversity has led some scholars, like A F K Ukah, to speak of African Christianities in the plural, to emphasise that 'different strands or traditions … may not be compatible one to another'. Hence the question of classifying African Christianity has become highly complicated, as the recent dynamics and new realities disrupt previous classificatory approaches.

***

Pentecostal/Charismatic Christianity

The explosion of Christianity in Africa today has been largely attributed to the Pentecostal/Charismatic tradition. According to Adriaan Van Klinken's essay, 'African Christianity – Developments and Trends', Pentecostal Christianity in Africa is often considered to have come in three waves: the spiritual or prophet-healing churches discussed above from the early 20th century, the churches resulting from American Pentecostal denominations' missionary work from the first half of the 20th century such as the Assemblies of God and the Apostolic Faith Mission, and the wave of so-called Pentecostal-Charismatic or the term preferred here, neo-Pentecostal churches (from the 1970s–1980s) which has recently attracted so much scholarly attention. The boundaries between these categories are not clear-cut: some African Independent Churches (AIC) have historical connections with American Pentecostalism have recently reinvented themselves in a neo-Pentecostal style. Africa has gradually shifted from their traditional holiness teaching to the prosperity gospel, and their leaders have become part of the global Pentecostal jet-set––characteristics generally associated with neo-Pentecostalism. However, fluid the boundaries may be, neo-Pentecostal churches (henceforth, NPCs) as part of their politics of self-representation often draw a clear line between themselves and the earlier AICs which they label, and sometimes bluntly demonise, as syncretistic.

Neo-Pentecostalism itself is an umbrella term for a variety of churches that began to emerge in the 1970s–1980s in various parts of the continent, especially in the urban areas where they are highly visible in the public space with large church buildings, accommodating thousands if not ten thousands, with billboards advertising their message. The popularity of the NPCs is a signal that Christianity in Africa has entered a new phase. Often-mentioned characteristics are these churches' global orientation and their advocating of a break with 'African tradition', their participation in transnational circuits, their strong missionary drive, the extensive use of modern media including radio, television, and the internet, the practice of 'spiritual warfare', and the worldly orientation reflected in the emphasis on prosperity and success as divine blessings for believers. Speaking in tongues--often considered a key characteristic of Pentecostalism--is not always required in these churches.

Much research on neo-Pentecostalism in Africa focuses on its socio-cultural, economic, and political dimensions, exploring the links of these churches and their programme of born-again conversion to modernity, globalisation, and neoliberal capitalism as well as their response to the crisis of the post-colonial nation-state, their contribution to development, and impact on gender relations. Detailed studies have been conducted on churches in various countries such as Ghana, Nigeria, and Zimbabwe, examining their fast growth and (inter)national proliferation over the past few decades, their expanding imperium with church-related businesses and universities, their media presence, and political affiliations, etcetera. These studies highlight the transnational networks and discourses of which these churches are a part, but at the same time show how the NPCs present local appropriations of the Christian faith in their specific socio-cultural and political contexts. Likewise, in spite of the rhetorical break with 'the past', the popularity of NPCs is related to their spiritual worldview that very much resembles traditional ones: it does not ignore spiritual realities such as witchcraft and evil spirits but, through a discourse of demonisation and practices of deliverance, these realities are preserved and 'the past', in fact, is kept alive. Precisely these complex dynamics of (dis)continuity and modernity, and of locality and globalisation, makes neo-Pentecostalism such a fascinating religious phenomenon in contemporary Africa.

***

Africanising Christianity

Dirk Van der Merwe in his work, 'From Christianising Africa to Africanising Christianity: Some hermeneutical principles', mentions that things have drastically changed in the post-colonial period. Africa seeks its own unique religious identity and now attempts to become a full contributor to world Christianity. Over the past few decades, many publications have emphasised the necessity for change and proposed ways to change. After decolonisation, the need for an African reformation grew even stronger. There is a belief that African Christian identity will be safeguarded only when the Christian faith is construed in terms of traditional cultural categories.

One of the ways for an African Christian identity is the inculturation of Christianity. Culture is an indispensable part of being human. It denotes the various patterns of the thoughts, actions, and feelings of human beings. Culture can be compared with a prism through which people view the whole of their experience. Inculturation presents and re-expresses the gospel in configurations and expressions proper to a particular culture. This course of action results in the reinterpretation of both the gospel and culture by being faithful to both. Anything less is considered syncretism and not a synthesis – the juxtaposition of non-communicating meanings. The Christian transformation of a particular culture takes that culture seriously. It does not overwhelm that culture, but rather reinterprets it. This process results in the enrichment of the true meaning of that culture. During such a transformation process it is important to remain faithful to both Christian traditions and to the authentic values of African Christianity. Cultural fidelity can only be achieved if there is a deep understanding of both Christian dogma and the tradition of faith and African culture.

Between the First World War and the emergence of political independence, several denominations sought to consolidate their enterprises just as many religious entrepreneurs hatched various 'Christianities' out of a vibrant religious culture. The two world wars and economic depression created so much disquiet that the pace of revivalism and religious innovation increased. Wade Harris, for instance, trekked across Liberia and the Ivory Coast to the Gold Coast, preaching and healing. His ministry benefited the mainline churches and inspired charismatic movements. In the Congo, Simon Kimbangu prophesied that the global disorder signalled that God was shifting the baton from whites to blacks. His imprisonment did not deter the growth of his movement. In the 1930s the Balokole Movement spread from Rwanda through the Congo into Uganda, Kenya, Tanganyika, and Sudan. It urged repentance, holiness ethics, and a closer relationship with Jesus. Examples could be multiplied to show that, just as the wars increased African confidence and shifted the vision of cultural nationalists to the quest for political independence, so were the efforts of missionaries to consolidate denominationalism confronted by intensified, subversive, indigenous initiatives. Missionary response to nationalism was informed by a number of factors including individual predilection, the negative racial image of Africans, some liberal support, and regional variations as those in the settler communities responded with fright and built bulwarks with apartheid laws. As the wind of change gusted more brutally, it became clear that the missions had weak roots: few indigenous clergies, a dependency ideology, undeveloped theology, poor infrastructure, and above all, little confidence in their votaries.

From the 1950s, the Roman Catholics led in the hurried attempt to train indigenous priests. Missions conceived opportunities to waltz with nationalists because the educated elites were products of various missions and their control of power could aid their denominations in the virulent rivalry for turf. This strategy implicated Christianity in the politics of independence. Matters went awry when the elite grabbed the politics of modernisation, mobilised the states into dictatorial one-party structures, castigated missionaries for under-developing Africa, promoted neo-Marxist rejection of dependency syndrome, and seized the instruments of missionary propaganda such as schools, hospitals, and social welfare agencies.

***

A Paradigm of Hospitality

A paradigm shift in African Christian historiography is a call for an African interpretation of the life of the church in Africa. Andrew F Walls commenting on Kenneth Scott Latourette's monumental work *A History of the Expansion of Christianity*, argues that 'since his time, much fundamental research has been conducted on the primary sources, oral and written, new perspectives have been taken up in which Africans, Asians and Latin Americans figure as the principal agents of Christian expansion'. He also says that 'modern African Christianity is not only the result of movements among Africans but has been principally sustained by Africans and is to a surprising extent the result of African initiatives'. Even the missionary factor must be put into the perspective that histories of missions written by missionaries and their protégés is often hagiographic. He calls for a new African Christian historiography that examines African initiatives without neglecting the roles of various missionary bodies.

Hospitality is a perennial value in Indian and African culture. The question is whether it will stand the test of time in the context of modernisation. Strangers and visitors in a city are definitely suspects. Yet the Gospel has to challenge this inhibition. The parable of the friend in need in Luke 11:5-8 can be taken as an example. There are three characters: The guest who arrives unexpectedly and not at the right time, the host who goes to wake up another friend at midnight, and the householder who naturally grumbles. The unifying factors are the person in need, centred values, and flexibility of time. Going out of the way to help a guest is expected in Indian and African culture despite the limits and threats of urbanisation. In the parable of Good Samaritan in Luke 10:29-37, the issue is not about doing bad things but neglecting to do good as well. The stranger, foreigner, and outsider really become the 'neighbour' and the commandment is 'Go and do likewise'. The story of the last judgment in Matthew 25:31-46, draws attention to reflect on the correct situations of feeding the hungry, giving drinks to the thirsty, welcoming the stranger, clothing the naked, and visiting the sick and those in prison.

Hospitality is a way of life that is intimately bound up with personal relationships and community in African life. There are African proverbs and sayings about the guests. The Swahili proverb 'A Guest is a blessing' has diverse variations in different African languages. John Mbiti says, 'Hospitality and tender care are shown to visitors, strangers, and guests. In the eyes of African peoples, the visitor heals the sick (African proverb). This means that when a visitor comes to someone's home, family quarrels stop, the sick cheer up, peace is restored and the home is restored to new strength. Visitors are, therefore, social healers – they are family doctors in a sense'.[7]

***

Resolution Attempts Past and Present

Prince Conteh in his work, *African Religion and Christianity*, states that the tension between African Religion and Christianity has been described as the 'African Christian problem'. He discusses the issue of African Christians clinging tenaciously to their traditional religious beliefs and customs, combined with their reluctance to give them up in favour of Christianity, and the resulting conflicts between African Religion and Christianity, which is common to many parts of Africa. In sermons, teachings, discussions, and songs, the Church continues to dismiss traditional practices as heathenism and in some places has refused to encourage any form of dialogue with African traditionalists.

Conteh went on, for many decades, scholars, the Church, and ecumenical organisations have been attempting to find answers to the African Christian problem. It has been noted that Africa has enough tools and expertise to evolve a viable form of Christianity for African Christians. However, this task is complicated by the lack of a clear consensus among African theologians/religionists/missiologists and the Church as to appropriate methods/approaches of dealing with the African Christian problem.

Analysing Mbiti's theological constructs for African theology and Kato's critique of those constructs, Eitel evaluates and contrasts their thoughts, African theology, as formulated by Mbiti, is context dominant and lends itself to the capricious whims of a syncretistic amalgamation of African traditional religions and Christianity that is neither African nor Christian. Kato, however, approached culture with the absolute standard of priori truth. His theocentric emphasis requires the Bible to dominate the contextualisation process. Scripture critiques culture and never the reverse.

Rogers, using Young's article as a point of departure, categorised African Christian theologians into two main groups based on the differences in their hermeneutical perspectives. The first group, which Rogers calls the 'Old Guard', is 'somewhat at variance on the degree to which dialogue between Christianity and traditional religion is useful'. The second group, which he calls the 'New Guard', does 'not have such dialogue as a major theme on their theological agenda'.

Some scholars have been working to provide contextual Christologies that are relevant to African Religious (AR) worldviews. The work of Jesus has been compared and contrasted with African traditional healers. Jesus has been referred to as: 'Ancestor/Proto-Ancestor', 'our "brother-ancestor" in fullness', 'the great ancestor, our ancestor par excellence', and 'an intermediary spirit between God and people', 'Priest', and 'Chief'. Part One of the edited works of Schreiter surveys African Christologies, and Part Two discusses the different perceptions of Jesus in Africa. Other scholars have published valuable guidelines for dialogue between AR and Christianity.

In ecumenical spheres, in recognition of the African Christian problem, the All-African Council of Churches (AACC) sponsored the first conference of African theologians in Ibadan, January 1966 on the theme, 'Biblical Revelation and African Beliefs'. From that time, most African theologians say something about the encounter between the two religions. The AACC continues to promote dialogue between Christians and members of other faith communities. This dialogue is however promoted to a greater degree with Islam than with AR.

After Vatican II and the apostolic message *Africae terrarum*, a series of consultations and publications on AR was carried out by the PCID. The Roman Catholic Church's theological evaluation of other religions has gone all the way from disregard and rejection which characterised much of Christian tradition, through a guarded acceptance and openness, to a positive assessment and recognition of salutary values.

Since the development of the 'Guidelines on Dialogue with People of Living Faiths and Ideologies' in Chiang Mai 1979, the WCC continues to take significant steps towards facilitating inter-religious relations and dialogue. At the recently concluded Critical Movement conference in June 2005, which brought together 130 participants of different faiths including indigenous religions, the WCC manifested its commitment to be involved in the present and future of interreligious relations and dialogue. The joint project for Africa—IRRD of the WCC and the PCID of the Vatican—continues to make provision for the discussion of various aspects of African religiosity and culture. The project held a Francophone meeting in Dakar, Senegal in 2002, and another for Anglophones in Addis Ababa, Ethiopia in 2004.

There are many AICs, and more are still rising, that represent creative indigenization of the gospel more fully on African soil. Some of these churches seem to be catering to the needs of many Africans and are therefore attracting an impressive following. Most of their church buildings are being expanded to accommodate more worshipers. The different schools of thought and approaches in dealing with the African Christian problem are reflective of the three basic typologies – exclusivism, inclusivism, and pluralism. Without a doubt, the ongoing discussions about the relationship between African Christianity and the gospel suggest that there is still work to do in the area of relating the Christian message to African cultures.

***

Homosexuality

According to Van Klinken, perhaps the most recent trend is that African Christianity in the 21st century has increasingly become the site of controversies over issues of homosexuality and sexual diversity. While for most of the 20th century, homosexuality was hardly a major issue for Christian churches or political leaders anywhere in Africa, in the past one or two decades this has changed dramatically. In many different African countries, from Nigeria to Zimbabwe and from Uganda to Cameroon, church leaders have publicly spoken out against the acceptance of homosexuality and the recognition of 'gay rights', Christian politicians have proposed anti-homosexuality legislation, and the popular opinion among the general public is that homosexuality is both 'un-African' and 'un-Christian'. Biblical texts and arguments dominate the societal and political debates, illustrating that in contemporary Africa the Bible has become 'a site of struggle' where the debate on homosexuality is being fought.

As much as the politicisation of homosexuality in Africa is a recent phenomenon, it is important to remember its historical background in the sexual politics of missionary Christianity and colonialism. In the case of former British colonies, the penal code criminalising same-sex practices is a residue of the colonial period and reflects the values of 19th century Victorian Christianity – even though that clause is now ironically defended as protecting 'African values'. It is only recently, however, that the legal prohibition of homosexuality has been actualised, and that efforts are being made to broaden its scope and increase the penalties for offences.

First, after the end of Apartheid in 1994, South Africa adopted a new constitution that explicitly outlawed discrimination on the basis of sexual orientation, which finally led to the legalisation of same-sex marriage in 2006. Prominent Christian leaders, including the high-profile Anglican Archbishop of Cape Town, Desmond Tutu, supported the idea to acknowledge and safeguard the human rights of gay and lesbian people in the new 'rainbow nation'. In response to these progressive moves, political and religious leaders in other African countries distanced themselves from South Africa, making homosexuality a public issue. In South Africa itself, there was also a lot of resistance, as became clear in the protests against the legalisation of same-sex marriage that were supported, if not mobilised, by popular Christian voices.

Second, on the agenda of the 1998 Lambeth conference––the decennia meeting of all Anglican bishops––were two issues that turned out to be highly divisive: the ordination of clergy in same-sex relationships and the blessing of same-sex partnerships. A number of African bishops such as Peter Akinola of Nigeria became the leading voices, effectively protesting against the 'unbiblical' stances of churches in 'the West', and in the process, they made homosexuality a key political issue also in their own churches and societies. The crisis in the global Anglican Communion has been interpreted as a reflection of the new realities in world Christianity, with a conservative global South that now outnumbers and overrules liberal churches in North America and Western Europe. This interpretation ignores some of the complexity, such as the distinct position of the Anglican Church of Southern Africa and the emergence of both conservative and liberal South-West alliances, but undeniably the current controversy in the Anglican Communion illustrates some crucial dynamics in contemporary global Christianity.

In addition to these two factors, the recent concern with homosexuality in African Christian circles must also be understood in relation to some of the developments discussed above, particularly the competition between Christianity and Islam in Africa and the rise of Pentecostalism. It is easy to imagine how African Christian leaders, especially in countries like Nigeria, who are critically aware of Muslim proselytising strategies, feel the need to speak out vociferously against homosexuality, to prevent their Christianity from being associated with a 'morally degraded West'. Pentecostalism has further contributed to public debates over homosexuality, the emergence of popular homophobia, and the introduction of new anti-homosexuality legislation in various African countries. Not only does it put a great emphasis on issues of sexual morality as part of its programme of born-again conversion, but also rejects homosexuality out of a literalist reading of scripture. More importantly, it presents a political theology in which global politics of homosexuality and 'gay rights' are framed in a dualist scheme of good versus evil, God versus the devil, and in which the Christian character of the nation needs to be protected against international pressure imagined as satanic forces. Making homosexuality a major issue in public debate, Pentecostals also make it difficult for other churches to take a more nuanced position as this could easily be used against them in a highly competitive religious market. Yet there are several courageous Christian leaders in Africa – most famously Desmond Tutu in South Africa, but also Bishop Christopher Senyonjo from Uganda and pastors from various denominational backgrounds who provide pastoral support to LGBT people and address homophobia from a Christian perspective. This illustrates, again, the different theological strands and trajectories in African Christianity and how these impact the ways in which Christianity engages with public and socio-political issues.

All Nations Full Gospel Churches International (ANFGCI): A Case Study

In her doctoral dissertation, Cynthia narrates the story of ANFGCI as an insider. She states that in an era of confusion, there is always a remnant who walks pleasing to God. One of the most significant developments in Ghanaian Contemporary Christianity is the globalisation of ministries. A number of the ministries in Ghana can be found in Canada among the diaspora. Founders of charismatic churches and even Classical Pentecostals have started branches in North America, in the UK, and even in Australia. Wherever Ghanaians immigrate to, the Pastors of the churches they patronised while in Ghana expect them to be missionaries by initiating a branch church of the church they left in Ghana.

Some ministries in Ghana insist that their members do not join a different church when they migrate. These churches expect members to eventually form a branch church, even if they initially go to other churches. Rev Dag Heward-Mills' Lighthouse Chapel International has established a number of churches, and so has Agyin Asare's Perez Chapel International. Interestingly enough the Classical Pentecostal churches and the Mission churches have had even more success in establishing branch churches in Toronto, Canada. The Church of Pentecost (CoP), the Assemblies of God, the Catholic Church, the Presbyterian Church, the Methodist Church, and other neo-Pentecostal churches have branch churches or affiliation with the founding/main churches in Ghana. Other people have started their own ministries through church splits which have become an unfortunate trend with most of the contemporary churches both in Toronto and in Ghana. The Ghanaian diaspora in Toronto, Canada has mirrored contemporary Ghanaian Christianity in an uncanny way.

***

Toronto in the 1980s

Thirty years ago, there were not as many Ghanaian immigrants in Toronto, and neither were there any churches to cater to these immigrants. Many of the immigrants at that time came to Toronto as foreign students with the aim of completing their education and then returning to Ghana. Ghana was young then, it had many jobs awaiting those who returned home upon completing their degrees. However, this trend changed as more and more immigrants found Canada to be an economic haven; the focus of the tide of economic and refugee immigrants quickly changed to North America. Canada became a soft entry to the 'land of milk and honey', not only for the educated, but also for the semi-literates, those with basic education, and some illiterates.

As the Ghanaian community grew, the need for a place of worship where they would feel loved and accepted became a challenge to many. Many would lose their enthusiasm for church when they did not receive the type of worship they were familiar with in Ghana. Many found the language barrier a challenge; it became difficult, as these Ghanaians could not attend the established churches found in Toronto. In an effort to manage these complications, some Ghanaians initiated prayer groups or fellowships with friends of like faith. Eventually, many churches were established by them.

In his article, Mensah posits that the churches that were founded in Toronto gave Ghanaians a space to worship and affirm their ethnicity. Although he argues that such churches invariably promote the creation of ethnic enclaves that hinder immigrants from assimilating into Canadian society, the reality is that these ethnic churches shielded the immigrants from racism, alienation, and cultural inattentiveness. These churches also helped new immigrants to adapt to life in Toronto. In his book about immigrants in Toronto, Cecil Forster discusses the importance of the church to immigrants (in this text, he is writing specifically about ANFGC):

'The church tries to provide services that are not available elsewhere not so much to challenge the wider society but to make the black community more self-sufficient within the existing society. On Sunday for example, two of its daytime services are in the Twi language of Ghana. Many who might have difficulty with the dominant culture and language can find refuge in this church where their culture and language flourish and are important at least once a week. And all night from nine o'clock every Friday night, the church throws its doors open to anyone needing a quiet moment for prayer, an opportunity to get their lives, a chance to reflect on the challenges of living in this country. Just as important, by opening its doors, it offers black youths a chance not to be elsewhere, not to be in other places still open at all hours of the night, not to be in those places that expose them to temptations'.

The same sentiment is expressed by Harvey Kwiyani who reiterates that the African immigrant congregation is not just an outcome of the need to create a home away from home where they can 'liturgise in their language and eat African food' but rather the immigrant churches have emerged out of the necessity to negotiate the racism that the African immigrant faces in the congregations of their host countries. The church thus became a place of respite after a week of discrimination by Canadian society, whether in the workplace or in the educational institutions they had become a part of.

Samuel Donkor tells a life-changing moment when he considered the importance of the church for discipleship. He stresses that 'evangelism is the means but church planting is the goal or end' to fulfil the Great Commission. This point buttresses Bosch's opinion that it is 'impossible to talk about the church without at the same time talking about mission'. He maintains that disciples are made in church and not in the Bible schools. Bosch quotes Gensichen that the 'missionary dimension of a local church's life manifests itself, among other ways when it is truly a worshipping community; it is able to welcome outsiders and make them feel at home; it is a church in which the pastor does not have the monopoly and the members are not merely objects of pastoral care; its members are equipped for their calling in society; it is structurally pliable and innovative, and it does not defend the privileges of a select group'.

People need the camaraderie that comes with worshipping with people of like faith. The other points of the ANFGC Mission Statement promote the nurturing and discipling of the Christian. Samuel puts in place certain rules to promote a multicultural environment where non-Ghanaians would not feel alienated when they joined the church. This is because, although his first convert was a Chinese man, the core people he started the church with were Ghanaians. By doing so, he ensured that the church did not become a 'club' catering only to Ghanaian immigrant Christians. Worship in the vernacular was not encouraged. English was the main language of operation, and posters were created to remind Ghanaians to be mindful of other nationals in their interactions at church. However, to accommodate the Ghanaians who had a challenge with the English language, a Twi service was conducted as a second service for them.

Samuel Donkor was determined from the onset to build a congregation that was not mono-ethnic so he also made sure that the leadership reflected the ethnic composition in the congregation. These policies were effective because presently, the church in Toronto boasts of 60 different nationalities, and this is a reflection of other ANFGC congregations in North America. The Board of Directors for ANFGC presently comprises one Nigerian, two Ghanaians, and a Trinidadian. He considered Canada as the logical base for launching a global ministry. He believes that the different countries represented in the congregations in Canada can afford the possibility of penetrating their countries of origin in spreading the Gospel. To date, there have been such openings in many countries including Trinidad, Jamaica, Costa Rica, Portugal, Norway, Liberia, Ivory Coast, and Angola where ANFGC churches have been established.

Meeting the people on a weekly basis in his apartment, Donkor followed the Scripture Union method of ensuring members went to one of the established churches in the area on Sunday. The difference between conducting a fellowship and starting a Church was evident. The fellowships can operate without a specific vision, goal, or purpose and do not require commitment on the part of the attendees. The fellowship seekers search for fulfilment when their local church is not adequately feeding them and equipping them to do the work of the ministry. There is however the need to belong to a local church for pastoral care with a pastor. In 1985, the fellowship moved from Donkor's apartment to a Community Centre, and in January 1986 the fellowship became ANFGC with 23 members. In 1987, ANFGC moved to a shared accommodation with a Lutheran Church where its services were held in the afternoons. The Ghanaian immigrants argued that establishing the church was a way of self-enrichment because they were ignorant of the fact that, unlike Ghana, one cannot misappropriate church funds for too long; the Canada Revenue Agency (CRA) does regular audits and can deregister charities where misappropriation of church funds is found. This was a case of a prophet being hardly recognised amongst his own people.

***

All Nations Today

Today, ANFGC has become a church planting organisation. True to its name, many nations are represented in the Toronto church, which is the headquarters of the 102 branch churches established in five continents, namely Africa, North America, South America, Europe, and South-East Asia. ANFGC has 19 churches in Ghana, but the reverse missionary efforts have seen the establishment of ANFGC churches in different cities and provinces in Canada. In Canada, apart from the Toronto branch, ANFGC has branches in Ottawa, Montreal, Windsor, London, Oakville, Mississauga, Ajax, Cambridge, Kitchener, Markham, Oshawa, Hamilton, Montreal, Halifax, Vancouver, Edmonton, Calgary, Winnipeg, Monton, Charlottetown, Barrie, Saskatoon, Guelph, and Quebec.

Pentecostal and/or charismatic churches tend to lean primarily towards one of the Charismatic-triads: Prosperity, Deliverance/Healing, and Prophetism. Some of these churches can properly be labelled 'Prosperity churches' as their central theme is acquiring, living, and expounding substantial wealth, and health. Some are also known as 'Deliverance ministries' because their central and defining focus is on deliverance. Other churches or ministries are known to be 'Prophetic ministries' because they focus on prophecy and their founders are known as prophets. In all the churches, however, one common characteristic is their dependence on the 'Faith movement'. Paul Gifford prefers to use the term 'victorious living' for the Ghanaian charismatic churches because they stress rituals ensuring success in all of 'this-worldly' realities like fertility, spouses, children, and crops.

The phrase 'Full Gospel', according to Asamoah Gyadu, is used to emphasise the centrality of the Bible in the definitions of the faith of charismatic churches as opposed to the Mission churches who were 'not Biblical enough'. He adds that the 'reservations concerned in particular the lack of emphasis on the experiences of the interventionist ministry of the Holy Spirit in the application of the Biblical promises and the practical appropriation of biblical truths'. Churches with such a designation thus embraced all the movements that seemed to have characterised Pentecostalism in general.

***

All Nations University

The ANU in Koforidua, Ghana is a result of Samuel Donkor's aspiration to make a contribution to the nation of Ghana. Under his leadership, the diaspora in Toronto, specifically ANFGC, accepted the challenge to build a university in Ghana, and after many consultations with the Ministry of Education and other people from North America, the National Accreditation Board (NAB) in Ghana gave him the authority to establish the university in May 1996. After years of groundwork, ANU opened its doors with 37 pioneering students in two programs on 4th November 2002. To date, ANU has 13 accredited undergraduate programs and has enrolled about 4000 students in the fields of Business Administration, Engineering, Computer Science, and Biblical Studies with a Graduate School. The vision of ANU is to provide quality higher education that endorses development in a vibrant Christian atmosphere. ANU is committed to total personality development where students are trained intellectually, socially, morally, and spiritually. As part of its social responsibility, the ANU has made it possible for women in the community to access free literacy education, ICT training, and basic business skills as part of empowering women to contribute to society.

ANU is increasingly becoming the university of choice not only for Ghanaians but also international students; it has attracted students from countries including Angola, Benin, Cameroon, Chad, Congo, Gabon, Gambia, Ivory Coast, Kenya, Liberia, Nigeria, Rwanda, South Sudan, and Togo. ANU has academic links with many renowned institutions locally and internationally. These include Kwame Nkrumah University of Science and Technology (KNUST), Kumasi, Ghana; University of Western Ontario Ivey School of Business in Canada; Kyushu Institute of Technology (KYUTECH) in Japan; Indian Institute of Technology (IIT), Dhanbad, Indian School of Mines (ISM), and the Sam Higginbottom University of Agriculture, Technology and Sciences (SHUATS), India.

The idea of a private Christian university in Ghana was a novelty, which has now been emulated by several prominent charismatic churches. Valley View – an Adventist University was the first to receive a charter, followed by Central University, Ashesi University, All Nations University, Methodist University, Pentecost University, and Evangelical Presbyterian University. Cephas Omenyo and Abamfo Atiemo maintain that the establishment of universities by charismatic churches is a drift towards elitism. They believe that the establishment of these universities is causing a drift of the semi-educated, and illiterate Ghanaian from the Classical Pentecostal churches and charismatic churches to the Prophetic movement which is presently drawing in the crowds in Ghana with prophetic charisma. The Prophetic movement, with 'prophets' who present themselves as having great anointing or spiritual power, and as such, capable of performing miracles has been documented. Commenting on the relationship between the Bible and the Spirit in African Pentecostal hermeneutics, Allen Anderson observes:

'One presupposition that conditions this hermeneutical approach is the emphasis on the experience of the Holy Spirit that is common to the Pentecostals, including African Pentecostals. The Bible is used to explain the experience of the working of the Holy Spirit in the church with supernatural "gifts of the Spirit", especially healing, exorcism, speaking in tongues, and prophesying although there are sometimes differences between the churches in the practice of these gifts'.

***

Schism of All Nations

ANFGC experienced a major division by a group of pastors with some members in their churches in 2011. The administrative structure in ANFGC at that time made it easy for the main perpetrator to influence some of the pastors under his authority. There were three districts at that time namely the Western District, the Eastern District, and the African District. Each district is led by a Superintendent who reports to the Denominational Pastor. The leader of the Eastern District was able to influence some of the pastors in that district to split their churches, taking with them the most influential members of their congregation. In each branch, however, there were people who decided to remain with the organisation, and as such did not follow those who left. This brought about divisions in families and even in marriages. Some members were so disillusioned that they gave up going to any church altogether. The emotional toll was heavy, as was the financial toll on the organisation. Pastors who had not been trained by ANFGC had to be employed to cover the shortfall. Since those branch churches were not able to support the newly appointed pastors financially, the organisation had to provide the affected branches with financial assistance until those churches regained stability.

One of the reasons given by the pastors involved in the split was their aversion to the transfer policy of ANFGC. After the split, the transfer policy was altered so that instead of pastors being transferred after three years at any station, the duration of the stay before the transfer was extended to four years. Pastors believed that the four years would give them a better chance of establishing a church before transfer. Also, four years accommodated those with younger families better. Another move to curtail any further split was the education of members; hitherto only pastors were educated on the reasons why pastors are transferred, but obviously, the split indicated that the general membership of the churches needed to know the rationale behind transfers and the evils that follow splits. Again, to promote transparency as to how the organisation is run, the operations department (plus the accountants) travel to all the branches each year to educate members on the financial status of the organisation.

Members have embraced the above attempts as steps in the right direction and lessons from the split. Only four branches were affected by the split namely Ottawa, Ajax, Montreal, and Halifax.

Church membership can be volatile, but with the right education, there is always a core group that will remain faithful and loyal to the church and to the leadership. The reality is that not everyone will stay in a church, but as some leave for whatever reason, others join. It is important that the church does not forget its mandate to go into the world and make disciples, and know that it is the Lord who adds to the church daily those who are being saved. Identifying schisms as a danger facing charismatic churches, Larbi blames splits on authoritarianism, doctrinal nuances, and unashamed personality clashes. He states:

'The structure of neo-Pentecostal churches itself seems to engender authoritarianism and dictatorial tendencies. Since the leader, as it often happens is the one who, it is thought, receives God's mandate to carry out a particular mission. He, by reason of this fact, becomes the central figure in the whole drama. The founder's word is the final, making no room for equally important views of their associates. Often the control system for containing dissents does not exist or has weak roots as the founder almost always controls the arbitration machinery to his advantage. Sometimes the social gap between the founder and other key ministers creates dissatisfaction among the associates. All these factors make schisms a regular pattern'.

As much as Larbi's reasons given for splits are legitimate, they lack objectivity. It presupposes those splits are only a result of disagreements or conflicts in the system. He also betrays his opinion on the structure of charismatic churches. Acknowledgement of the imperfection of human nature and the desire of some people to be in control should also be considered as a cause for church splits. Some people need to be number one and will never be satisfied playing second fiddle. A church may split when a member or an associate pastor seeks to manipulate people and/or events for his own ends. Many reasons may be given by the perpetrator of the split, but the bottom line for the reasons given stems from pride and selfishness. Splits may be blamed on the simplest issues: a) it may be a preferred interpretation of doctrine emphasised and promoted by a subset group, b) it may be a desire of someone who believes he is better qualified with more anointing than the founder and/or leadership, and as such promotes himself and gains a following, or c) it may even be a difference of opinion as to how the worship or music and other things should be.

Endnotes

[1] Peter, C B, 'African Hyphenated Christians - an Alternate Model of Theologizing in Africa', Moi University, Kenya, Nordic Journal of African Studies 3(1): 100–113 (1994)

[2] Reese, Robert. 'John Gatu and the Moratorium on Missionaries'. Missiology, vol. 42, no. 3, July 2014, pp. 245–256, doi:10.1177/0091829613502143

[3] Donkor, Samuel H B, 'A Historical And Theological Study Of Evangelism And Church Planting Based On The Great Commission With Special Reference To All Nations Full Gospel Churches International (ANFGCI)'. Unpublished PhD Thesis, Gospel & Plough Institute Of Theology, SHUATS, 2018

[4] Gyimah, Cynthia, 'The Study Of Contemporary Practices In Ghanaian Christianity'. Unpublished PhD Thesis, Gospel And Plough Institute Of Theology, Faculty Of Theology, SHUATS, 2018

[5] Lecture on African Christianity by Rev Dr Samuel H Donkor, D Min, PhD in the Faculty of Theology

[6] https://www.academia.edu/43896731/Christianity_in_Africa_A_Beacon_of_Hope_for_Christianity_in_Europe

[7] Mbiti, John.S, 'The Forest Has Ears', Peace Happiness and Prosperity I, 7.7, 1976, p 23.

■■■

8

Telling the Truth

'I present my fiction as though it were truth; you present your truth as though it were fiction'.

There is a tale told of the great English actor, William Charles Macready. An eminent preacher once said to him: 'I wish you would explain to me something'. 'Well, what is it? I don't know that I can explain anything to a preacher'. 'What is the difference between you and me? You are appearing before crowds night after night with fiction, and the crowds come wherever you go. I am preaching the essential and unchangeable truth, and I am not getting any crowd at all'. Macready replied: 'This is quite simple. I can tell you the difference between us. I present my fiction as though it were truth; you present your truth as though it were fiction'.

I had an opportunity to preach in the Chapel of Regent's Park College after 38 years in October 2018. One of my former Professors in Oxford from 1979-82, asked me for a copy of my sermon. I was elated because he said that he would place that copy in the Angus Library of the College for posterity. The honour was because I had attempted to blend three stories: the story of Abraham, the story of Serampore, and the story of my life in my sermon. History is made up of stories. Stories, not in the sense of fiction, but in the sense of narratives that recount the events, movements, ideas, and lives that have shaped religions and nations. We base our shared life around the story of the Bible. However, there are so many more stories that we hear and live together. Each story grows and shapes and sometimes even transforms the way we understand how God works in the world. The church-shopping syndrome allows us ease into worship communities where we only listen to stories that mirror our own. However, the question is that we do not have to be imprisoned in our comfort zones. Stories from around the world are just a mouse click or a library trip away or maybe even a walk to the corner of the street.

In Old Testament studies, scholars have identified the several conventions of Hebrew storytelling and in the process offered fresh readings of many classic stories, readings that both make sense of longer narrative sequences and articulate larger theological themes. In the story of Jacob, there is a contrast between his former and latter self. Before birth, an oracle said of the twins, 'The older will serve the younger' (Genesis 25:23). When Jacob usurped Esau's blessing, Isaac blessed Jacob by saying, 'May the sons of your mother bow down to you' (27:29). In the course of the story, tension surfaces. At the Jabbok, the reader hears 'your servant' and 'my lord' in the mouth of Jacob as he stands in the presence of his older brother Esau. And the reader sees Jacob 'bow down' before his brother. The one who had seized a blessing from his older brother was now ready to give it back! A different Jacob offers gifts: 'Take my blessing' (33:11).

Preaching has two foci: 'what the sermon aims to say' and 'what the sermon aims to do'. These two aspects direct the form that the sermon takes. The foundation of preaching the word of God was laid for me at home just by reading the Bible, sharing in Sunday Schools and in Youth Fellowships. In our church, the youth fellowship had a trajectory of different names: *Khadagadhari* (bearer of swords) for the boys, *Alokbahi* (bearer of light) for the girls, and later both became Youth Fellowship and subsequently, 'Christian Endeavour' by which it is popularly known till date in our church and in India. In the beginning, the then Pastor of my church, Rev Surykant Behera from Cuttack, shaped the foundation of the youth fellowship. He was a Pastor of a different kind. He knew how to preach well, how to paint the best, and not least, to cook well. He never married. All the children of the church were like his children. I still remember that he taught me the first Odia alphabet. He was a very good Sunday School teacher and Youth Leader as well.

One of the stories he used to tell us was about Mary Jones, the daughter of a weaver who was born into a poor Welsh family in December of 1784 and lived in Llanfihangel-y-Pennant, Abergynolwyn, in the UK. Her parents were devout Calvinistic Methodists and she herself professed the Christian faith at eight years of age. Having learned to read in the circulating schools organised by Thomas Charles, it became her burning desire to possess a Bible of her own. The nearest copy was at a farm two miles distant from her little cottage, and there was no copy on sale nearer than Bala – 26 miles (42 km) away; and it was not certain that a copy could be obtained there. Welsh Bibles were scarce in those days. Having saved for six years until she had enough money to pay for a copy, she started one morning in 1800 for Bala, and walked the 26 miles over mountainous terrain, barefoot as usual, to obtain a copy from Rev Thomas Charles, the only individual with Bibles for sale in the area. According to one version of the story, Mr Charles told her that all of the copies which he had received were sold or already spoken for. Mary was so distraught that Charles spared her one of the copies which were already promised to another. In another version, she had to wait two days for a supply of Bibles to arrive and was able to purchase a copy for herself and two other copies for members of her family. According to tradition, it was the impression that this visit by Mary Jones left upon him that impelled Charles to propose to the Council of the Religious Tract Society the formation of a Society to supply Wales with Bibles.

It will not be true to say that I remember the full story of Mary Jones as told in detail above but I do remember that Mary Jones had purchased a copy of the Bible. Rev Surykant Behera inculcated the idea that I must make an effort to save money to buy an Odia Bible for myself, like Mary Jones. He also introduced me to the idea from childhood to memorise scripture and ensured I bought the Odia Bible from my own savings. For that, he gave me a 'small earthen pot' to save money. I do not remember the exact amount but one thing I know is that when that box was almost full, he made me go with him to Cuttack about 35 miles from where we lived, to meet the missionary from whom I could buy the Bible. The pot was broken in her presence and to my surprise, I found that the amount covered the exact cost of one Odia Bible.

I had the privilege of sharing the Word of God in our small youth fellowships in the church when I was in high school but not in the church as I was not baptised. The opportunity to preach the Word of God at church was given immediately after my baptism on 14th April 1968, when I was 18 years old. My father used to take me on Sundays with him to nearby churches, where if he used to preach in one church then I was expected to preach in another nearby. I also began receiving invitations to preach in other churches in Odisha before beginning my theological education in 1971, which was a rare opportunity for me.

My preaching was spontaneous as I was brought up in a tradition that taught me never to write a sermon down. Obviously preaching in my mother tongue still comes naturally to me till today and it is spontaneous except that I note a few points on a piece of paper. The first sermon, I was told to write down was the sermon class in Serampore College when I was a student. However, while preaching in the College Chapel in 1972, as part of the sermon appraisal class, I never looked at the script that I had submitted to the practical ministry tutor. Eventually, since 2006, I began writing sermons in a diary with a date and place, which included some in note form and some full script. Therefore, I thought of incorporating a few selected sermons for posterity as a memory.

The Great Korean Revival 100th Anniversary Conference was scheduled in August 2007 and to my pleasant surprise, I received an invitation to attend the same. The Conference, arrangements, and the address by the General Secretary of WCC as well as interaction with participants was remarkable. I had also received an invitation to preach in the Sunday Evening service followed by the Conference. Over dinner on Saturday, a friend reminded me that I was expected to preach on Sunday evening and asked me about the church where I had been invited. I said I did not know anything only their name—Myung Sung Presbyterian Church—and somebody would come to take me there. My understanding was that normally Sunday evening services had low attendance as the morning service was crowded and I had prepared a sermon accordingly. Imagine my surprise when he said that I was going to preach at the largest Presbyterian Church.

Myung Sung Presbyterian Church is the largest Presbyterian Church, was founded in 1980, and is located in Myung-il-dong, Seoul, South Korea, with its Prayer Sanctuary in Wonju. It has over 30 church plants, including Myung Sung First Presbyterian Church, founded in 2004, and Myung Sung Second Presbyterian Church, founded in 2006, along with an additional ten 'screen' (video) churches. The founder and current senior pastor of the church is Dr Kim Sam-Whan. It has a membership of 100,000 but was founded in 1980 by Kim Sam-Whan with only 20 members.

I struggled overnight to rewrite the entire sermon. The ordeal began when a deacon picked me up from the hotel before service and took me to have a meal with church deacons in an exclusive hotel prior to church. I was served 'sushi'. I had never heard such a name nor had eaten such a meal before. Sushi is a Japanese dish where the appetiser consisted of thinly sliced raw fish that you had to eat with a sauce. While sharing my experience later with my son Ashis, he smiled, knowing how I would have responded in that situation.

The Sunday service was fully packed with an overflow of screens and a colourful and melodious choir of about 1200. It was and is an unforgettable memory. Given below are my sermon notes for what I spoke that day.

I. Theme: On the Way Together: Text: Luke 24:13-32

'If you want to walk fast, walk alone; if you want to go long way, walk together'

Myung Sung Presbyterian Church, South Korea, August 2007

Walking is a good exercise. The African saying 'If you want to walk fast, walk alone; if you want to go long way, walk together' is meaningful. It is essential to find space to walk in a city where people live in the pigeonholes of high-rise apartments. In cities, people drive to nearby parks and walk, a common sight each morning. In villages, it is a privilege to find such pollution-free space for a walk and enjoy the beauty of nature that makes us sing 'Then sings my soul, my saviour God to thee, how great thou art'. We walk to keep our body fit, which is a gift from God. Walking is also a spiritual exercise. Walking with God as well as walking with people of God. Walking alone is easy as we make decisions on our own but walking together is difficult. Our call is to walk together as 'People of God'.

The Lucan narrative in chapter 24:13-32 is a beautiful story of walking together. The story is called 'On the Road to Emmaus'. Two of the disciples were going to a village called Emmaus, about seven miles from Jerusalem. Jesus Himself joins them as they are talking. He joins the conversation, which is very interesting. 'What are you discussing together as you walk along?' (v.17). One of them called Cleopas, asks Him, 'Are you only a visitor to Jerusalem?' (v.18). 'Do you not know what happened?' He questions, 'What things?' (v.19), they respond telling Him about Jesus of Nazareth. Jesus is asking a question about Himself, despite being the subject of the conversation. Jesus is told that some of the women amazed them when they said Jesus was alive (v. 22). When Jesus sits at the table, he breaks bread and gives it to them, then their eyes are opened (v. 30).

Today, we fear strangers as we do not know them and they are difficult to entertain. In the Lucan narrative we find that the two disciples showed love for the stranger; they did not ignore him. They did not try to ditch him. They allowed him to come alongside them and join them on their journey. The word for loving the stranger is *philoxenia* and the word for fear of the stranger is *xenophobia*. These two disciples practised *philoxenia,* which means they 'loved the stranger'. What those disciples modelled is very unlike the way our society sees the stranger. The prevalent attitude today is what we call *xenophobia* which means 'fear of the stranger'.

There is also a certain tension between being 'the guest' or 'the host'. I don't know if Jesus was feeling any of this awkwardness but as we move along in the Lucan text we see Jesus, who began as a stranger, was then welcomed as a guest into their home, eventually becoming the host. As they sat down to eat, He took the bread and blessed it. Then He broke it and gave it to them. Suddenly their eyes were opened, and they recognised Jim. At that moment He disappeared! In Luke 24:30-31 Jesus is the host whenever we come to the Lord's Table or Communion. When we partake of the broken bread and the cup, we experience the real presence of Christ. When we hear the words, 'This is my body which is broken for you' and, 'This is my blood shed for the forgiveness of your sins', it is Christ who is present and active as the host. The question for us today and always, is: Will we see Jesus as the stranger/guest/host?

The narrative in Luke 24 is on the way to Emmaus. Two disciples of Jesus had started out for home. There was no reason to stay in Jerusalem any longer. The Lord they loved was dead and buried. Cleophas and another follower of Jesus were sad. Their hopes in Jesus had been crushed. It was dangerous for Jesus' disciples to be seen in Jerusalem, and it was a long journey home. It would have seemed to have been the longest journey home they had ever taken. They were met by someone they thought to be a stranger. He did not seem to be weighed down with sorrow and was making better progress on the road. If Emmaus was their home, they might have wondered why a stranger was making haste to go to their little town out in the middle of nowhere.

Luke lets us know that this supposed stranger was actually Jesus. Either the disciples were so lost in spirit that they did not recognise Him, or more likely, Jesus prevented them from recognising Him. He notices the look of these two disciples and asked them why they were so gloomy. Cleophas could not believe that this 'stranger' on the Jerusalem Road to nowhere did not know what had happened there. With all the commotion, they thought, how could anyone not know what had happened to Jesus? Jesus continued to play the role of a stranger to draw out what He wanted from them. They responded that they had believed that Jesus of Nazareth was going to be the Prophet who would deliver Israel from Roman bondage. Instead, Jesus had been crucified and was now dead and buried. Luke then tells us that Jesus began to show them from all of Scripture the texts that spoke of both His passion and resurrection. Wouldn't we certainly like to know ourselves the Scriptures He shared with them?

When they got to Emmaus, Jesus acted as He would travel further. What place could be beyond nowhere? The two disciples knew that travel at night was dangerous, especially if one was going to the nothing beyond nowhere. They also knew the requirements of hospitality to strangers that the Law of Moses commanded, so they bid this stranger stay with them. Jesus took food with them, which is proof to us that He was no ghost. He was really alive.

The Lucan story describes one element of the opening of the eyes. There is another opening of the eyes story in Numbers chapter 22. The story is about Balaam - the Prophet, Balak - the king of Moab, and most significantly the donkey. Balaam was expected to curse the people of Israel (v. 10) instead the story moves in a different direction, which can be a nice 'aide-memoire' to set the agenda for a Living Theology. The donkey saw the angel of the Lord standing in the road with a drawn sword in his hand. So the donkey turned aside out of the road and went into the field. Balaam struck the donkey, to turn her back. Then the angel of the Lord stood in a narrow path between the vineyards, with a wall on either side. And when the donkey saw the angel of the Lord, she pushed against the wall and pressed Balaam's foot against the wall. So, he struck her again. Then the angel of the Lord went ahead and stood in a narrow place, where there was no way to turn either to the right or to the left. When the donkey saw the angel of the Lord, she lay down under Balaam.

However, the climax of the narrative in Numbers is the conversation between the man of God and the donkey. Then the Lord opened the mouth of the donkey, and she said to Balaam, 'What have I done to you, that you have struck me these three times?' And Balaam said to the donkey, 'Because you have made a fool of me. I wish I had a sword in my hand, for then I would kill you'. And the donkey said to Balaam, 'Am I not your donkey, on which you have ridden all your life long to this day? Is it my habit to treat you this way?' And he said, 'No'. The question is can a donkey speak?

In observing the 100thAnniverssary of the Great Korean Revival, we remember the great Pyongyang Revival of 1907. We are thankful to God for the initiative taken by the Korean Church in the formation of peace and unification of the Peninsula. Walking together on the way towards peace and justice is not an easy road, but it is one nation's vision for common solidarity. It requires patience, especially learning to listen to each other and to God. How do we walk or continue to walk, despite the hurdles that have come our way so far? This is an important question. Our Christian faith affirms the presence of God, who is always ever-present and accompanies us. The tragic part is we, as humans sometimes cannot recognise Him like the two disciples on the road to Emmaus could not recognise the resurrected Jesus. Sometimes knowing God too well, we may travel a wrong path like Balaam and cannot see or perceive the presence of God. The irony of the story in Numbers is that the man of God could not see the Angel but the donkey could. How strange was that?

While we walk with God as an individual, it is equally important to note the beauty of our journey. On the way together, miracles do happen if we believe in Jesus of Nazareth. We are in the age of high technology. Perhaps we must learn to listen to the voice of God through small voices from the margin or the initiatives of nondescript actors like the donkey speaking to a man of God.

I am reminded of a story of a Kangaroo and a Camel who had an interesting conversation. A stubborn kangaroo kept escaping from his enclosure at the zoo, and this left the zoo officials concerned. Knowing that the kangaroo could leap really high, the officials put up a 10-meter fence. Surprisingly, the kangaroo was out again by the next morning, and he was found roaming about the zoo. To prevent the kangaroo from getting out again, the officials put up a higher fence – this time, a 20-meter fence. This was, however, not able to stop the kangaroo as he got out yet again. This caused the officials to raise the fence forty meters high. Shortly after the 40-meter fence was put up, a camel in the enclosure next to the kangaroo asked how high he though they'd be willing to go. The kangaroo replied, 'About a thousand meters, unless somebody starts locking the gate at night'.

It is very important to be watchful while walking together. Our calling is to walk in the footsteps of our Lord and Saviour Jesus Christ, to be a witnessing community here and now. Paul reminds us in Ephesians 4: 17-25 in the context of Christian conduct. 'Be renewed in mind and spirit, put on the new nature created in God's likeness which shows itself in the upright and devout life, called for by the truth' (Ephesians 4:24). The command is to learn to walk together. The mandate of God is crystal clear. 'Lord has told you, O man, what is good; and what does the Lord require of you but to do justice, and to love kindness, and to walk humbly with your God?' (Micah 6:8).

It is said that Rabbi Yehoshua once asked Elijah about the future: 'When will the Messiah come?' Elijah answered, 'Go and ask Him, Himself'. Rabbi Yehoshua was amazed: 'You mean I could find Him, talk to Him—now? Where is He?' Elijah said, 'You can find Him at the gates of Rome'. 'How will I recognise Him at the gates of Rome?' asked Rabbi Yehoshua. Elijah told him, 'There He sits among the lepers whom you will find unwinding all of their bandages at the same time and then covering their sores with clean bandages. The Messiah is the only one who unwinds and rewinds His bandages one at a time, thinking, "I want to be ready at a moment's notice if I am called'". Rabbi Yehoshua travelled from the cave of Rabbi Shimon bar Yohai all the way to Rome – a journey that seemed to take him only a few steps. He was not frightened by the strong gates of the enemy nor the pitiful condition of the lepers. Keeping in mind Elijah's advice of how to identify the Messiah in the most unlikely of places, among the most wretched of people, he quickly spotted the one poor sufferer who was unwrapping and rewrapping only one sore at a time. Rabbi Yehoshua approached him and said, 'Peace be upon you, my master and teacher'. The leper looked knowingly at him and replied, 'Peace be upon you, son of Levi'. Rabbi Yehoshua asked him, 'When will the master come?' 'Today', said the leper. Rabbi Yehoshua returned to Elijah in the blink of an eye. Elijah said to him, 'What did the Messiah say to you?' Rabbi Yehoshua replied, 'He said, "Peace be upon you, son of Levi"'. Elijah said, 'Ah! As to your first question to me, he assured you that both you and your father have a place in the world to come'. Rabbi Yehoshua said, 'But he lied to me, saying, "Today I will come". He has not come'. Elijah said, 'No, he did not say that he would come "today". Rather, he was quoting a Psalm to you: Today – if only you will listen to His voice' (Psalm 95:7) (Babylonian Talmud, Sanhedrin 98a).

More recently, in the television series *Joan of Arcadia*, a teenage Joan Girardi sees and speaks with God and performs tasks that she is given, tasks that often may seem strange but are for the greater good. The title song for the series is Joan Osbourne's 'What if God Was One of Us'. God appears in the form of various people including small children, teenage boys, elderly ladies, transients, or passers-by.

II. Theme: Homecoming: Text: Isaiah 52:7-10; John 1:1-14

Christmas Service, 2011, Khordha Baptist Church

Pope Julius authorised 25th December 353 AD to be celebrated as the birthday of Jesus. Professor Charles Follen lit the candles on the first Christmas Tree in America in 1822. Nobody then would have thought that the celebration of Christmas with decorations would become so elaborate and commercial. However, today we need to recall to our memory a profound truth of Christmas. Christmas is one of the greatest festivals based on the Truth of Incarnation which we may call the 'Homecoming of God'. God came down from heaven and was born in a manger but we have failed to acknowledge Him.

The way we are running the world does not seem to be terribly successful right now. The narrative of the homecoming of God in the Gospel according to John has been woven together with five elements of the Old Testament: a) the Word of God: heavens were made, He spoke and things happened; b) the Wisdom of God: the Lord created me at the beginning of His works (Proverbs 8:22); c) the Law of God: God gave Israel the law, not as a set of instructions but a written mode of His presence; d) the Temple of God: God's presence in the pillar of cloud by day and fire by the night, dwelling in the tent and temple of Jerusalem; and e) the Spirit of God: God-breathed and human became a living being. Our Living God, creator God, the God of Israel is not an 'upstairs' God but 'downstairs'. Therefore, we say that Christmas is the 'Homecoming of God'. All the above five themes are knitted together in relation to 'the Messiah' who was equipped with God's Spirit to bring God's Judgement into the world, speaking words of power, teaching and embodying wisdom, upholding the law, and blessing and re-building the temple.

The story of Christmas according to John is about the 'Word becoming flesh' and being 'Tabernacled' among us. The word in both Hebrew and Greek for 'Tent' is 'Tent- Pitching God'. God dwells and has pitched His tent in our world today; a world full of confused young people, lonely old people, loads of money hoarded by a few, and market meltdowns. How can one wish everybody a peaceful Christmas because it hardly ever is. Yet, in the midst of the mess, there is always a blessing. The story of the first Christmas, centres around unexpected pregnancies, unplanned journeys, lack of boarding facilities, and migration to Egypt after birth for fear of violence.

We have to tell the story. In other words, 'we have a story to tell to the nations'. But the question is how do we convey a message that is unrelated to the messenger who conveys it. Billy Graham tells of a time in the early years of his preaching ministry when he was due to lead a crusade meeting in South Carolina and he needed to mail a letter. He asked a little boy in the street how he could get to the post office. After the boy had given him directions, Billy said, 'If you come to the Central Baptist church tonight, I will tell you how to go to heaven'. The boy replied, 'No thanks, you don't even know how to get to the post office'.

The story of Christmas is eternal and powerful and has transformed millions of lives around the world. The story of Christmas is for one and all. An economist returned to visit his old college. He was interested in the current exam questions papers. To his surprise, he found that the question papers are exactly the same ones which he had answered. The reply was, 'The questions are always the same, only the answers change'. We often have a problem with time. We get used to things the way they are, and we want them to stay that way. We are nostalgic for what seems a happier time in our lives. Although we long for certainty, living in time means living in uncertainty about what the future will be.

One main constraint of our time is violence. It has not changed in the course of history. Cain killed his brother Abel. God asked him where was his brother Abel. His answer was that he did not know. 'Am I my brother's keeper?' Violence makes us constantly fearful. We don't know where the threat is as it is an enemy who is willing to risk everything. The former Prime Minister of Pakistan Benazir Bhutto was buried in a graveyard near the grave of her father Zulfikar Ali Bhutto. Thousands of mourners packed the streets as the assassinated former Prime's coffin was driven through the streets. There was ransacking and burning of churches in the Kandhamal district of Odisha on the eve of Christmas. We need to strongly condemn the communal violence against the tribal and Dalit Christians, including the destruction and desecration of Christian churches and places of worship in the Kandhamal district of the Odisha.

Our God is a loving and forgiving God. The breadth, length, and depth of God are rich in mercy and lavish in grace. The challenge is to act in response to that love shown on the Cross. The Archbishop of York, Dr Sentamu captured headlines around the world when he shaved his head, moved into a tent inside, and began a fast in an act of 'public witness' to call for peace in the Middle East. He also carried outdoor full-immersion baptism of new Anglican converts at Easter. More charismatic statements of Christian witnesses can be expected from him.

A Baptist pastor and civil rights leader was assassinated on 4th April 1968. About 40 years before he had preached a sermon. 'Which of you who has a friend, will go to him at midnight and say to him, "Friend, lend me three loaves; for a friend of mine has arrived on a journey, and I have nothing to set before him?"' (Luke 11:5-6). This text served as a basis for the contemporary problems of his time and the role of the church is grappling with them. His sermon was that as it is midnight in the parable, it is also midnight in our world. The darkness is so deep that we can hardly see which way to turn. Midnight is the hour when people do not follow the Ten Commandments but desperately seek to obey the 11th commandment: 'Thou shall not get caught'. According to the ethics of midnight, the cardinal sin is to be caught and the cardinal virtue is to get away. It is all right to steal if one is dignified about it. We in the 21st century are definitely clever. A rich old man was on his death bed and desperately wanted to take some of his money with him. He called his priest, his doctor, and his lawyer to his bedside. 'Here's 30,000 cash to be held by each of you. I trust you to put this in my coffin when I die so I can take all my money with me'. At the funeral, each man put a sealed envelope in the coffin. After returning from the funeral the three were talking. The priest suddenly broke into tears and made a confession: 'I had only put 20,000 into the envelope because I needed 10,000 for the renovation of the church'. 'Well since we are confiding in each other', said the doctor, 'I only put 10,000 in the envelope because we needed a new machine at the hospital which cost me 20,000'. The lawyer was shocked. 'I am ashamed of both of you', he exclaimed. 'When I put my envelope in that coffin, I put my personal cheque for the full 30,000'. Midnight is a confusing hour when people forget to distinguish between right and wrong.

The most inspiring word is that no midnight remains for long. Our eternal message of hope is that dawn will come. Change happens but it happens when we are ready to be human. Not to use our suffering as another weapon against each other, not to argue about whose sufferings are worse, but to recognise the same love and the same loss. We believed that the most radical and total change in the history of the world happened when God began to speak to us in the voice of a human, not the voice of a monarch or a philosopher but the inarticulate voice of a child in a manger. When we start hearing the voice of God in the cries of the people around us, then the dawn is near. Faith in the dawn arises from the faith that God is good and just. When we believe this, we know that the contradictions of life are neither final nor ultimate. We can walk through the dark night with the conviction that all things work together for good for those that love God. Even the most starless midnight may herald the dawn of some great fulfilment. The dawn will come. Disappointment, sorrow, and despair are born at midnight, but morning follows. 'Weeping may endure for a night', says the Psalmist, 'but joy cometh in the morning' (Psalm 30:5).

Christmas is all about the Homecoming of God. Home-making involves a myriad of aspects: staying together as a family, making friends, welcoming neighbours, building community, cultivating a garden, learning cooking, making space for the handicapped in our society, and learning to cope with difficult situations. Yet, what is most important in home-making is that is crowded with possibilities. The basis of this journey is that although we are loved by God, we have to take up our cross and follow Him.

Difficulties and suffering go deep in life. They tempt us to try magical quick-fix solutions which do no justice to the depth of the problem. If deep suffering could be dealt with by formulas, techniques, and problem-solving mentality, then our society should have been able to progress in coping with war, poverty, debt, violence, addiction, family break-up, injustice, and a multitude of other miseries. The ministry of Jesus was about healing which involved love, trust, compassion and forgiveness, and radically inclusive hospitality. If there is to be the real thing, it needs to be measured by its ability to sustain. There comes a point when the question does change. We do not ask how to avoid a particularly difficult situation but rather, what it is for.

The handicapped raise issues that are real. They are people with different experiences of life that are often painful. They do not communicate well in words. Some have badly damaged brains. How can they be part of our home-making? How can they come to church at least once a year and sit with us? There are also practical questions about running such places as Shanti Bhavan. The most interesting part of these communities is the interaction of faces without words: so much is shared by looks, glances, frequent smiles, and laughter. Touching is more basic in this community:

dressing, feeding, caring, bathing, and playing. We need to learn to be gentle as well as firm, in touching the handicapped. The screams of some of them in pain awaken much pain in me. I am reminded of a prayer by St Paul. 'I kneel in prayer … that through faith, Christ may dwell in your hearts in love. With deep roots and firm foundations may you, in company with all God's people, be strong to grasp what is the breadth and height and depth of Christ's love, and to know it, though it is beyond knowledge' (Ephesians 3:14, 17-19).

III. Theme: A Forgotten Story: Text: John 20

All Saint's Cathedral, Nagpur

The famous Evangelist Dwight Moody was about to begin service during one of his campaigns, when an usher handed him an envelope and disappeared. He opened it assuming it to be a request for prayer but found the word, 'Fool' written on it. He looked at his audience and said, 'This is most unusual. I have been handed a message which consists of one word "Fool". I find this to be most unusual. I have often heard of those who have written letters and forgotten to sign their names, but this is the first time I have ever heard of anyone who signed his name first and forgot to write the letter'. It is not the majority but only the minority who can make an unpleasant situation, pleasant, and an unusual situation, extraordinary.

We are here today on 22nd July, a day which Roman Catholic, Eastern Orthodox, and Anglican traditions consider to be a feast day for Mary Magdalene, a saint. She is also commemorated by the Lutheran Church with a festival on the same day. We in the CNI have set the theme for today as 'Mary Magdalene'. Magdala was a town on the western shore of the Sea of Galilee. Mary Magdalene has been the subject of much debate, an exemplar for discussion, and a social parable. In Luke 8:2, Mary Magdalene is one among others who provided resources for the ministry. It also says that seven demons were cast out of her.

'On the first day of the week, at early dawn, they went to the tomb taking the spices, they had prepared … returning from the tomb they told all these things to the eleven and all the rest. Now it was Mary Magdalene and Joanna and Mary the mother of James and the others with them who told these things to the apostles' (Luke 24:1, 9, 10). John says in chapter

20:1&2 that the first witness to the tomb was Mary Magdalene. She ran and went to Simon Peter and the other disciple, the one whom Jesus loved, and said to them, 'They have taken the Lord out of the tomb and we do not know where they have laid Him'. Mary was the first witness of the resurrected Jesus, and although at first she could not recognise Him, when He called her name she remembered. The woman who sat at the feet of Jesus, brought an alabaster box of ointment, washed His feet with tears, and anointed them with ointment in Luke 7: 36-50 was Mary of Bethany, Martha's sister. Among the women who were looking on the crucifixion were Mary Magdalene and Mary mother of James (Mark 15: 40-41). It may not sound startling to us in the 21st century but to say that women were the first witnesses to the resurrection of Jesus, is itself revolutionary. How can we also believe that Mary came from Magdala, a thriving centre of the fishing industry?

Where do we begin our story today? A 19th century woman in 1858, a daughter of a Brahmin priest, saw her father growing old, blind, and die of starvation, followed by her mother and her older sister. She and her brother left and then her brother died. Eventually she got married but 19 months later her husband died, leaving her with one daughter. She went to the UK in 1883 at the age of 25, then to the USA where she formed an association. After five years, she came back to India and started a mission for widows, helped them during the famine of 1896, and translated the Bible into Marathi. She was Pandita Ramabai, founder of the Mukti Mission in Pune, which is still active today, providing housing, education, vocational training, etc. for many needy groups including widows, orphans, and the blind

Let us come to the 20th century. A 19-year-old girl from Kolkata with courage and a spirit of adventure crossed a distance of 42 miles in water in 16 hrs and 20 minutes on 29th September 1959, famously becoming the first Asian woman to swim across the English Channel. It was an eye-opener for the rest of the world who until then believed that Indian women rarely ventured outside their kitchen garden. She was Arati Saha (1940 – 1994). In 1960, she became the first Indian sportswoman to be awarded the Padma Shri, the fourth highest civilian honour in India. Born in Calcutta, West Bengal, British India, Arati was initiated into swimming at the early age of four, and her talent was spotted by Sachin Nag. She was inspired by the Indian swimmer Mihir Sen to attempt to cross the English Channel.

Mary Magdalene, chosen by the Lord to be the first witness of the resurrection can easily be missed. According to Josephus, a 1st century Jewish historian, a credible witness must be someone with a good past life, not a slave, and not a woman. Yet, the Saviour not only first appears to Mary, but also to several other women who likewise had come to care for the Lord's body (Matthew 28:8-10). In a world where women were looked down upon and not valued, this powerful story teaches us that Christ does not see us for our worldly credibility, status, race, or gender, but instead sees our level of faith and devotion to Him. In the darkest of moments, these women had stayed by Jesus' side, supporting Him, caring for Him, even burying Him. Now they are the first to have seen His light. All of us have dark moments in our lives when we feel sorrow and despair. Like Mary who went to the tomb on a Sunday morning expecting to see the dead body of the Lord, we too may feel that all hope is lost. Yet on that Easter morning, Mary found the living resurrected Messiah! He came to her just as the Saviour comes to those who seek Him. In those dark moments when all seems lost, and our eyes are filled with tears, we too can hear our name, called by the Good Shepherd who knows us like no other. He brings light and joy to overcome even the darkest of days. Like Mary, we too can be witnesses of the living resurrected Messiah. Like Mary, we too can tell all who will hear of the glorious news of the Gospel. He has risen. Jesus Christ is raised from the dead! Come and see.

IV. Theme: The Call of Wisdom:Text: Proverbs 8:35

Whoever finds me finds life, and receives favour from the Lord'

English Baptist Church, CNI, Cuttack

The Proverbs usually convey truisms (self-evident truth). Yet, with a little imagination, they lend themselves quite easily to witty sayings. A legacy of my English teacher in school was the encouragement to be creative with axioms. They have created ripples of amusement in various get-togethers. Maxims such as 'Marriages are made in heaven but unmade on earth'; 'No man can serve two masters unless both are generous paymasters'; 'Dead people tell no tales, only their biographers do', and more. Greek wisdom was concerned with speculation and cosmogony. Hebrew wisdom was interested in the revealed will of God and the observable order that God placed in the universe. Proverbs in the Bible conveys a wide range of meanings including the idea of comparison, a code of behaviour, and the discovery of hidden truth. Israel has a long tradition of pre-Solomonic sages (1 Kings 4:30); wise men—a class of experts—who were on par with the priests and the prophets in the pre-exilic period (Jeremiah 18:18).

Life sometimes teaches us hard lessons although they are good learnings. I came across the following story in a newspaper. A wife says to her husband, 'You seem to have completely lost your balance of mind after retirement. Nothing interests you except newspapers and books. This year is our first in our own house after retirement and I had planned a grand celebration for the festival. Please go to market and buy some necessities'. The husband replies, 'All these years, the celebrations were organised by others. People would start coming home with gifts but today it is already 2 pm and nobody has come to wish us'. Depressed with this change of fortune, he reaches for the spirituality column in the newspaper and reads this:

'A donkey was carrying idols of the gods on his back for an important annual religious *puja*. When he passed through the villages, villagers bowed down to the idols but the donkey thought that they were bowing to him and was thrilled with this new-found respect. After depositing the idols, his master loaded vegetables on him and they began their return journey. This time nobody paid any attention to the donkey. The donkey started braying to invite the attention of the villagers, but they became irritated with the non-stop noise and started beating the donkey'. All of a sudden, the husband is enlightened. He realises that all the gifts and respect he has received were not meant for him but for his position.

The Christological interpretation of Proverbs chapter 8 has existed for centuries (1 Corinthians 8:6; Colossians 1:15-18; Hebrew 1:1). 1 Corinthians 1:24 specifically says that 'Christ is the power of God and the wisdom of God'. 'The Lord possessed me at the beginning of his work, the first of his acts of old. Ages ago, I was set up, at the first, before the beginning of the earth' (Proverbs 8:22-23). The issue was raised by Arius in the 4th century

AD and discussed with a resolution in the Council of Nicaea in 325 AD. For God's people, it is the plea, the place, the purpose, and the possibility of wisdom. Wisdom is also separating the myth from reality. The saying goes that the 'Ostrich is a peculiar bird, which when faced with danger, buries its head in the ground'. This notion is so prevalent, that these large birds have become synonymous with people who refuse to face their problems head-on. However, today, the belief that ostriches stick their heads in the sand has been proven to be a myth. The first thing to consider is that ostriches have small heads relative to the size of their body. So, when they bring their heads close to the ground to nibble at the grass, they may look like they are disappearing entirely. Also, ostriches don't build nests for their eggs. Instead, they dig holes in the sand to keep their eggs. While the eggs are incubating, both male and female ostriches will take turns using their beaks to rotate them, thus possibly creating the illusion that they are burying their heads in the sand. Now we know that ostriches are far more sensible than we've given them credit for. When they do sense danger, their first response is to remove themselves from the situation at a quick clip. An ostrich can sprint at up to 70 kilometres an hour on their long, powerful legs. Instead of using their wings for flight, they are used as 'air rudders', which help them run – allowing them to zigzag, brake, and turn quickly as they sprint away

The secret to success in life is found in our choices; the choices that we make in life. However, the path to success is to trust in the Lord. The basic assumption in Proverbs is the providence of God. God is at the centre of life. The words of Jesus provide the richest mine of profoundly spiritual proverbs. 'Everyone then who hears these words of mine and does them will be like a wise man who built his house on the rock' (Matthew 7:24). It is both hearing and doing the words of Jesus. When you do, you are like the person who builds on a firm foundation and are not easily moved. The wise man is one who benefits from doing the right thing with knowledge. 'The Son of Man came eating and drinking, and they say, "Here is a glutton and a drunkard, a friend of tax collectors and sinners." But wisdom is proved right by her actions' (Matthew 11:19).

V. Theme: Galilean Breakfast:Text: John 21:9-14

St George's Cathedral, CSI, Chennai & Church of God, Cuttack

The story begins with the Sunday worship at St George's Cathedral in Chennai with the bishop of the diocese. There was a full crowd and different arrangements had been made on the campus. After the preaching, the bishop invited everyone to have a 'Galilean Breakfast'. It was a lovely scene as we were served fish fry and bread. I have never forgotten the lovely worship in the Cathedral followed by the fellowship on the campus with the people. John narrates in chapter 21 that when the disciples reached land, they saw a charcoal fire with fish laid out on it and bread. Jesus said to them, 'Bring some of the fish that you have just caught' ... Jesus took the bread and gave it to them and so with the fish. This was now the third time that Jesus revealed Himself to the disciples after He was raised from the dead.

Looking at the story of the resurrection, I was reminded of an incident from 2010. The 2010 Copiapó mining accident, also known as the Chilean mining accident, began on Thursday, 5th August 2010, with a cave-in at the San José copper-gold mine, located in the Atacama Desert 45 kilometres north of the regional capital of Copiapó, in northern Chile. The accident trapped 33 men 700 meters (2,300 ft) underground. The miners were trapped approximately 5 kilometres from the mine entrance. They survived for a record 69 days. All were eventually rescued on 13th October 2010 over a period of almost 24 hours. After the last miner was winched to the surface, the rescue workers still underground held up a sign before the camera stating 'Mission accomplished Chile' to the estimated more than 1 billion people watching the rescue on live television around the world. After all 33 miners were rescued, almost all were in good medical condition, and expected to recover fully. Two miners had silicosis, one of whom also had pneumonia, and others had a dental infection and corneal problems. One of the survivors testified, 'I was with God and with the devil - and God took me'. No one in recorded history has survived so long trapped underground.

The story of resurrection is not fiction but a reality. In gospel narratives, all four gospels mention women going to the tomb of Jesus, but only Mark mentions the three that this tradition interprets as bearing the name Mary: Mary Magdalene, Mary the mother of James, and Mary Salome (16:1) whereas Matthew says that Mary Magdalene and 'the other Mary' went to see the tomb (28:1). Luke speaks of Mary Magdalene, Joanna, Mary the mother of James, and adds 'the other women' (24:10). John mentions only Mary Magdalene (20:1), but has her use the plural, saying: 'We do not know where they have laid Him' (v.2).

How do we look at Easter? The conversation. v.10 – They went home. v.1 – Mary went first. v.9 – They did not understand the scripture. v.13 – Somebody has taken. v.15 – if you have taken.v.16 – v.22 – Receive the Holy Spirit, v.19 – We are now reading the story backwards like a rear mirror. John 21: 7 'Therefore that disciple whom Jesus loved said to Peter, "It is the Lord"'. v.12 – Jesus said to them come and have breakfast. v.13 Jesus took the bread and gave it to them, and so with the fish. The Galilean breakfast ends with a mandate to Simon Peter, 'Simon, son of John, do you love me more than these?' (21:15). The commission after breakfast is 'You follow me' and do not worry 'if it is my will that he remains until I come, what is that to you' (v.22).

On 27th May 2010, the Former Chief Justice of India M N Venkatachaliah stated that we were entering a time that would leave no mark of resemblance with the present. Twenty-five years from now we would not know what the present was like. We were entering the most confusing time of our life. Chetan Bhagat in *One Night @ The Call Centre* sarcastically notes that a dynamic young, skilled, articulate professional works through the night under US time, pretending to be familiar with a climate and a culture that he has never experienced. He enjoys a unique lifestyle: a cocktail of premature affluence and westernisation that has been transplanted to an Indian setting. The instructor teaches the call centre trainees the formula 10=35 i.e. a 35-year-old American's brain and IQ is the same as a 10-year-old Indian's.

The story of breakfast in John 21 is a story of the shaping of the mind of the disciples. It should be read along with the story of the feeding of the 5000 where Jesus told His disciples, 'You give them something to eat'. How do we follow Jesus today? How do we recognise Him on the way to Emmaus? The story of Jacob wrestling in prayer (Genesis 32:30) and seeing God 'face to face' (33:10). Ezekiel 47 refers to water flowing from the temple. Joel 3:18 says a fountain shall come forth from the house of the Lord. Revelation 22 talks about the river of life. A river that makes glad the city of God, trees on the river bank bring forth fruit and its leaf is a medicine for healing. To recognise Jesus is to perceive the reality in our own context here and now.

A Rabbi once asked his students: 'How do we know when the night has ended and the day has begun?' The students thought they had grasped the importance of the question. After all, there are prayers, rites, and rituals that can only be performed at night and others that belong only to the day. So, it is important to know when night has ended and the day has begun. The first and brightest of the students offered an answer: 'Rabbi, when I look out at the fields and I can distinguish between my field and the field of my neighbour, that's when the night has ended and the day has begun'. A second student offered his answer: 'Rabbi, when I look from the fields and I see a house, and I can tell that it's my house and not the house of my neighbour, that's when the night has ended and the day has begun'. A third student offered another answer: 'Rabbi when I see an animal in the distance, and I can tell what kind of animal it is, whether a cow or a horse or a sheep, that's when the night has ended and the day has begun'. Then a fourth student offered yet another answer: 'Rabbi, when I see a flower and I can make out the colours of the flower, whether they are red or yellow or blue, that's when night has ended and the day has begun'.

However, the Rabbi retorted, 'No! None of you understands! You only divide! You divide your house from the house of your neighbour, your field from your neighbour's field, you distinguish one kind of animal from another, you separate one colour from all the others. Is that all we can do – dividing, separating, splitting the world into pieces? Isn't the world broken enough? Isn't the world split into enough fragments? Is that what Torah is for? No, my dear students, it's not that way, not that way at all'. The shocked students looked into the sad face of their Rabbi. 'Then, Rabbi, tell us: How do we know that night has ended and the day has begun?' The Rabbi stared back into the faces of his students, and with a voice suddenly gentle and imploring, he responded: 'When you look into the face of the person who is beside you, and you can see that person is your brother or your sister, then finally the night has ended and the day has begun'.

Every day is Resurrection Day for a follower of Christ. Every day we should celebrate the fact of the resurrected Saviour. We must be challenged to rise above apathy and mediocrity and soar to greater heights. When the disciples met the resurrected Jesus, as far as the world was concerned, nothing had changed. Tiberius was still the emperor in Rome. Pontius Pilate was still the governor of Judea. The Sadducees and the Pharisees were still fighting among themselves. Jerusalem was still Jerusalem. As far as the world knew, nothing had changed, everything was exactly the same. Yet the resurrection of Jesus made a difference. It made a difference in the lives of the disciples of Jesus. The men and women who followed the resurrected Christ were never the same again. To them every morning was an Easter sunrise! Thus, Paul could write, 'Thanks be to God who gives us the victory through Jesus Christ, our Lord'. Looking at the early church one notices that it had a spirit of excitement and joy in serving the Lord and advancing the Kingdom of God throughout the world. The Holy Spirit used them and sent them throughout the known world spreading the gospel. They were ready and willing to serve anywhere and go to any area the Lord chose to send them. 'So when they had finished breakfast, Jesus said to Simon Peter, "Simon, son of John, do you love Me more than these?" He said to Him, "Yes, Lord; You know that I love You". He said to him, "Tend My lambs"' (v.15).

VI. Theme: A Wedding Homily Text: Genesis 18: 1-15, I John 5:1-12, Matthew 3:13-17

St Mark's Cathedral, Bangalore

On three occasions within our extended family, I was invited to share a homily during the marriage ceremony. These were nephews and nieces who were born and brought up before our eyes. The first one was Ritu (Namrata) and Deepak on 24th May 2013 at St Mark's Cathedral, Bangalore. Usually, a fairy tale ends with the phrase 'they lived happily ever after'. This may be because fairy tales regard marriage as the 'climax'. On the other hand, 'Our faith sees the wedding day, not as the place of arrival but where the adventure really begins' (Archbishop Dr Robert Runcie). The poet Edwin Muir says 'where each one asks from each, what each most wants to give'. 'Love is patient and kind; love does not envy or boast, it is not arrogant or rude. It does not insist on its own way; it is not irritable nor resentful. It does not rejoice at wrongdoings but rejoices with the truth. Love bears all things, believes all things, hopes all things, endures all things' (1 Corinthians 13:4-7). Jesus was invited to a wedding at Cana in Galilee where Mary, the mother of Jesus was also present. Mary could have told herself it was none of her business whether the host had enough wine or not. But Mary had a heart of concern that led to Jesus' first miracle in His ministry and the only one recorded in the Gospel according to John.

There have been defining moments in life – first day of school, first job, and other defining moments. But today is the beginning of a day for both of you together. One thing you must know, in the words of Psalmist, 'you are crowned with glory and honour'. Many people in a relationship try to change the 'other person' without changing themself. It reminds me of a joke. After learning that her husband did not share the same beliefs as she did, a new bride cried to her mother, 'Mum, what should I do? How can I change his thinking? He says he does not believe in hell!' The mother replied, 'Now that you're married to him, the both of us will make him believe in hell'. The point is that you are not called to change the other person, but change yourself and build a relationship through conversation.

Some people assume that men are more intelligent but that is not so. Three men walking along, came upon a river in spate. They needed to get to the other side. One prayed 'God give me the strength to cross the river'. So, God gave him big arms and strong legs to swim. The next man prayed, 'Please God give me the strength and ability to cross the river'. God give him a rowing boat and he was able to cross the river. The third man seeing how it worked out for the other two, also prayed saying, 'Please God give me the strength, ability, and intelligence to cross the river'. This time God turned the man into a woman. The woman took a map from her handbag, found a bridge across the river, and walked to the other side'.

From this day, your relationship with God and with one another within the relationship of two families bonded together needs to be explored and experienced day by day as you walk together. It is possible if we trust only in God. The most appropriate word on the occasion of a wedding is 'love'. And that is certainly apt because it is love that causes two people to commit and give themselves to each other for the rest of their lives. Much can be said to define and describe love. All would agree that the most important element is not so much what is *written* or *said*, but what is *done*. In this sense, we can say that the word love is shown and proven by what we do – not by what we think or say. One of the best descriptions would be to say that if you loved someone, you wished and did for them what you would wish and do for yourself. I do believe that this covers all the important aspects of love. Love causes two people to give themselves completely to each other in marriage. Everything else about marriage flows from this fact. The need for fidelity, permanence, and unity in marriage all flow from this. Yes, it is quite a commitment that two human beings take upon themselves when they give themselves to each other for the rest of their lives. That certainly has to be one of the main reasons why the Church wants us to surround this act of ceremony with our highest form of honour and glory and invoke God's help and blessing. Marriage should be transformative as husband and wife make one another their work of art. It is possible to be transformed as long as we do not harbour ambitions to reform our partner. There must be no coercion if the Spirit is to flow; each must give the other space and freedom. If the reality of God fades from our lives, then there is corresponding inflation of expectations from the other that leads to complications. When we surrender to God in giving ourselves to each other in love, then there is fulfilment and completion. H W Jurgon, a sociologist claims that married couples talk with one another 70 minutes a day in the first year of marriage, this drops to 30 minutes a day in the second year, then only to 15 minutes a day in the 4th, typically hardly share any small talk in the 8th year, and they become nearly silent with one another. Please do not do that.

VII. Theme: A Wedding Homily 'Quick to Listen, Slow to Speak and Slow to Anger':Text: James 1:19

Union Church, Bhubaneswar

The second occasion was the marriage of our nephew Lipu (Saurav) and Simi on 27th December 2019 at Union Church, Bhubaneswar. The story goes that once, during a wedding rehearsal, the groom approached the vicar with an unusual offer. 'Look, I will give you £2000 if you will change the wedding vows. When you get to me and the part where I am to promise "to love, honour and obey", please leave that part out'. On the wedding day, when it came time for the groom's vows, the vicar looked at the young man and said, 'Will you promise to prostrate yourself before her, obey her every command and wish, serve her breakfast in bed every morning, cook the food all your life, and promise that you will not ever even look at another woman as long as you both shall live?' The groom gulped and looked around and said in a tiny voice, 'Yes'. Then he leaned towards the vicar and hissed, 'I thought we had a deal'. The Vicar put £2000 into his hand and whispered back, 'She made me a better offer'.

A wedding can be a spectacular affair. To produce a perfect moment in life, some become nervous. A spectacular wedding does not assure successful marriage. Marriages that will last and make people happy are referred to as marriages that are made in heaven, but which still need to be lived on earth. Therefore, listening is a virtue that is rare nowadays but is a requirement for a successful marriage. James in his letter gives some practical advice: 'Know this, my beloved brothers; let every person be quick to hear, slow to speak, slow to anger' (1:19). Everyone should be quick to listen but slow to speak and anger. How profound is the statement?

Listening is an engagement. The priority in homemaking is listening to God. Both of you together engage in a conversation with God. 'Hear O Israel, the Lord our God, the Lord is one' (Deuteronomy 6:4). The commandments are to be on your hearts, impress them on your children and talk about them. The next priority is listening to parents. The love and care of your parents are of prime importance and are never to be forgotten. The modern tendency, which sometimes varies and is sad to hear, is that after marriage children forget their parents. The joke is that the same boy who until marriage used to ask his mother for advice, in one night after marriage, will say 'I will consult my wife and let you know'. What a dramatic change and a mysterious miracle that happens overnight. It is perfectly human and understandable but that does not mean one should be ungrateful to one's parents. The final priority is listening to each other. You are not called to impose your view upon the other. Marriage is a relationship for life where conversation is very important.

The foundation of a successful life is in family. What is taught in the family is never forgotten. During World War II, countless Jewish parents gave their children to Christian neighbours with the understanding that they or their relatives would take the children back if they survived. In May 1945, Rabbi Eliezer Silver and Dayan Grunfeld from England were sent as Chaplains. They were told that many Jewish children had been placed in a monastery in Alsace-Lorraine. But the Priest said there was no way to know who was Jewish as their names could be Miller—a German name—, or Markovich—a Russian name—, or Swersky—a Polish name. One of the Rabbis had a brilliant idea. He said they would return that evening when the children would be asleep in the dormitory.

In the evening, the Rabbis walked through the aisles reciting the *shema* (hear), the Jewish confession of faith from the book of Deuteronomy that was a daily prayer in ancient Israelite tradition. It's the equivalent of the Lord's prayer in the Christian tradition. *Shema* is an affirmation of Judaism and a declaration of faith in one God. The obligation to recite the *shema* is separate from the obligation to pray and a Jew is taught to say *shema* in the morning and night. 'Hear O Israel, the Lord our God, the Lord is One' (Deuteronomy 6:4). One by one, the Jewish children burst into tears and started reciting it. The Priest had succeeded in teaching the Jewish children how to say Mass and the Lord's Prayer but had not succeeded in erasing these children's memories of their Jewish mothers, now murdered, putting them to bed every night with *shema* on their lips.

To listen is to perceive and not take things for granted. Hearing is an important part of discipleship for our engagement in society. There are competing voices, some are dominant, some are marginalised, and some are silent. We are accustomed to multiple voices in our commercial and corporate world. Normal human error is to take certain things for granted. The story of the consultant from the study of current ecumenical structures and relationships as presented by Jill Hawkey to the WCC Central Committee on 18th February 2005, is very educative. 'In New Zealand, people tell the story of a old high-country farmer, sitting up in the hills with his sheep all around him, when suddenly a helicopter lands close by. A very expensively dressed man jumps out, clutching a state-of-the-art laptop computer. 'Good- day' says the young man to the farmer. 'I'm here to help. If you like, I can tell you exactly how many sheep you have. I will use the latest satellite technology to calculate this and in return, all you have to do is give me one sheep'. 'Alright then' says the bemused farmer. So, the man sets up his computer, types in furiously looking around the hills at the thousands of sheep. After a few minutes, he says, 'Okay. I'll just put my payment in the helicopter and then I'll tell you the findings'. He comes back and says, 'You've got 12,892 sheep'. 'That's amazing' says the farmer. 'Absolutely right. Now, if I tell you what your job is, can I have my sheep back?' 'Okay then', says the man smugly. 'What's my job?' 'You're a consultant', says the farmer. The man looks amazed. 'How do you know that?' 'Easy', says the farmer. 'I didn't ask you to come here, you've told me something I already know, and that's my dog, not a sheep, you've just put in your helicopter!'

VIII. Theme: A Wedding Homily 'What Do You Have That You Did Not Receive? Text:1 Corinthians 4:1-7

Union Church Bhubaneswar

The Third homily was at Union Church, Bhubaneswar on 16th April 2021 at the wedding of our niece, Munki (Magnolia) and Satya. The wedding was special because due to Covid-19, the number of guests both at the wedding and the reception had been limited as per the prescribed guidelines. About 15 years earlier when I entered CMC Vellore Campus for the first time to meet the Director, I was reminded of one verse – 'What do you have that you did not receive? If then you received it, why do you boast as if you did not receive it?' This verse—with its various perspectives—has been a reminder in my journey of faith and it should be in your journey too, Munki and Satya, as you begin together from today. It is a journey that must move toward remembering the grace of God that has sustained you in the past and shall sustain you in the days to come. I, myself recall the journey that my wife and I have completed only yesterday – 46 years together now.

The first question is where will you go? The direction or the goal of life each day must be set by the grace of God. The direction is very important and you both must not deviate from the path. The story goes that Einstein was once travelling from Princeton on a train when the conductor came down the aisle, punching the tickets of every passenger. When he came to Einstein, Einstein reached in his vest pocket. He couldn't find his ticket, so he reached into his trouser pockets. It wasn't there either, so he looked in his briefcase but couldn't find it. Then he looked in the seat beside him. He still couldn't find it. The conductor said, 'Dr Einstein, I know who you are. We all know who you are. I'm sure you bought a ticket. Don't worry about it'. Einstein nodded appreciatively. The conductor continued down the aisle punching tickets. As he was ready to move to the next car, he turned around and saw the great physicist down on his hands and knees looking under his seat for his ticket. The conductor rushed back and said, 'Dr Einstein, Dr Einstein, don't worry, I know who you are. No problem. You don't need a ticket. I'm sure you bought one'. Einstein looked at him and said, 'Young man, I too, know who I am. What I don't know is where I'm going'. Do not forget to begin the day with God as individuals and as a family. Life has become very hectic but carve a little time to be together with God in a day.

We all played the game of hide-and-seek as children, but we tend to play the same game with God and that is unwanted and very dangerous. God knows us, what we think, and what we do. We stand before God as we are and cannot change the role by pretending to be someone else. When Albert Einstein was making the rounds of the speaker's circuit, he usually found himself eagerly longing to get back to his laboratory work. One night as they were driving to yet another rubber-chicken dinner, Einstein mentioned to his chauffeur (a man who somewhat resembled Einstein in looks and manner) that he was tired of speechmaking. 'I have an idea, boss', his chauffeur said. 'I've heard you give this speech so many times. I'll bet I could give it for you'. Einstein laughed loudly and said, 'Why not? Let's do it!' When they arrived at the dinner, Einstein donned the chauffeur's cap and jacket and sat in the back of the room. The chauffeur gave a beautiful rendition of Einstein's speech and even answered a few questions expertly. Then a supremely pompous professor asked an extremely esoteric question about anti-matter formation, digressing here and there to let everyone in the audience know that he was nobody's fool. Without missing a beat, the chauffeur fixed the professor with a steely stare and said, 'Sir, the answer to that question is so simple that I will let my chauffeur, who is sitting in the back, answer it for me'.

The letter of Paul to the Corinthian church is a reminder of their calling to follow Jesus. The text has three questions: a) For who sees anything different in you? b) What do you have that you did not receive? c) If then you received it, why do you boast as if you did not receive it? The Corinthian church was gifted but grace was not in proportion to gifts. Being puffed up in their own minds made their own opinions the most important to them. Paul begins with the pointed question – who sees anything different in you? A question that is normally not asked and even if asked, is usually brushed aside. What is it that makes you special above and beyond anyone else? What qualities do you have that other Christians lack, giving you the right to judge?

Today I will request both of you to just remember the following two questions only:

What do you have that you did not receive? If then you received it, why do you boast as if you did not receive it? These questions will set a parameter for the agenda of your life to be always thankful and grateful, first to God and then to your fellow human beings and creation. How often we do not notice the micro amid the macro that brings joy and happiness in our lives in the midst of crisis and difficulties. The Covid-19 pandemic has altered all our perspectives. We have lost our near and dear ones. People are without food. Our worship pattern has changed. Perhaps now we have begun learning how to pray and worship God after being confined in our own homes for months. The digitisation of teaching and learning and also worship is not the same as we do in person. 'Be still and know that I am God'.

Acknowledge God in all your ways and lean not on your own understanding. An atheist was walking through the woods. 'What majestic trees! What powerful rivers! What beautiful animals!' he said to himself. As he was walking alongside the river, he heard a rustling in the bushes behind him. He turned to look. He saw a 7-foot grizzly bear charge towards him. He ran as fast as he could up the path. He looked over his shoulder and saw that the bear was closing in on him. He looked over his shoulder again, and the bear was even closer. He tripped and fell to the ground. He rolled over to pick himself up but saw that the bear was right on top of him, reaching for him with his left paw and raising his right paw to strike him. At that instant, the atheist cried out, 'Oh my God!' Time stopped. The bear froze. The forest was silent. As a bright light shone upon the man, a voice came out of the sky. 'You deny my existence for all these years, teach others I don't exist, and even credit creation to cosmic accident. Do you expect me to help you out of this predicament? Am I to count you as a believer then?' The atheist looked directly into the light, 'It would be hypocritical of me to suddenly ask you to treat me as a Christian now, but perhaps you could make the bear a Christian?' 'Very well', said the voice. The light went out. The sounds of the forest resumed. And the bear dropped his right paw, brought both paws together, bowed his head and spoke: 'Lord bless this food, which I am about to receive from thy bounty through Christ our Lord. Amen'.

All gifts that we have are only a gift from God including the breath that we take. We need wisdom in discerning the will of God. May God bless you both.

IX. Theme: Generation after Generation: Abraham and Sarah: Text: Deuteronomy 8:1-6

Serampore College Bi-centenary (1818-2018) celebration, 19th October 2018
Regents Park College Chapel Service, Oxford, UK
All Nations Full Gospel Church, Toronto, Canada, 14th October 2018
Spiritual Convention, Simlabari, West Bengal, 22nd November 2019

The story is told about a boy who was just eight years old when a concentration camp was liberated in 1945. He was hiding among the dead bodies when he saw the American soldiers entering the gates of the camp, unsure if they were friend or foe. The Chaplain of the US Third Army, climbed off his jeep to examine the carnage. Suddenly he caught sight of the boy hiding behind. Shocked to see a sign of life there, he picked Lau up and hugged him tightly in a warm embrace, while tears of sadness and joy poured from his eyes. 'How old are you my son', he asked in Yiddish, from behind his tears. 'What difference does it make how old I am?' Lau responded suspiciously. 'Anyway, I am older than you'. 'Why do you think that you are older than I am?' Rabbi Schacter asked, now smiling. 'Because you laugh and cry like a child', Lau replied. 'I have not laughed for longer than I can remember and I cannot even cry anymore. So, which one of us is older?'

The story is an essential part of self-identity. To remember is human and to forget also is human but to be ungrateful is almost inhuman. I entered this College Chapel about 39 years ago as a student. We lived first for three years and later for four years in Oxford. The hospitality and friendliness at Regents is indelibly linked with the nostalgia of the past. I had never dreamt at that point that one day, I would be surrounded by my old friends one of whom is now the Principal and the other the Dean and in the presence of my old teacher Rev Dr Paul S Fiddes. Similarly, my memory also retraces my time at Serampore, of my association of 18 years as well as the privilege of living in Carey House. It is a joy also to have the presence of the Principal of Serampore College and my former student Rev Deepankar Haldar.

The story of God's engagement is recorded in the Old Testament. The story of Abraham and Sarah is an inseparable part of the story of Israel. Abraham has become the archetype of all who accept the call to go out into the unknown. Now we can understand and comprehend how a cobbler called William Carey responded when he heard a call to come to India to preach the gospel to heathens. The same cannot be equated with the modern-day tribe of Non-Resident Indian (NRI) Pastors/Theologians /Ecumenists who also claim to have a call to migrate from India to the comfort zones of our world. The call to serve in India has a tale. Timothy Gorringe in his book *Redeeming Time* states, 'To do theology in India is not to do theology at 120°Fahrenheit as it has been romantically described, but to take part in a struggle between death and life' (Deuteronomy 30:19).

The Deuteronomy account in chapter 8 reminds the people of Israel of their story: 'Remember your Lord'. It has two aspects: 'Do not forget' and 'do remember'. 'Do not forget' is in the heart and 'Do remember' is in action. They encompass every area of life. Every relationship has two components: i) reaching out – doing positive actions, and ii) the element of restraint – holding back from any action that might destroy a relationship.

The story of Abraham and Sarah accrues a different significance when the story of Hagar and Ishmael is included. Here we see God speaking to a woman—a slave girl—for the first time in the Torah. We witness the journey into the wilderness and the command to return and submit to Sarah. Hagar means 'the stranger', which connects with the later commandment to love the stranger as yourself (Leviticus 19:23). She is the only person in Scripture to name God, 'You are El-roi (אל ראי), the God who sees me'. Similarly, Ishmael's name means 'God hears', and it is his destiny as the one who 'shall live at odds with all his kin', who later in Genesis 25:9 appears as a dutiful son to Abraham and his brother Isaac at Abraham's burial.

The story of Hagar and Ishmael is unfortunately used as stereotypes of Islam and hostility between Islam and Israel. There is an explicit New Testament interpretation of the story of Hagar in Galatians 4:21-5:23. 'These women are two covenants. One woman, in fact, is Hagar from Mount Sinai, bearing children for slavery. Now Hagar is Mount Sinai in Arabia and corresponds to present Jerusalem, for she is in slavery with her children. But the other woman corresponds to the Jerusalem above; she is free and she is our mother'.

The story of the Serampore Trio, the Cobbler-Weaver-Printer, despite its humble beginnings, is the grand narrative of the modern protestant mission in India. But there could have been no Serampore mission without Tranquebar and the work of Zeigenbalg. It was the king of Denmark, Frederick the Fourth, who after reading an appeal for help from the widow of a Danish soldier in Tranquebar, decided to send two German missionaries, one of whom was Ziegenbalg. The Serampore College was established in 1818, empowered to grant degrees by the Incorporation of the Royal Charter of the King of Denmark in 1826.

The mere absence of a comma between 'Asiatic' and 'Christian' in the report could have led the British evangelical public to believe that the student body was much more 'Christian' in composition than ever was the case; John C Marshman rectified this 30 years later when he inserted a comma. Christopher Smith makes a very good observation that in reality, the college had two rather different personae by which it appealed to contrasting constituencies. In India, it functioned as an Arts and Science College, while to mission supporters in the western world it was portrayed as a school designated 'to train Indians to replace Europeans completely as missionaries, and so to create a truly indigenous church'.

Today perhaps Serampore story needs to be read along with other emerging stories. One such story is that of Sam Higginbottom. A person who graduates from Princeton University in 1903, commits to go un-ordained to India to do evangelistic work. He becomes a guest of the Principal of a Christian College in Prayagraj (Allahabad) and accompanies him while he attends the Presbyterian Synod in Punjab. But there he is given the order to return to Prayagraj (Allahabad) to teach economics. Seeing the context, he changes his mind but he is told, 'If you think we ought to be teaching scientific, modern farming as a missionary method, why do you not return to America first, study the subject, and see if folks in America back your faith with their money'. He goes back in 1909, reads Agriculture and comes back to start the first Agriculture Institute in India in 1910. Nobody had ever thought at that point, the same Institute could now become the Sam Higginbottom University, offering Theology as a full-fledged Faculty—called Gospel and Plough—along with Faculties of Agriculture, Engineering, Humanities and Sciences.

Sometimes, what we most need, appears only if we have eyes to see. God caused a spring to appear right where Hagar and Ishmael needed it – or perhaps God opened Hagar's eyes to see the spring which was already there. When we place ourselves in Hagar's shoes, this becomes a story about miracles and gratitude. In the changed and changing scenario of India today, in remembering past stories, there is a need to charter a new path. The basis of that remembrance could be in the words of St Paul – 'what do you have that you did not receive? If then you received it, why do you boast as if you did not receive it?' (I Corinthians 4:7). Remembering their stories, we need to venture into the unknown, knowing that God is there. We have a collective responsibility to account for before future generations; to value the precious legacies we have inherited for their benefit. Expect great things from God. Attempt great things for God.

X. THEME: 'SEARCH ME O GOD AND KNOW MY HEART': TEXT: PSALM 139

English Baptist Church, CNI, Cuttack

Yeshu Darbar, & University Chapel, SHUATS

Perhaps no other game is as well known among children of every generation as the game called 'Hide and Seek'. The person seeking must find the others who have hidden themselves in which case the searcher wins or they win if they are not found. As we grow older, we continue to play hide and seek with each other and also with God. Then it is not a game any longer but our lives depend on the outcome. 'Humans have a tendency to hide unless they are caught'.

Psalm 139 is a beautiful piece of poetry. The Psalmist comes to God with absolute openness and honesty. The words of the Psalmist should also become our prayer today, expressing words and thoughts to God that are truly our own. The Psalmist says to God, 'You are a hiding place for me' (32:7). The human tendency is to run away from God. Rabbi Mendel Futerfas was an outstanding hero who survived Stalin's Gulag, a network of forced labour camps by order of Vladimir Lenin that reached its peak during Joseph Stalin's rule from the 1930s to the early 1950s. English-language speakers also use the word *gulag* to refer to all forced-labour camps that existed in the Soviet Union, including camps that existed in the post-Lenin era. He was able to leave Russia and reunite with his wife and children in London. One activity prohibited in the Gulag was playing cards. Inmates managed to smuggle cards in which the guards could not catch despite surprise inspections. Eventually, the Rabbi was told the secret. As soon as the guards entered, the inmates, who were professional pickpockets, would slip the cards into their pockets. But before they left, they would slip them back out.

Perhaps the most interesting testimony is by Corrie Ten Boom in her book *The Hiding Place*. Cornelia Arnolda Johanna 'Corrie' Ten Boom (15 April 1892 – 15 April 1983) was a Dutch Christian watchmaker and later a writer who worked with her father, Casper Ten Boom, her sister Betsie, and other family members to help many Jews escape from the Nazis during the Holocaust in World War II by hiding them in her home. One room of their home became a hiding place for Jews and the Dutch underground church. She believed her actions were following the will of God. They were eventually caught, and she was arrested and sent to the Ravensbrück concentration camp. Her most famous book, *The Hiding Place*, is a biography that recounts the story of her family's efforts and how she found and shared hope in God while she was imprisoned at the concentration camp. After she was freed, she began a worldwide ministry, which took her to 60 countries in the next 33 years and testified to God being her hiding place.

Years after she had left the concentration camp, Corrie went back to visit Ravensbrück and found something amazing: 'Corrie learned that her own release had been part of a clerical error; one week later all women her age were taken to the gas chamber'.

Isaiah 45:15 says that 'Truly, you are a God who hides, O God and Saviour of Israel'. God is not a hidden God but He is a God who unveils the meaning and purpose in our lives that goes beyond our understanding. Psalm 139 falls into four parts: vs. 1-6 Omniscience: 'You know when I sit down and when I rise up; You search out my path and my lying down. Even before a word is on my tongue, behold, O Lord, you know it altogether. Such knowledge is too wonderful for me; it is high; I cannot attain it'. vs. 7-12 Omnipresence: 'Where shall I go from your Spirit? If I ascend to heaven, you are there. If I make my bed in Sheol, you are there! If I dwell in uttermost parts of sea, even there your hand shall lead me and your right hand shall hold me. Even the darkness is not dark to you, the night is bright as the day'. vs. 13-18 Omnipotence: 'I am wonderfully made, you knitted me together in my mother's womb, your eyes saw my unformed substance, how precious to me your thoughts, If I would count them, they are more than sand'. vs. 19-24 Inescapable response: 'Do I not hate those who hate you? Do I not loathe those who rise up against you?'

A mirror reflection sometimes brings back memories. In Marianne Wiggins' *Almost Heaven,* the central character is Melanie John, a middle-aged woman in the psychiatric unit of a medical college who is suffering from hysterical amnesia – partial memory loss resulting from shock and psychological disturbance – brain injury. She was with her husband and four children in a car when she got out to recover a paper that had flown out of the window. That was when she saw a vehicle slam into the rear of her car with her family. The car explodes and her husband and four children are killed instantly. The last 20 years of her life are erased from her memory. She remembers the days 20 years before – her graduation, law school but not after that. Without the stories of the intervening 20 years, she has no way of knowing, no meaning of the present, no meaning of the future. The story is a journey to recovering memories, the pain of loss, and regaining a sense of self-identity.

The parable of the lost sheep, the lost coin, and even the story of the Garden of Eden' are all about God seeking humans. Humans have a tendency to hide unless caught. But the human story of hiding is a serious game when the player knows what he is doing. There is a story about an economist who would take money from his left-hand pocket and transfer it to his right-hand pocket. Then he would take the money from his right-hand pocket and put it in the left-hand pocket. In an attempt to make both pockets feel as though they were full, at least momentarily. Someone pointed out that he was really playing a zero-sum game in that the total amount remained the same. 'I know that', replied the economist. 'But my right pocket and my left pocket don't'. People are out to destroy other people because they cannot accept themselves for who they are. Often, we wish to be smarter, stronger, faster, better, or have a different career which is tied to our identity. With maturity, we grow to accept ourselves. Society continues to put tremendous pressure on our youth to be someone besides ourselves, tempting us to put on a mask.

The contrast between God's way of doing things and our way is never more accurate than in the area of human change and transformation. The story of Jonah is not only interesting but depicts human character – God told him to go to Nineveh and tell people to repent. What did Jonah do? He ran from God and tried to hide. Jacob came to a place where he had just one lousy stone for a pillow (Genesis 28:11). The sun had set. The old bag of tricks with his elder brother were useless. Yet, well before daylight, Jacob is wide awake declaring, 'This is an awesome place, the house of God and the gate of heaven' (v.17). Jacob's face to face encounter with God at Peniel taught him to hide in God. The Psalmist in 32:7 says 'Lord, you are my hiding place. You will protect me from trouble'. Life is full of challenges, failures, successes, and tragedies. Having a relationship with God does not make us immune to suffering. The hymn puts it in context: 'Rock of Ages, cleft for me, let me hide myself in thee'. To hide in God – the place and circumstances where He keeps us safe in Him may not be comfortable by human standards. Whether pleasant or painful, it fits His plan for growth.

We live in a paradox of our time. Wider freeways – narrower viewpoints. Spend more – have less. Buy more – enjoy less. Bigger houses – smaller families. More conveniences – less time. More degrees – less sense. More knowledge – less judgement. More medicine – less wellness. Stay too late – get up too tired. Read too little – Watch more. Multiplied possessions – reduced values. Travel all the way abroad to have holidays – do not cross the street to meet a neighbour.

But we also have good stories. Let me end with some lines from the well-known poem *Footprints in the Sand* by Margaret Stevenson:

Lord, you said once I decided to follow you,
You'd walk with me all the way.
But I noticed that during the saddest and
most troublesome times of my life,
there was only one set of footprints.

I don't understand why, when I needed You the most, You would leave me.

He whispered, "My precious child, I love you and will never leave you
Never, ever, during your trials and testings.
When you saw only one set of footprints,
It was then that I carried you".

XI. Theme: Telling the Truth and Living the Truthtext: Isaiah 54:2

New Road Baptist Church, Oxford, UK, 21st October 2018

'Enlarge the place of your tent and let the curtains of your habitations be stretched out; hold not back, lengthen your cords and strengthen your stakes'. (Isaiah 54:2)

A story is told about Menno Simons, one of the founders of the Mennonite tradition. He was often pursued by the authorities who wanted to try him for heresy and burn him. Once he was travelling by a coach on the roof because all the seats inside had already been taken. It was halted by armed men on horseback. 'Is Menno Simons in there?' They shouted. Menno looked inside and asked, 'Is Menno Simons in there?' The passengers said no. So he turned to the armed men and said, 'They say he is not there'. The armed men rode off and Menno Simons survived. The Mennonite Confession of Faith today reads that 'We commit ourselves to tell the truth, to give a simple "yes" or "no"'. The issue is complex and it will be an oversimplification to debate in what circumstances we would be allowed to tell a lie. Nevertheless, we are expected to be 'truthful persons – living the truth' so that we may be capable of telling the truth. In other words, truth-telling should be a way of life.

Today we commit to memory the story of the Serampore Trio: William Carey, Joshua Marshman, and William Ward in order to indwell the story of telling the truth and living the truth. It was an integral part of the life and witness of Serampore missionaries in their own context. A memory of the Serampore Trio is worth narrating. A desolating disaster occurred on 25th March 1812. It was the Serampore fire. 'The immense printing office, two hundred feet long and fifty broad, reduced to a mere shell. Sanskrit dictionary, two grammar books, ten translations of Bible, type sets for printing in 14 different languages. The loss was immense. Carey walked over to the smoking ruins. The tears stood in his eyes. "In one short evening", said he, "the labours of years are consumed. How unsearchable are the ways of God! I had lately brought some things to the utmost perfection of which they seemed capable, and contemplated missionary establishment with perhaps too much self-congratulation. The Lord has laid me low, that I may look more simply to Him"' (Life of William Carey: Shoemaker and Missionary by George Smith, 1909).

Carey had grossly underestimated what it would cost him to come to India. Carey's early years were miserable. 'I am in a strange land. No Christian friend, a large family, and nothing to supply their wants. But he also retained hope: "Well, I have a God and His word is sure"'. In October 1799, things finally turned when he was invited to relocate to Serampore, a Danish settlement, near Calcutta. He came under the protection of Danes, who permitted him to preach legally. By the time Carey died, he had spent 40 years in India and his mission could count only 700 converts in a nation of millions. According to our modern-day church growth theory, his mission was a total failure but today we are gathered in New Road Baptist Church to celebrate that failure which has laid an impressive foundation of Bible translation, education, and social reform.

She was a 14-year-old student when she was asked, 'What will you do when you get out of here?' 'I know one thing I will not do', she told her friends emphatically, 'I will not be a missionary in India like my parents'. Later she received a cable saying, 'Come immediately, your mother is ill and needs you'. So, Ida came to India for a short visit. One day, there was a knock on the door. A young Indian stood there, tall, grave, and dignified. 'I desperately need your help. My wife is dying in childbirth'. 'It is my father you want', she replied. 'No, I cannot take a man'. The same scene was repeated two more times that evening. In the morning she sent a servant to find out what had happened and learnt that all three young women had died. Troubled but resolute, she wrote a letter to her friend saying she was returning to America to study to be a doctor. In 1899 she graduated and after raising funds to build a hospital, she returned to India and began with a small clinic where she treated women. She was Ida Scudder the founder of Christian Medical College (CMC) Vellore. Now CMC Vellore is celebrating 100 years of medical education in India. 9000 outpatients knock on the doors of CMC every day. One new campus is already functioning 20 kilometres away and the second one is expected to begin in 2020. How unsearchable are the ways of God?

A commitment to living the truth requires taking risks. Some would say avoid risks but 'Not to take a risk when it is time to take a risk is the biggest risk of all'. What prevents us from making a decision is the fear of change. Fear of change implies a loss of control and power that results in resistance to change. For William Carey, the directive to broaden, to stretch, and to reach beyond based on Isaiah 54:2 was clear, and this expansive vision of the gospel ended with the motto 'expect great things from God and attempt great things for God'. Truth is an integral part of listening and rooted in innocence but not in ignorance. People are searching for answers to complex questions in a rapidly changing world. To tell the truth, may be easy but living the truth calls for a change of heart and mind. Living the truth means to follow the footprints of Jesus of Nazareth with non-negotiable values. What prevents us from enlarging the place of our tent is the fear of change. But a call to enlarge the vision is always overwhelming. Crossing boundaries needs us to step out in faith.

It is important to note that the community which Jesus calls and sends is a community of those who have burned their boats, who are on the road, who face the possibility of suffering. This community is constituted by the command to follow (Mark 1:7) in a hard and narrow way which involves the denial of security. It is summed up in the words of Jesus: 'If any man would come after me, let him deny himself and take up his cross and follow me' (Mark 8:34). Nicholas Thomas Wright writes, 'When Jesus Himself wanted to explain to His disciples what His forthcoming death was all about, He did not give them a theory – He gave them a meal with a story about His own life. The night He was betrayed He took the bread and gave it to His disciples saying, "This is My body broken for you"'.

We are called to deny ourselves, take up our cross and follow Him. When we do that, He will lead us to a place of peace and contentment in any circumstance. The Lord can show us what we need to see by His Spirit, who will provide the understanding of who He is and how we can use our personal, spiritual, and physical gifts to more effectively serve others. Being a true servant is seeing people as opportunities for a relationship. Being able to see them through the eyes of Christ fills us with a sense of His presence within the depths of our hearts. 'Let each of you look not only to his own interests but also to the interests of others. Have this mind among yourselves, which is yours in Christ Jesus, who, though He was in the form of God, did not count equality with God a thing to be grasped, but emptied Himself, by taking the form of a servant, being born in the likeness of men. And being found in human form, He humbled Himself by becoming obedient to the point of death, even death on a cross' (Philippians 2:4-8).

XII. Theme: What Do You Have That You Did No Receive? Text: 1st Corinthians 4:1-7

Sunday Service, 18th March 2018, CMC Vellore Auditorium

Our association with CMC varies from the time to time. In some cases, from student days to faculty, whether inside or outside, as patients, well-wishers, staff and students, there is an emotional attachment. According to Jewish tradition, two rabbis once debated the question 'How do you know when the night ends and the day begins?' The first rabbi said the night ends and a new day begins when you can tell the difference between a blue thread and purple thread. The second rabbi said, 'The night ends and a new day begins when you can see the face of your brothers/sisters'. This is the hope of a new dawn.

The Corinthian church was gifted but grace was not in proportion to gifts. Being puffed up in their own minds made their own opinions the most important to them. Paul begins with the pointed question – who sees anything different in you? A question that is normally not asked and even if asked, is usually brushed aside. What is it that makes you special above and beyond anyone else? What qualities do you have that other Christians lack, giving you the right to judge? The text has three primary questions: a) For who sees anything different in you? b) What do you have that you did not receive? c) If then you received it, why do you boast as if you did not receive it?

Reading the signs of our times is very important in our journey of faith. The wrong reading may end in disaster. A story goes that some missionaries established a very big hospital and put up a board in front of it. On the left side they drew pictures of sick people and on the right side pictures of people who were healthy and smiling. The idea was to convey that sick people enter the hospital, but in the end, they leave it healthy and happy. Unfortunately, scripts in Northern Africa and the Middle East are read from right to left. Therefore, the locals interpreted the board to mean that healthy and happy people entered the hospital but left being sick. Why would anyone go to the hospital then?

To search for a heart of wisdom is the search for discernment. It requires taking a step of faith. 'Elijah climbed to the top of Carmel, bent down to the ground and put his face between his knees. "Go and look toward the sea", he told his servant. And he went up and looked. "There is nothing there", he said. Seven times Elijah said, "Go back". The seventh time the servant reported, "A cloud as small as a man's hand is rising from the sea"' (1st Kings 18:41-44). The Psalmist in Psalm 90:1-12 reminds us 'To count our days', Abraham left Ur in Mesopotamia, because God called him to found a new nation. He obeyed the commands of God unquestioningly, from whom he received repeated promises and a covenant that his 'seed' would inherit the land. At Hebron, Abraham purchased the Cave of Machpelah as a burial place for his wife, Sarah, from Ephron the Hittite (Genesis 23). According to the final chapter of the Book of Deuteronomy, Moses, who led the people of Israel out of Egypt and wandered in the wilderness for 40 years, ascended on Mount Nebo to view the land of Canaan, which God had said he would not enter. Moses died in Moab. He was granted only a distant vision of land and was not allowed to enter the promised land.

During World War II, countless Jewish parents gave their children to Christian neighbours with the understanding that they or their relatives would take the children back if they survived. In May 1945, Rabbi Eliezer Silver and Dayan Grunfeld from England were sent as Chaplains. They were told that many Jewish children had been placed in a monastery in Alsace-Lorraine. But the Priest said there was no way to know who was Jewish as their names could be Miller—a German name—, or Markovich—a Russian name—, or Swersky—a Polish name. One of the Rabbis had a brilliant idea. He said they would return that evening when the children would be asleep in the dormitory.

In the evening, the Rabbis walked through the aisles reciting the *shema* (hear), the Jewish confession of faith from the book of Deuteronomy that was a daily prayer in ancient Israelite tradition. It's the equivalent of the Lord's prayer in the Christian tradition. *Shema* is an affirmation of Judaism and a declaration of faith in one God. The obligation to recite the *shema* is separate from the obligation to pray and a Jew is taught to say *shema* in the morning and night. 'Hear O Israel, the Lord our God, the Lord is One' (Deuteronomy 6:4). One by one, the Jewish children burst into tears and started reciting it. The Priest had succeeded in teaching the Jewish children how to say Mass and the Lord's Prayer but had not succeeded in erasing these children's memories of their Jewish mothers, now murdered, putting them to bed every night with *shema* on their lips.

What good is a dream unless executed? What good are thoughts unless used to benefit others? What good is happiness unless shared? What other nation is so great as to have their gods near them, the way the Lord our God is near to us whenever we pray to Him? And what other nation is so great as to have such righteous decrees and laws as this body of laws I am setting before you today? (Deuteronomy 4:7-8). An artist was once asked to paint a picture of a dying church. To the astonishment of many, instead of painting an old run-down building, he painted a fancy, rich-looking church building with the best of everything inside: carpet, padded pews, stained glass windows, and a grand piano. But outside the church, a box sat on the table, covered with cobwebs, which had the inscription: 'Offering for mission'.

I was listening to the 'Chai 3:16' story on 14th January 2018 in the Cathedral of Redemption, New Delhi by Benny Prasad. Chai is pronounced *Hai* and stands for 'Life' in Hebrew and 3:16 refers to John 3:16, the most popular Bible verse that speaks about 'eternal life'. There are 808 million young people below the age of 35 in India. Sadly, Bengaluru, where Chai 3:16 is located, has been called the suicide capital of India for quite some time. One of the main reasons is because of educational and parental pressures. Most of the time the value of the child in our culture is based on their academic report, hence these days a lot of them are unable to meet their families' expectations, resulting in suicidal tendencies. We hardly have any counselling centres but every corner has a tuition centre. This shows that education is valued more than life itself. Chai 3:16 is a non-commercial 400-seater cafe, where chai is served and the price of chai is decided by the students from different parts of society from the all over world. As we listen to the problems of students, we should spend 80% time listening and 20% time talking. Our role is to value them and love them.

The story below emphasises the importance of what we say and what we do. A local businessman opened a bar. A group of Christians from a local church were concerned and planned an all-night prayer meeting to ask God to intervene. It so happened that lightning struck the bar and it burned to the ground. The owner of the bar sued the church claiming that the prayer of the congregation was responsible for the fire but the church hired a lawyer to argue in the court that they were not responsible. The presiding judge, after his initial review of the case, stated that: 'No matter how the fire started, one thing is clear. The bar owner believed in the power of prayer but the Christians did not'.

XIII. Theme: In Season And Out Of Season Text: Psalm 121, John 17: 6-19, 2 Timothy 4:1-8

Gospel and Plough Institute of Theology, Valedictory Service, 16th May 2019

This sermon was preached during the valedictory service in 2019, but I never thought that it would be my final sermon at GPIT because in the following years, due to Covid-19, there was no valedictory service and also

I resigned in 2021 from my service. In 1936, Kenneth Latourette wrote a book entitled *Mission Tomorrow*. In 1947, he co-authored a book entitled *Tomorrow Is Here*. The title of these two books speaks about man's attitude. People say tomorrow, God says tomorrow is here. One of the illusions of life is that the present hour is not critical, but the truth is that the decisive time is now, whatever time it is. One of the things that amazes me about children is their optimism. Eyes filled with wonder. Hearts filled with hope. Minds flooded with dreams. It does not matter how unrealistic and improbable they might be. They are convinced, they can grow up to be spiderman\ superman. Unfortunately, age causes hopes and dreams to fade.

Is there anything too hard for God? What will you do? Ravi Zacharias told a funny story of a little boy who wanted a bicycle. After watching a high church service on TV, the boy prayed: 'Lord, if it is in Your sovereign will and in Your eternal plan that I can get myself a bicycle – in Your time and according to Your will – would you please get me a bicycle. In Jesus name, I pray. Amen'. But no bicycle arrived for him. The next day he watched a prosperity gospel preacher, and decided to pray: 'Lord, I declare my need for a bicycle! And I declare that it will be a nice blue-coloured bicycle and delivered to my home within 24 hours. I lay claim to it, Amen!' Again, he waited in vain for a bicycle to arrive. So, he decided to do things his own way. He walked off into the woods with a statue of the Virgin Mary taken from his home. He then prayed, 'Dear Jesus, if you ever want to see your mother again…'

A pastor asked his congregation to guess and write the number of beans in a jar. Then he asked them to write their favourite songs. When the lists were complete, he first revealed the exact number of the beans and the students compared their guesses with the actual number. When he asked which song was closest to being the right one, all protested that there was no right answer. A person's favourite song is purely a matter of taste. Similarly, when you decide what to believe in terms of your faith, is it more like guessing the number of beans or choosing a favourite song. Choosing one's faith is more like choosing a favourite song.

Doing your best is more important than being the best. Are you wasting time or investing in time? One of the common refrains we hear from those who have reached the pinnacle of success is that of the emptiness that stalks their lives. That sort of confession is at least one reason why the question of meaning is central to life's pursuit. After his second Wimbledon victory, Boris Becker surprised the world by admitting his greatest struggle was with suicide. Jack Higgins the author of *The Eagle Has Landed* has said that, as a small boy, he had known, 'When you get to the top, there is nothing there'.

'Today after all is the tomorrow you worried about yesterday'. The key question to keep asking is are we spending our time on the right thing? Because time is all you have just now! *The Last Lecture* is a book co-authored by Randy Pausch—a professor of computer science and design at Carnegie Mellon University in Pittsburgh, Pennsylvania—and Jeffrey Zaslow of the Wall Street Journal. The book speaks about a lecture Pausch gave in September 2007 entitled 'Really Achieving Your Childhood Dreams'. It has been translated into 48 languages and has sold more than 5 million copies in the United States alone. 'What wisdom would you try to impart to the world if you knew it was your last chance?' A month before giving the lecture, Pausch had received a prognosis that the pancreatic cancer with which he had been diagnosed a year earlier, was terminal.

You have spent three years as an undergraduate, two years as a post-graduate and some of you even five years if you continued from UG to PG. But now you will be entering into the unknown. Be assured that God will be with you. Be sure of where you are going and which path you are following. *The Road Not Taken* by Robert Frost is an interesting poem.

Two roads diverged in a yellow wood,
And sorry I could not travel both
And be one traveller, long I stood
And looked down one as far as I could
To where it bent in the undergrowth;

I shall be telling this with a sigh
Somewhere ages and ages hence:
Two roads diverged in a wood, and I—
I took the one less travelled by,
And that has made all the difference.

May I encourage you in the words of St Paul – 'I charge you therefore before God and the Lord Jesus Christ, who will judge the living and the dead at His appearing and His kingdom: Preach the word! Be ready in season and out of season. Convince, rebuke, exhort, with all longsuffering and teaching' (2 Timothy 4:1,2). The question is what kind of Gospel will you preach? In the bright morning sunlight of 24th March 1980, a car stopped outside the Church of the Divine Providence. A lone gunman stepped out, unhurried. Resting his rifle on the car door, he aimed carefully down the long aisle to where El Salvador's archbishop, Oscar Arnulfo Romero, was saying mass. A single shot rang out. Romero staggered and fell. The blood pumped from his heart, soaking the little white disks of the scattered host. Romero's murder was to become one of the most notorious unsolved crimes of the cold war. I like the following quotation: 'A church that does not provoke any crisis, preach a gospel that does not unsettle, proclaim a word of God that does not get under anyone's skin or a word of God that does not touch the real sin of the society in which it is being proclaimed: what kind of gospel that?'

XIV. Theme: Prepare the Way: Text: Mark 1:1-8

Candlelight Service Sunday, Allahabad Bible Seminary

In 2018, during a consultation, I heard the testimony of a lady in CMC Vellore. She was barely a 7 year old when she was paralysed from the neck downwards. She went from Ayurveda to Christian faith healers to *vaidhyam* in Vellore, and began to walk but with a limp as one leg was shorter than the other. Eventually she migrated to the UK with her parents, in search for a better life and not least, a husband. She was introduced to a young doctor, Kumar Jesudasan, who decided to marry her despite her infirmities. She returned to India with her husband who worked in a leprosy hospital and their family life was full with two adorable sons and one daughter. It was a breath of fresh air and happiness and contentment and she looked forward to a happy future for the rest of her life. But life turned out to be different. Liver failure and a terminal illness led to the passing away of her husband at the age of 47. She had a severe fracture and post-polio syndrome. That was followed by breast cancer at age 60. The witness concluded that she continues to write and speak in seminars and consultations and was invited as a 'Peace Consultant' to the WCC meeting on peace and reconciliation.

She testified that the brand of suffering had changed direction toward those who were suffering. The road she walked on now was one she would never have chosen on her own. It was going to be a slow journey with many challenges, of that she was certain. All she knew was that 'He would walk with me'. 'One may be cured but not healed or one may be healed but not cured'.

Mushrooms grow in the dark; darkness that soothes us to sleep. Rich earth where seed germinates and wombs that provided first nourishment. Thomas Wilson, Chairman of IBM three generations ago had said that the world market is for five computers. Steven Jobs and Steve Wozniak, founder of Apple Computer, invented Apple vacuum tubes in a small box. They offered it to Atari and to Hewett-Packard. Steve sold his Volkswagen and calculator for $1300. McDonald's founder, Ray Kroc offered to sell half his shares at $25,000 but no one accepted. All these stories tell a different tale of the beginning of these success stories.

Prepare the Way. Mark is the gospel with the unusual beginning which has no narrative story of the birth of Jesus. It begins with 'My messenger' who will prepare the way, that too a voice in the wilderness. John appears baptising in the wilderness and proclaiming a baptism of repentance for the forgiveness of sins. All the countries of Judea and Jerusalem were going out to him and were being baptised in the River Jordan. A prophet emerges in the wilderness. What was the image? He was clothed in camel's hair, wearing a leather belt, and eating locusts and wild honey. What did he preach? That after him came one who was mightier than him, the strap of whose sandals, he was not worthy to stoop down and untie. He was baptising with water but the one after him would baptise with the Holy Spirit. How did the story end? He faced a violent death when he was beheaded by Herod Antipas. Yet Jesus named John the Baptist as the greatest man born of woman.

We live in a time where spectacle is preferred over substance and noise is often mistaken as informed debate. To stay on course is to prepare the way to receive the Lord and Saviour Jesus Christ. The celebration demands an acknowledgement of the presence of God in our midst which some of us deny. The story of an atheist and bear is an interesting anecdote. An atheist was walking through the woods. 'What majestic trees! What powerful rivers! What beautiful animals!' he said to himself. As he was walking alongside the river, he heard a rustling in the bushes behind him. He turned to look. He saw a 7-foot grizzly bear charge towards him. He ran as fast as he could up the path. He looked over his shoulder and saw that the bear was closing in on him. He looked over his shoulder again, and the bear was even closer. He tripped and fell to the ground. He rolled over to pick himself up but saw that the bear was right on top of him, reaching for him with his left paw and raising his right paw to strike him. At that instant, the atheist cried out, 'Oh my God!' Time stopped. The bear froze. The forest was silent. As a bright light shone upon the man, a voice came out of the sky. 'You deny my existence for all these years, teach others I don't exist, and even credit creation to cosmic accident. Do you expect me to help you out of this predicament? Am I to count you as a believer then?' The atheist looked directly into the light, 'It would be hypocritical of me to suddenly ask you to treat me as a Christian now, but perhaps you could make the bear a Christian?' 'Very well', said the voice. The light went out. The sounds of the forest resumed. And the bear dropped his right paw, brought both paws together, bowed his head and spoke: 'Lord bless this food, which I am about to receive from thy bounty through Christ our Lord. Amen'.

While preparing the way, let us be reminded of Joseph Mohr, born in Austria 1792, who was ordained as a Catholic priest in 1815. On 24th December 1818, it was discovered that the church organ was broken that put a damper on the carefully planned music for that night's Christmas Eve service. So, Joseph Mohr penned these lyrics and brought them to the organist Franz Gruber, who composed a simple melody for a guitar accompaniment. Supposedly, this song was first performed on that Christmas Eve in 1818, just a few hours after it was written. In 1863, nearly 50 years after being first sung in German, 'Silent Night' was translated into English by either Jane Campbell or John Young. Eight years later, that English version made its way into print in Charles Hutchins' *Sunday School Hymnal.* Today, 'Silent Night' is sung around the world in more than 300 languages.

'Silent night! Holy night,

All is calm, all is bright,

Round yon virgin mother and child!
Holy infant, so tender and mild,

Sleep in heavenly peace! Sleep in heavenly peace!'

This hymn has transcended the barriers of time and has spoken from generation to generation!

XV. Covid-19 Christmas: A Homecoming: Text: Psalm 137

'By the waters of Babylon there we sat down and wept when we remembered Zion'

Stories are an essential part of our self-identity. We live in a world of stories that tell how we came to be here and of ourselves. It is a treasure house of memory that transcends the boundary of time and still speaks. The educational role of the story is to challenge our presuppositions, upset our complacencies, and illuminate our imaginations with new truth. The experience of the past few months under COVID-19 has been challenging as well as liberating. It has been less characterised by attendance at church on Sunday, and more characterised by the prayer and service we offer each day. We have been compelled to become a different kind of church but hopeful and rooted in the offering of prayer and praise and overflowing in service to the world. By our service and by our love, Jesus Christ is made known, and the hope of the gospel – a hope that can counter fear and isolation, has spread across our land.

'By the rivers of Babylon— there we sat down and there we wept when we remembered Zion. On the willows there we hung up our harps. For there, our captors asked us for songs, and our tormentors asked for mirth, saying, "Sing us one of the songs of Zion!"

How could we sing the Lord's song in a foreign land? If I forget you, O Jerusalem, let my right-hand wither! Let my tongue cling to the roof of my mouth if I do not remember you if I do not set Jerusalem above my highest joy'. Psalm 137 relates the longing for Zion that dwelt in the hearts of the Jews when exiled in Babylon and also testifies that they did not forget the songs, or psalms, of Zion though they were far from their homeland. It is one of the best-known psalms that focuses on the traumatic experience of exile in Babylon. The psalm reveals the sufferings and sentiments of the people who probably experienced first-hand the grievous days of the conquest and destruction of Jerusalem in 587 BCE and who shared the burden of the Babylonian captivity. The psalm touches the raw nerve of Israel's faith. People in difficult situations have often found comfort in this song of the ancient Hebrew exiles.

Rivers of Babylon was a Rastafari song written and recorded by Brent Dowe and Trevor McNaughton of the Jamaican reggae group, the Melodians, in 1970. The lyrics are adapted from the texts of Psalm 19 and Psalm 137. The Melodians' original version of the song appeared on the soundtrack album for the 1972 movie 'Harder They Come', which made it internationally known. The dream of slaves for freedom was encapsulated and had a powerful liberating force through the story of the crossing of the Red Sea. All of our stories find culmination and significance in the story of Jesus of Nazareth. The story of Christmas manifests the very God in all mysteries of divine love. We have a story to tell to the nations that abiding truth is mediated through the story of the birth of Jesus. Discipleship is the only forum where one goes through learning and training through life to carefully treasure the riches one possesses. Memories can also lead to despair if tied to dark moments of hatred and depression. Therefore, memory is double-edged but the power is unquestionable.

Pope Julius authorised 25th December 353 AD to be celebrated as the birthday of Jesus. Professor Charles Follen lit the candles on the first Christmas Tree in America in 1822. Nobody then would have thought that the celebration of Christmas with decorations would become so elaborate and commercial. However, today we need to recall to our memory a profound truth of Christmas. Christmas is one of the greatest festivals based on the truth of Incarnation which we may call the 'Homecoming of God".

Our time does not seem to be terribly successful right now. The narrative of the homecoming of God in Luke chapter 2 has been woven together with elements of the Old Testament: 'Behold, my servant shall act wisely; he shall be high and lifted up, and shall be exalted' (Isaiah 52:13). The Gospel writer puts it beautifully saying, 'And the angel said to them, "Fear not, for behold, I bring you good news of great joy that will be for all the people. For unto you is born this day in the city of David a Saviour, who is Christ the Lord. And this will be a sign for you: you will find a baby wrapped in swaddling clothes and lying in a manger' (Luke 2:10-12). Living God, creator God, the God of Israel is not an 'upstairs' God but 'downstairs'. The Word became flesh and 'tabernacled' among us. The word 'tabernacle' is derived from the Latin word meaning 'tent' or 'hut'', the Hebrew word 'Mishkan' meaning 'dwell', 'rest', or 'to live in', and the Greek word 'skene' meaning 'tent'.

We live in a difficult time that nobody had ever imagined. The world has come to a standstill. In that context, I read a story of a person's visit to Starbucks. 'Stood behind a customer. The customer gave an order for coffee. Decaf Grand, sugar-free vanilla, non-fat latte with extra foam, milk heated to 140°F (milk becomes sweet and delicious). I stood in line, started to think, maybe I want 140° coffee. My choice of milk temperature up to that point has been catastrophically naïve. Suddenly his choice made me unhappier about my own. I began to covet. I was not sure what I wanted. I became anxious and indecisive. I was not sure to commit either to my choice or to his'. Not choosing becomes a lack of trust in God so we must be wise.

How shall we celebrate Christmas in the context of COVID-19 and what shall we say to the world about Jesus of Nazareth? Can we ever be sure to wish everyone a peaceful Christmas in the midst of suffering, uncertainties, anxiety, and bereavement when a total of 1.11 million, as of 18th October 2020, have left the world. Our story in the Bible involved Mary embarking on a journey to Jerusalem for a census during the last stage of her pregnancy, no room at the inn, a place in the stable among animals, and also migration to Egypt for the protection of the baby.

The most inspiring word in the midst of our midnight is the message of hope that dawn will come. Change happens when we are ready to be human. Not to use our suffering as another weapon against each other, not to argue about whose sufferings are worse, but just to recognise the same love and the same loss. We believe that the most radical change in the history of the world happened when God began to speak to us in the voice of a human, not the voice of a monarch or a philosopher but the inarticulate voice of a child in the manger. When we start hearing the voice of God in the cries of the people around us then the dawn is near. Faith in the dawn arises from the faith that God is good and just. When we believe this, we know that the contradictions of life are neither final nor ultimate. We can walk through the dark night with the conviction that all things work together for good for those that love God. Even the most starless midnight will herald the dawn of some great fulfilment. The dawn will come. Disappointment, sorrow, and despair are born at midnight, but morning follows. 'Weeping may endure for a night', says the Psalmist, 'but joy cometh in the morning'.

Christmas is all about staying together as a family, making friends, welcoming strangers as neighbours, building community, cultivating a garden, learning cooking to share food, making space for the marginalised, learning to cope with difficult situations. Home-making is crowded with possibilities because we are loved by God but must take up our cross and follow Jesus. Difficulties and suffering go deep in life. They tempt us to try magical quick-fix solutions which do no justice to the depth of the problem. If deep suffering could be dealt with by formulas, techniques, and problem-solving mentality, then our society should have been able to progress in coping with war, poverty, debt, violence, addiction, family break-up, injustice, and a multitude of other miseries. The ministry of Jesus was about healing which involved love, trust, compassion and forgiveness, and radically inclusive hospitality. If there is to be the real thing, it needs to be measured by its ability to sustain. There comes a point when the question does change. We do not ask how to avoid a particularly difficult situation but rather, what it is for.

The sea of migrant people shown on Indian television during the COVID-19 pandemic was an eye-opener for all of us. We never understood their pain and suffering. The present unemployment around the world, economic slowdown, lack of health care and even access to health care for one and all, those who are physically challenged, terminally ill, and the elderly who are homebound, raise issues that are real. Confused young people, lonely old people, and market meltdown are ground realities. All convey a different message but also opportunities to think and to hear those voices. Some have an empty stomach, some a damaged body, and some mind and spirit. How can all be part of our home-making of *oikoumene*, 'the whole inhabited world', in 2020? How can they come to Church and sit with us if churches aren't fully open and pray with us saying 'Thank you God'? There are also practical questions. The most interesting part of interaction and interface with each other is shared looks, glances, frequent smiles, and laughter. Touching is part of healing and is a basic need in our community but we are all deprived of that during the pandemic because we have to wear a mask and maintain social distance.

I am reminded of a prayer by St Paul. 'I kneel in prayer ... that through faith, Christ may dwell in your hearts in love. With deep roots and firm foundations may you, in company with all God's people, be strong to grasp what is the breadth and height and depth of Christ's love, and to know it, though it is beyond knowledge' (Ephesians 3:14, 17-19). May God bless us to walk humbly with Him this year.

The faculty of a college were having their annual meeting when suddenly an angel appeared. Turning to the Dean, the Angel said, 'I will grant you one of the three choices – infinite wisdom, infinite wealth, or infinite health'. The Dean thought for a minute then asked for wisdom. 'So be it', said the angel and disappeared. In the silence that followed, the Dean sat thoughtfully, saying nothing and staring off into the distance. Finally one of the faculty members exclaimed, 'Do you have anything to say? What words of wisdom can you give us?' The Dean replied, 'I should have taken the money'.

Some of us represent the head without a heart. The only connection is intellectual. It is easy to become a sceptic or cynic. Some represent the heart without the head. When a simple question is asked, a simple answer should suffice. Still others represent the one who does not know how to ask or is not interested enough to ask, with no connection either to the head or heart. The danger is that many of us belong to this category.

One notorious answer comes from Voltaire, the 18th century French polymath, who wrote: 'If God did not exist, it would be necessary to invent him'. Because Voltaire was a trenchant critic of organised religion, this quip is often quoted cynically. But in fact, he was being perfectly sincere. He was arguing that belief in God is necessary for society to function, even if he didn't approve of the monopoly the church held over that belief.

■■■

9

Becoming

'I dare to dream greatly; I dare to fail greatly. I dare to tolerate the ashes of my unfulfilled dreams, for I may dream again. I dare not tolerate the ashes of my unfulfilled life, for I may never live again'

Philippos Syrigos

One common question that is normally asked is what you want to be when you grow up. Becoming is not just about achieving a certain aim but also being forward moving. The journey of life continues until my God calls me back home, but the story that I set out to narrate in this memoir is now complete. There is power in allowing myself to be known and heard, in owning my story, and in being willing to know and hear others. This is how we become. My pace of work remains more or less the same but has taken on a different form. Ideas tend to influence us through multiple sources and they often get reinforced over time in mysterious ways. Needless to say, the formative periods in a joint family, struggling to live and learn through hardship, but cherishing family values have been inspiring as well as rewarding. I have tried to narrate the experiences of my life with joy and tears.

The words of Martin Luther King Jr are so profound when one thinks of unfulfilled dreams: 'So many of us in life start out building temples: temples of character, temples of justice, and temples of peace. And so often we do not finish them. Because life is like Schubert's Unfinished Symphony. At so many points we start, we try, and we set out to build our various temples. And I guess one of the great agonies of life is that we are constantly trying to finish that which is unfinishable. We are commanded to do that.

And so we, like David, find ourselves in so many instances having to face the fact that our dreams are not fulfilled … let us notice first that life is a continual story of shattered dreams'.

The journey of life takes mysterious turns and everybody has a story to tell. The Former Archbishop Rowan Williams, in his sermon for Romero, on 25th September 2017 narrated a story. 'Two Welsh countrymen sat in a pub discussing the recent death of one of their neighbours. "How much did he leave?" Asked one of them. The other lifted an eyebrow and replied "Everything"'. Exactly 40 years earlier, on 25th September 1977, Archbishop Oscar Romero in his weekly mass had provided an extended and more theological version of that comment. In this homily, he had reflected on the biblical notion of property. Property, he said, in Jewish and Christian scripture, was something that was lent to the user, never absolutely given. Always to be used, rented from God. And so, he says, the truth is that the rich pay rent for the land whose use they are given for a time, to the poor. In a just world, that is how we should conceive property. We are given something through which we are set free to discharge our debt to the poor. Because if our God is with the poor, then when we serve the poor, we serve God. When we recognise our indebtedness to the poor, we pay our rent to God for the land we use. And in that perspective, he went on to say, 'We are all of us beggars together'. No one simply owns at another's expense. Everyone is caught up in exchange. Those who are wealthy – in this world's terms – are those who have been given the privilege of using the things of the world for the flourishing of their neighbour. Beggars together we become rich almost together. 'A church that does not provoke any crisis, preach a gospel that does not unsettle, proclaim a word of God that does not get under anyone's skin or a word of God that does not touch the real sin of the society in which it is being proclaimed: what kind of gospel is that?' (Oscar Romero).

Since April 2021, my wife and I began a different phase in our lives as we settled down in our hometown in Odisha. We have a roof overhead which was built only by God's grace. We began doing things together that we had not done for quite a long time – sweeping, cleaning, washing, cooking, gardening, and in addition to these, my wife continued her hobby of looking after the cats and dogs of the street and visiting our neighbours. Someone rang me to find out about our well-being. When I asked him, what I should do now after retirement, his comment was, 'You have a fulfilled life'. That was when I began wondering how to assess a 'fulfilling' journey. I cannot even begin to imagine where I began when I was struggling to complete my education, but I ultimately studied at Oxford and Birmingham University with a family scholarship, have been married for 47 years with good health, and have a lovely family of sons, daughter-in-law, and three lovely granddaughters. We have still not come to terms with losing our elder daughter-in-law. The mobile phone rings more often as our children call to find out about our well-being, we meet our younger son, granddaughter, and daughter-in-law in London through Skype every Sunday, and most interestingly we regularly receive handwritten letters from our two granddaughters Aavisha and Davinia.

The words of Jurgen Moltmann are quite motivating. He himself came to faith at a prisoner of war camp at the end of World War II. His life had been permanently stamped by his circumstances, and he sought meaning, answers, and hope. Moltmann speaks with great enthusiasm about these early days of his faith journey. Every idea was new and every concept exciting. In Opening Dialogue[1], Moltmann says the reading of Scripture was fresh and engaging. 'My image of theology is not "a safe stronghold is our God". It is the exodus of God's people, on the road to the promised land of liberty where God dwells. For me, theology is not an inner-church or postmodern dogmatics, designed only for one's own community of faith. Nor is it for me the cultural study of the civil religion of bourgeois society. Theology springs out of a passion for God's kingdom and its righteousness and justice, and this passion grows up in the community of Christ. In that passion, theology becomes imagination for the kingdom of God in the world and for the world in God's kingdom'.[2] In The Diary of Private Prayers, the 20th century theologian Donald Baillie says: 'For it is little that I have the power to do or to ordain. Not of my own will am I here, not of my own will shall I soon pass hence. Of all that shall come to me this day, very little will be such as I have chosen for myself'. Hard words for some who are hyper-spiritual. Thankfully Baillie goes on to pray: 'It is Thou who dost keep in Thy grasp the threads of this day's life and who alone knowest what lies before me to do or to suffer. But because Thou art my father, I am not afraid'.

A final touch to this memoir was given during the two months summer holiday in Shillong with our elder son and two granddaughters in July-August 2021. Shillong is a hill station in the north-eastern part of India and the capital of Meghalaya, which means 'The Abode of Clouds'. It is said that the rolling hills around the town reminded the British of Scotland. Hence, they would also refer to it as the 'Scotland of the East'. The first incident was a meeting and conversation with Dilip Mukerjea. Dilip Mukerjea is the owner and managing director of Braindancing International and Buzan Centre Singapore Pte Ltd. His best-selling works include Superbrain, Brainfinity, and Braindancing. An unusual conversation about 'Brain Dancing' being a beautiful gift from God began in the market square in Shillong while we were waiting for some takeaway and culminated at his home. 'Your brain is a hypnotically beautiful garden, abloom with possibilities. It is creatively flamboyant, interflowing with a rich blend of vivid imagery and vibrant prose. Buoyant when aroused, it is capable of a fascinating spectrum of moods: chaotic, random, violent sometimes, often uncontainable, a pandemonium of creative effusions … yet it can also be dazzling, all-embracing, enchanting, and restorative. Your brain garden is a universe ablaze with a battalion of "brilliance", a salute to what you were born with, who you are capable of being, the legacy you can leave humankind'.[3]

The second incident was the evening family prayer with our son and granddaughters. I had heard the prayer of our younger granddaughter when she was about five, but surprisingly, even at the age of 12 the prayer has not changed although her mother had left the world six years before: 'Jesus, be with mummy, keep her safe every night, every morning, every evening, and every afternoon'. That simple, beautiful acknowledgment of her presence every day baffled me. Then I saw a post on Facebook on 8th August 2021 by our elder son on his 45th birthday. 'There's been a missing ingredient during my birthday celebrations over the past 23 years. I didn't have to think long and hard to figure it out. I've not had the pleasure of the presence of my parents during these important transitions into a new year. But this year, I've been blessed to wake up, see them in flesh and blood and enjoy the warmth of their hugs and blessings. It's incredible how grateful I am to experience their support through the best and worst of days. As senior citizens, they braved the pandemic to travel from Odisha to Shillong to stay with us. They adjusted to what we have to offer and the life we lead in Shillong. They took over the kitchen and it's been one sumptuous meal after another since Friday leading up to the birthday. They quickly took charge of the proceedings (to be mentioned later) for the day and organised a smooth celebration. Wisdom dictates that one should "Count your blessings" and they definitely top the list. This birthday is truly about the presence and power of parents. Thanks, Dhirendra Sahu and Manjusree Sahu. You'll never truly know how reassuring and rejuvenating your presence has been here. Watching them spoil my daughters, quietly going about fixing little problems, and tweaking things in that old school manner is a lesson in itself. These moments are priceless and precious'.

Institution building is a laborious and lengthy process. We live in a time of quick-fix solutions where short-sightedness overrules vision. Corruption and lust for power are not static and are a panacea for all ills, spreading and destroying the vitals of the system. If they continue, inefficiency, and irrationality impede the decision-making process. The academics and intellectuals played a vital role in offering a dissenting voice and moral force but instead, they too have rapidly agreed to be co-opted into the system. The founder of any organisation/ movement has a clear calling and vision. No one is more passionate about the cause. Yet the founder's passion rarely translates to subsequent generations of leadership. Brenan Manning while addressing a retreat of evangelical pastors of large churches said: 'The greatest idol I find in leaders is ambition'. The allure of success, growth, and the modern virtue of branding and image may lead to a dangerous situation for both the leaders and the organisation itself. Fred Smith said, 'Our platforms become the gallows upon which our humility is hanged'.[4] He says when we begin to see our priority as a growing ministry instead of a faithful one, we sow the seeds of drift. The 20th-century variety of leaders/gurus comprise more worldly gentlemen/ women, both in the best and the worst sense. The basic question—why do people go to them or even follow them—still remains unanswered. Billy Graham, according to all accounts, lived a life consistent with the values he taught. Early in his ministry, he identified that spiritual enthusiasm does not make you immune to greed, pride, lust, and ambition.[5] He gathered together influential individuals to create a board of accountability, those with authority to supervise the decisions of the evangelism team. Even Graham submitted to the board, not trying to tiptoe around them or find loopholes for his own benefit. He needed people who could tell him the truth at all times, even when it was uncomfortable.

One unfinished agenda in my life is the Barefoot Trust, a registered charity founded in memory of my Barefoot Pastor. Initially, it was known as the 'Birendra Foundation' but later we changed it to 'Barefoot Trust'. It was dormant for a while and normally any dream, especially charitable family trusts, end when overseas grants are discontinued or after the demise of the founder. Therefore, I was not hopeful about the future. However, the moral and practical support from our younger son Ashis in recharting the discourse despite being in London, and the active engagement of our older son, Bibhu, in taking full responsibility as Managing Trustee, brought new hope with a breakthrough in 2017-18. Bibhu has taken up the challenge and does the work now, based in Shillong, while we hope to continue the work in Odisha. 'We ourselves feel that what we are doing is just a drop in the ocean. But the ocean would be less because of that missing drop' (Mother Teresa).

The basic issue is choosing the path of faithfulness over being successful in our own small endeavours, whether in the family, church, organisations, institutions, or society. It demands intentionality, courage, and resolve. One lesson that I have learned is to cope with the bitter pain of betrayal, not by the enemies but by friends, colleagues, those whom you love and trust, and even people whom you have tried to help. When we forget that all we do flows out of our experience of the undeserved grace we ourselves have experienced, we lack motivation and endurance. This memoir is a call for personal humility and accountability as well as institutional humility and accountability, for adaptability, and growth in our current context. Sometimes I wonder why our church and minority institutions are beyond the purview of public scrutiny in terms of auditing our finances. I am told it is difficult to misappropriate church funds in Canada for too long because the Canada Revenue Agency (CRA) does regular audits and can deregister charities where misappropriation of church funds is found. The ethical apathy of the public is worrisome and a cause for corruption. Evil triumphs by default. The only thing necessary for the triumph of evil is to do nothing good or remain silent, or to be on the fence, or become Pilate in washing our hands.

The most rewarding and unforgettable memory is the love, care, and appreciation that we received during my preaching ministry in the local churches, and the teaching ministry among the students. In the rural ministry, it is still a pleasure to sit on the floor with the people and share a simple meal together. Some people still ask me, can you sit cross-legged on the floor and eat and my answer is an affirmative, even at the age of 71. Our father taught us to pray only by kneeling during the family prayer every day. There is a sense of fulfilment which is invaluable. There is no regret in humbly following the footsteps of my Lord and Saviour. The earthly ministry of Jesus focussed on the kingdom of God. He explained the nuances of the kingdom using parables. The followers of Jesus continued to effect change by bearing witness to the life, death, and resurrection of Jesus. The community that gathers in the name of Jesus in each place is called to make a difference as per the values of the kingdom, which is in contrast to the prevailing values of the world. The contrast is perceived by combating greed with contentment, success with faithfulness, power-grabbing with humble service, and instead of conquering through might, the kingdom must gradually infiltrate the nations of the world like yeast. People with the power of the Holy Spirit have made a difference by 'serving the least', which is often one of the most neglected mandates of Jesus. The barefoot ministry of my father was a catalyst for individual, collective, and social renewal in a micro context. I greatly value such a legacy, not just to be remembered but cherished. One of the second generation members of the fruit of his ministry in a remote village of Odisha called me one day to remind me of the micro ministry that he did among people in unreached areas who were deprived of the benefits of the fellowship of the local church that we are used to receiving. It was a delight to hear that the ministry still continues with that vision and drive to move forward in that direction.

The organizational structure of the church can be redesigned for mission in any context to 'serve the least'. It is not a trendy act of benevolence but a lifestyle of authentic community and spiritual transformation. We often reduce serving to a once-a-month program or seasonal event before Christmas. One childhood memory that is still vibrant is of my father making a point to visit families in the evening on a regular basis. When we were looking forward to the celebration of Christmas, my father used to think of the people in the three small congregations that he had founded.

He would carry the homemade Odia snacks specially prepared for all of them and go by bus to those villages. He would stay overnight on the 24th and celebrate Christmas with them. We used to see him only on Christmas evening for dinner. I was delighted last year to accept an invitation from the younger generation of the same congregations to visit them on 24th and 25th December 2021, to worship and celebrate with the community, eat meals together, and preach in the three small congregations. Then I returned home after the Christmas morning service to have lunch and immediately travelled to another village nearby with my wife to preach in the afternoon Christmas service. This village church was the one that would invite me to preach every year when I came home for Christmas and visited my parents while I was in Serampore. Christmas 2021 was a fulfilment of a dream of being with the people at the micro-level.

A testimony that always helped me in my journey of faith is that of Canon Subir Biswas. As a theological student at Serampore College in 1971, I had the privilege of volunteering in the refugee camp under the leadership of Canon Subir Biswas of St Paul's Cathedral, Kolkata during the India-Bangladesh war. Canon Biswas was very concerned for the poor and he actively participated in many organisations. He was the founder of Urban Industrial Mission (Durgapur), Calcutta Urban Service, Kalikata Basti Pragati Sanstha (KBPS), and Antara Khelaghar: The Fellowship of the Handicapped. Thousands of Bangladeshi refugees will be forever grateful for all the help received because out of this massive relief operation, the Cathedral Relief Service was conceived and founded. He could infuse warmth and offered friendship to everyone who came in contact with him. His testimony is heart-warming and overwhelming: 'I was such a busy person, busy from early morning to late night. So busy that others could not approach me for help. "How could we disturb you?" I was doing great things for the kingdom of God, for justice, for truth, for the church, and for the poor. I had built a whole world around me which depended on me. And then came sudden illness and cessation of all activity. Lord, You are marvellous … In the midst of all the frustration and fear, you speak gently. "Be not afraid". Forgive us Lord when we build worlds which are dependent on us and not on you'.

'Memory is not wisdom; idiots can by rote repeat volumes. Yet what is wisdom without memory?'

Martin Farquhar Tupper

Endnotes

[1] Opening Dialogue: Jürgen Moltmann's Interaction with the Thought of Karl Barth, Jayne H. Davis, Review and Expositor, 100, Fall 2003

[2] Moltmann, Jürgen, Experiences in Theology, trans. Margaret Kohl, Minneapolis: Fortress Press, 2000, p. xx.

[3] Mukerjea, Dilip, Conquering Critical Thinking, Brainware Press, Singapore, 2018

[4] Smith, Fred, The Idol of Ambition, 18th April, Fred's blog

[5] Myra, Harold & Shelly, Marshall, The Leadership Secrets of Billy Graham, Grand Rapids, 2008, p 53, 57

■■■

Barefoot Trust

A Public Charitable Trust
Registered Under The Indian Trust Act 1882 (41141601460
12A:AACTB9876FE20214 – 80G:AACTB9876FF20220)

LOOK - LISTEN - LEARN - LIVE

ENABLING ONE'S IMAGINATION TO EMPOWER THE CREATION OF A SUSTAINABLE PLANET.

Mission Statement

To nurture collaborations towards an equitable ecosystem in order to leave positive visible footprints of change initiated by the disadvantaged at the micro and macro levels through enabling imagi-actions[1] that set the building blocks for the least of our brothers and sisters in society.

About Us

Education without Learning, Disability without Inclusion, and Food without Nutrition are prevailing issues that are being addressed by the Barefoot Trust. At the Barefoot Trust, our interventions are based on emerging trends from a learning culture founded on encouraging and enriching conversation, developing quality relationships, identifying opportunities for engagement, crafting strategy, igniting innovation, exercising servant leadership, catalysing entrepreneurship, and not least, staying relevant in the ever-changing context for a justifiable social presence in Odisha and Meghalaya. Our main focus areas are Education, Food, and Inclusion (disabled and other socially disadvantaged communities) based on the principles of sustainability.

Aim

- To look for exemplary alternatives and approaches to education, disability, and youth empowerment by working with dreamers and doers
- To listen to challenges relating to youth, women, and people with disabilities through dialogue
- To learn based on conversation, consensus, capacity-building, and partnership
- To live and let live by encouraging innovative livelihood and sustainable environmental practices

Objectives

- To embark on a journey of dialogue, counselling, and community building for peaceful co-existence
- To create awareness on Education, on learning how to learn, and new pedagogies for the local context
- To create an environment of equal opportunities for the vulnerable, marginalised, and people with disabilities

The Trust

Being barefoot is a reality of life in India that is multi-layered and multi-faceted. The Barefoot Trust was founded in the loving memory of Birendra Kumar Sahu, known in Odisha as 'The Barefoot Pastor'. We hold a legacy of dedication and commitment to serve with a simplistic lifestyle and a message that God loves one and all irrespective of caste, class, and colour.

Contact Address

Barefoot Trust
Nayakothi
State Bank of India Square
Khordha - 752055
Odisha, India
Mobile: 9935470860
Email: barefoot.trust@gmail.com
Account Name: Barefoot Trust
Name of Bank: ICICI
Account No: 242405001270
IFSC Code: ICIC0002424

Barefoot Trust
% Asian Confluence
Upper Nongrim Hills
Shillong - 703003
Meghalaya, India
Mobile: 7005845032
Email: barefoot.trust@gmail.com
Account Name: Barefoot Trust
Name of Bank: Indian Bank
Account No: 20392327666
IFSC Code: IDIB000L028

■■■

Glossary of Personal Work

Books

Conversation on Health & Healing. Delhi: ISPCK. 2019, Sahu, Dhirendra K. and Arul Dhas, eds.

Church of North India: A Historical and Systematic Theological Inquiry into an Ecumenical Ecclesiology. 1994. Frankfurt am Main: Peter Lang. pp xi + 354., Sahu, Dhirendra K.

Sound of Silence: A Festschrift in Honor of Bishop D. K. Sahu at his Shashti-Purti. Delhi: ISPCK, 2010, Tiwari, Ravi and Bibhudutta Sahu, eds.

United & Uniting: A Story of the Church of North India. 2001. Delhi: ISPCK., Sahu, Dhirendra K

Articles

"A Case Study on Identity: The Communion of Churches in India." In With a Demonstration of the Spirit and of Power, Faith and Order. Paper No 195, pp. 105-14. WCC. 2004.

"A Gathered Community of Witness & Service." In Global Christian Forum: Transforming Ecumenism edited by Richard Howell. pp. 130-139. Delhi: Evangelical Fellowship of India. 2007.

"A Search for an Inter-Cultural Ecclesial Identity." In Inter-Cultural Asian Theological Methodologies: An Exploration, edited by Samson Prabhakar. Bangalore: South Asia Theological Research Institute. 2002.

"A Vision for Education." Allahabad Theological Journal 6. 2016.

"Beyond Dialogue." NCC Review September 2005. p. 370.

"Building on What Unites: Overcoming What Divides." NCC Review CXX(2). 2000.

"Charting a New Paradigm of 'Do this in Remembrance of Me'." Allahabad Theological Journal 7. 2017.

"Christian Faith and Economic Justice: 20th Bishop Joshi Memorial Lecture." A Build Publication. November 1996.

"Christian Participation in Nation Building." CSI Life. 2005.

"Church of North India." In: Encyclopaedia of Christianity in India. pp. 319-326. Pune: St Paul. 2014.

"Commemoration Service Address." Convocation of Senate of Serampore. pp. 1-8. 2009.

"Congregational Empowerment for Dalit Liberation." NCC Review April 2007. p. 62.

"Diakonia: Servant of the Servant King." Footprints of Faith: A Festschrift. Prayagraj: SHUATS. 2016.

"Educating the Educated." NCC Review Jan-Feb 2007. p. 21.

"Episcopacy in the Church of North India." North India Church Review May 2001. p. 3.

"Eucharist and Ecumenical Movement in India." In Eucharist and Community: Beyond All Barriers. A Theological Forum in preparation for FABC 2009. pp. 77-89.

"Evangelical-Ecumenical: From Polarity to Convergence." NCC Review Jan-Feb 2003.

"Historiography: Perspectives and Prospects." All Nations University Journal of Applied Thought 7(1): p1-14. 2019.

"Human Sexuality: A Legal Perspective." Religion and Society. December 2009. pp. 37-44.

"Individuals, Institutions and Imagination." In Together with People edited by Samson Prabhakar. Bangalore: SATHRI/BTESSC. 2004.

"Interpreting the Interpreted: Story of Job." Allahabad Theological Journal. 2015.

"Living Theology@120°F ." *Living Theologies: Reflections from Diverse Specificities, CISRS*, 2021.

"Management: A Possibility for Transformation." In Christian Manager Dec-Jan 2005.

"Mapping the Oikoumene in India." NCC Review March 2006. pp. 22-34.

"Micro Ecumenism." In India: God of All Grace, edited by Joseph George. pp. 403-10. ATC&UTC. 2005.

"Ministry from the Margin." Indian Journal of Theology. 2005.

"Minority Within Minority: If we Talk the Talk, we have to Walk the Walk." In A Conversation on Health & Healing, edited by Dhirendra K. Sahu and Arul Dhas. Delhi: ISPCK, 2019.

"Mission and Ecumenism: An Opportunity & Challenge." In Shepherd of a Pilgrim People, edited by G. Sobhanam and V. Victor. pp. 40-46. Delhi: ISPCK. 2005.

"Mission and Ministry III: Challenges from the Ecumenical Movement." Bishop and Mrs S. K. Parmar Lecture Series. Jabalpur: LTC/ISPCK. 2007.

"Mission and Transformation." Canon Subir Biswas Memorial Silver Jubilee Celebration Lecture 1999. St. Paul's Cathedral and Cathedral Relief Service, Calcutta.

Mugabe, H. J. 1994. "A Response to the Paper: Salvation from an African Perspective." Indian Journal of Theology 36(1).

"Partners in Creation: A Forgotten Paradigm." Gurukul Summer Institute. April 1998.

"Pedagogy of Transformative Process." In Ripples: A Journey of CNI SBSS. Delhi: ISPCK. 2001.

"People of the Way." Allahabad Theological Journal I, 2014.

"Recognizing the Structure: A Possibility for Mission Today." In Church's Participation in Theological Education, edited by S. Prabhakar and M. J. Joseph. pp. 12-19. Bangalore: BTESSC. 2003.

"Repositioning Dalits & Tribals in Local Congregations: Mission Challenges." NCC Review August 2008. p. 332.

"Role of Church in Nation Building." NCC Review Nov. 2005. p. 494.

"Spirit of Ecumenism: Retrospect & Prospect." North India Church Review July 1996.

"Spirituality of Reconciliation: Theological Justification for Active Non-violence." In Towards a Culture of Peace in South Asia, edited by S. Prabhakar, pp. 53-66. Bangalore: BTESSC/SATHRI. 2004.

"Serampore Then & Now." Indian Journal of Theology 35(1). 1993.

"The Church of North India." In Encyclopaedia of Christianity in India, Pune: Jnana-Deepa Vidyapeeth. 2005.

"The Church of North India (United)." In Anglican Communion, edited by Ian S. Markham et.al. pp. 319-328. Oxford: Wiley-Blackwell. 2013.

"Theological Education in India: A Profile." In Building Communities for Celebration and Resistance compiled by V. S. Lall. 1998.

"Towards a Transformed & Transforming Community." Edited by E. Pradhan and S. Singh. pp. 38-44. Delhi: CNI-ISPCK. 2005.

"Toward a Transforming Church of North India." In: Church on the Move. Delhi: ISPCK. 2005.

"Towards an Understanding of Justice & Peace." In Mission with the Marginalized edited by Samuel W. Meshak. pp. 533-40. Tiruvalla: Christava Sahitya Samiti. 2007.

"Visionary Household of God." Bishop Thomas Mar Athanasius Memorial Lecture. Kottayam, Kerala, India, 21-23rd November 2003.

"What does the Lord require of us?" In: Lenten Lantern. p 1. NCCI. 2009.

"Wisdom - Folly: A Call for Discernment in Ministry." Allahabad Theological Journal. 2013.

INTERNATIONAL CONSULTATIONS / VISITS

- All Nations University, Koforidua, Ghana, 28th March-12th April, 2022
- All Nations Full Gospel Church visit, Toronto, Canada, 7th-17th October 2018
- Oxford Conference: Serampore College Bi-Centenary (1818-2018), Regent's Park College, Oxford, U.K., 19th-21st October 2018
- All Nations Full Gospel Church visit, Calgary & Toronto, Canada,18th June-2nd July 2016
- Executive Seminar on Human Resource Management, Galilee International Management Institute, Israel, 4th-15th December 2014
- 13th General Assembly of Christian Conference of Asia, Kuala Lumpur, Malaysia, 14th-21st April 2010
- Peace, Security and Development in South Asia, Bangalore, 30th-2nd April 2009
- Global Ecumenical Conference on Dalit Liberation, Bangkok, 20th-24th March 2009
- Sixth Congress of Asian Theologians, Iloilo, Philippines, 9th-13th February 2009
- Global Christian Forum, New Delhi, 8th-11th November 2008
- Eighth Consultation of United & Uniting Churches, Johannesburg, 29th-5th November 2008
- Asia General Secretaries Meeting, Bangladesh, 31st-3rd September 2008
- Consultation on Tradition & Modernity, Bangkok, 26th-28th July 2008
- Dialogue on Mission for South Asia, UTC, Bangalore, 29th-2nd April 2008

- Global Christian Forum, Limuru, Nairobi, Kenya, 6th-12th November 2007
- Consultation Role of Church for Peace and Unification in Korean Peninsula, Seoul, South Korea, 8th-13th August 2007
- Consultation on Proposed Ecumenical Alliance for Development, Bossey, Geneva, December 2005
- South Asia Regional Capacity Building Training, Bangladesh, August 2005
- South Asia Regional Capacity Building Training Kathmandu, Nepal, November 2005
- Ecumenical Enablers' Training Programme, Bangkok, February 2005
- Ecumenical Enablers' Training Programme, Sri Lanka, June 2005
- Second Anglican Contextual Theologian Consultation, Durban, South Africa, 2nd-6th August 2004
- Anglican Contextual Theologians Consultation, Cambridge, MA, USA, May 2003
- Dialogues between World Alliance of Reformed Churches and Disciples, Cambridge, United Kingdom, March 2003
- Pastoral visit to Andaman and Nicobar Islands, 8th-18th March 2003
- Seventh Consultation of United and Uniting Churches, Netherlands, September 2002
- International Consultation on Intercultural Methodologies, Sri Lanka, April 2002
- Dialogues between World Alliance of Reformed Churches and Disciples, Geneva, January 2002
- Dialogue between World Alliance of Baptist Churches and Anglican Communion, 18-21, January, Yangoon, Myanmmar, 2001
- Baptist International Conference on Theological Education, South Africa, 1993

NATIONAL CONSULTATIONS / SEMINARS

- Church Reformed: Always Reforming, ECC Bangalore, 25th-27th April 2017
- National Consultation on 'Diaconal Church in a Radically Changing India', CSI Canter, Chennai, 23rd-24th February 2015
- 'From Hostility to Hospitality': A Paper presented in Colloquium on People with Disability: Board of Theological Education of Senate of Serampore, Bangalore, 12th-14th November 2009
- Pre-Election Consultation on 15th Lokshava, New Delhi, 1st-3rd April 2009
- World Fellowship of Inter-religious Councils, Cochin, 4th-7th October 2008
- National Conference of Nurses League, CMAI, Secunderabad, 7th-9th November 2006
- Denominationalism vis-à-vis Ecumenism, Institute of Revisioning of Mission, HPD Center, Nagpur, India, 12th February 2003
- Keynote Address: A Consultation on Men & Women in God's Mission, Bishop Heber College, Tiruchirapalli, India, 14th-16th November 2001
- Theological Education in North India: A Consultation on Priority of Theological Education, BTE SSC, CNI Bhavan, New Delhi, 23rd-24th April 2001
- Keynote Address: Church in Dialogue, 37th North India Theological Students Conference, Rural Laity: A Ministry of Empowerment: Board of Theological Education of Senate of Serampore College, Cuttack, Odisha, 21st-25th April 1996
- Address on Ecumenism: All India Pastors' Conference, Kalimpong, West Bengal, 28th-31st July 1996
- Keynote Address: The Emerging Socio-Economic and Political Order in India: A Theological Response: North India Theological Students Conference, 1993

PASTORAL MINISTRY IN WIDE-RANGING CONTEXTS

- Diocese of Cuttack, CNI (1974-79)
- Association with Woodstock Baptist Church and New Road Baptist Church, Oxford, UK (1979-1982)
- Diocese of Calcutta, CNI (1982-1988)
- Baptist Missionary Society Deputation weekend ministry in different churches of UK (1979-82 & 1988-1992)
- Diocese of Calcutta and Barrackpore, CNI (1992-2000)
- Pastoral Ministry in Eastern Himalayas as a Diocesan Bishop of CNI (2000-2004)

ACADEMICS

- Teaching Theology at Serampore College (1982-1988), (1992-2000)
- SHUATS (2012-21)
- Supervised: Doctor of Philosophy (Theology) Dissertation - 13 Master of Theology Thesis - 8

ADMINISTRATION

- Dean (1993-1996) & Vice-Principal (1996-2000), Serampore College, India
- Registrar, North India Institute of Post Graduate Theological Studies
- General Secretary, National Council of Churches in India (2005- 2009)
- Dean, Faculty of Theology, SHUATS (2012-2021)

ADDITIONAL RESPONSIBILITIES

- Member of the Senate of Serampore College (1982-1988), (1993-2000), (2002-13)
- Editor: Indian Journal of Theology (1992-2000)
- Chairperson: Theological Commission & Commission on Mission of CNI (2001- 2004)

- Member of Synodical Board of Social Services of CNI (2001- 2004)
- Member of the Coordination Committee of Senate of Serampore (2002- 2005)
- Member of the Honorary D.D. Committee of Senate of Serampore (2002- 2003)
- Member of the Continuation Committee of United and Uniting Churches, WCC (2002-2008)
- Member of the Honorary D.D. Committee of Senate of Serampore (2008- 2009)
- Editor, NCC Review (2005- 2009)
- Joint Secretary of National United Christian Forum (2005-2009)
- Member of Council of Christian Medical College, Ludhiana (2013-16)
- Member of Council of Christian Medical College, Vellore (2005-19)
- Executive Committee Member of Christian Medical College, Vellore (2010-12)
- Member of Ad-hoc Nomination Committee for selection of Associate Directors, Principal & Director of Christian Medical College, Vellore (2011-12)
- Acting-Chairman, Vice-President, (2011-12) & President (2012-16), Trans-world Radio, New Delhi
- Acting Chairman, Council of Christian Medical College, Vellore (2017-18)
- Managing Editor, All Nations University Journal of Applied Thought (ANUJAT), Ghana (2019-present)

■■■

Family Tree

- Somanath Sahoo — Netramani Sahoo
  - Haribandhu — Kausalya
    - Gopinath — Netramani
      - Rabi Narayan — Mamina
      - Kabiraj — Mamata
    - Govinda
    - Binod — Harasa
      - Sanjaya — Suryakanti
      - Bijaya — Kusum
    - Sadananda — Nayana
      - Dhaneshwar — Sumitra
  - Birendra Kumar Sahu — Promodini Sahu
    - Dhirendra Kumar Sahu — Manjusree Sahu
      - Bibhudutta Sahu — Natashia D. Kharkongor
        - Aavisha Kharkongor
        - Davinia Kharkongor
      - Ashis Sahu — Agnes Smith
        - Aviella Sahu
    - Surendra Kumar Sahu — Mugdha Sahu
      - Sanjeeb Sahu — Anukta Dey
        - Sanyukta Sahu
      - Namrata Sahu — Ignatius Deepak Stanley
        - Daniel Edward Stanley
      - Sudeep Sahu
    - Prasant Kumar Sahu — Manmohini Nath
      - Sourav Sahu — Ripsina Rath
    - Dilip Kumar Sahu — Sarita Das
    - Pradeep Kumar Sahu — Phalguni Sahu
      - Satyaben Jena — Magnolia Sahu
        - Abir

www.ingramcontent.com/pod-product-compliance
Ingram Content Group UK Ltd.
Pitfield, Milton Keynes, MK11 3LW, UK
UKHW041858190726
13854UKWH00002B/967

9 789390 569823